MOUNTAIN MEN

MOUNTAIN MEN

*A History of the Remarkable Climbers and
Determined Eccentrics Who First Scaled the
World's Most Famous Peaks*

Mick Conefrey *and* **Tim Jordan**

DA CAPO PRESS

To Gaynor Scattergood and Grace Conefrey

Designed by Jeffrey P. Williams
Set in 11-point Centaur MT by The Perseus Books Group

Cataloging-in-Publication data for this book is available from the Library of Congress.

First Da Capo Press edition 2002
Reprinted by arrangement with Macmillan Publishers Ltd
ISBN 0-306-81129-4

Published by Da Capo Press
A Member of the Perseus Books Group
http://www.dacapopress.com

Da Capo Press books are available at special discounts for bulk purchases in the U.S. by corporations, institutions, and other organizations. For more information, please contact the Special Markets Department at the Perseus Books Group, 11 Cambridge Center, Cambridge, MA 02142, or call (800) 255-1514 or (617) 252-5298, or e-mail j.mccrary@perseusbooks.com.

1 2 3 4 5 6 7 8 9—06 05 04 03 02

CONTENTS

Introduction

'Where am I?' an American climber murmured, having taken a fall during a snowstorm on the second highest mountain in the world. 'What am I doing here?' His friends, seeing the cut on his head, diagnosed concussion; he was evidently confused. Yet, reading accounts of this expedition from 1953, and others like it, the non-climber begins to wonder if the blow on the head had simply brought the man to his senses. After all, what was he doing there? He was cold and tired and frightened. The rarefied air was difficult to breathe. Rocks would often come bounding down the mountain like shells—one of them had knocked a tin cup out of his friend's hand. It was an extremely dangerous way to spend the summer. Why hadn't he gone to the beach instead?

Dangerous sports are proliferating, and in many ways climbing a mountain was a much stranger thing to do fifty or a hundred and fifty years ago than it is today. When Victorian Englishmen began arriving in Switzerland to take up the latest craze of 'alpinism' they seemed to many of the local people to behave, and often look, like lunatics. The mountains were endured by those living beneath them, regarded at best as an avoidable source of danger, and at worst as a constant threat. It was difficult to understand the urgent need of their English visitors to scramble to the top of them, with champagne picnics in their knapsacks. Fifty years on, as the sport began to spread around the world and climbers from New York arrived in Alaska to attempt the highest peak on the continent, the local newspapers devoted long editorials to ridiculing them. It was said that they were already roped together when they stepped off the boat. A few years earlier, an Italian aristocrat had climbed a volcano in the territory and brought his iron bedstead with him. They seemed crazy, and a few of them were. In the remote mountains of Pakistan, one of the first English visitors grew so disgusted by the eating habits of a colleague that he chased him across the glacier with his revolver.

The man with the revolver was Aleister Crowley, who some years later achieved lasting notoriety as Britain's premier Satanist—'Great Beast 666' being one of his favourite cognomens. While many have heard of Crowley the Satanist, fewer know that in his time he was an exceptional and daring mountaineer who led some of the first climbing expeditions to the highest peaks in the world. At the turn of the last century an inquisitive promenader on the white cliffs of Dover might have peered gingerly over the precipice, and directly into the face of the Great Beast. It was where he liked to practise, clinging to the chalk like a bat, the sea swirling below him. His expeditions were failures and ultimately inconsequential in the story of the conquest of high mountains, but as we began to research *Mountain Men* and the television series it accompanies, characters such as Crowley loomed out of the pages of the history books. We soon realized that a comprehensive history of mountaineering, if it is possible at all, would be dry indeed: there are too many mountains, too many climbers, and too many stories to allow the best of them to be told in detail. Like Sisyphus, the poor reader would be trudging up and down for ever. The purpose here is to tell a series of very different stories from a century of climbing that begins with the Victorian enthusiasts and ends in the 1950s with the conquest of the great Himalayan peaks. The stories are about men rather than mountains or the technicalities of climbing; extraordinary men who had one thing in common, and in almost every other respect were different.

Some of the pioneers climbed for the same reasons people climb mountains today. But others were explorers in an age when remote mountain ranges represented the last uncharted regions of the globe. Some were motivated by patriotism, and some only by the desire for fame and money. One wanted to prove to the world that he could pray his way to the top of the world's highest mountain, while another, irritated by a comment from his local barman, was determined to show that he was neither too old nor too fat to climb.

The television series focused on the men who attempted the first ascents of three of the world's great mountains: the Matterhorn, which rises spectacularly from the border between Italy and Switzerland; McKinley, a vast dome of ice and snow in the heart of Alaska; and K2, in the remote Karakoram range of Pakistan, perhaps the world's most intimidating peak. The limitations of screen time excluded several of the stories told here. We have added chapters on Mont Blanc and Albert Smith, the theatrical impresario who more than anyone else was responsible for selling alpinism to the Victorian public, and on Maurice Wilson's solitary attempt on Everest in 1934, perhaps the most peculiar in the annals of mountaineering.

The first ascent of the Matterhorn in 1865 was a key moment. It is often cited as the end of the 'Golden Age' of alpinism but paradoxically the event brought more publicity to the sport than ever before. The driving force behind it was one of the most interesting and complex of all the Victorian climbers, Edward Whymper. He spent five years trying to reach the summit, and the rest of his life wishing that he could forget it.

No mountain has so strange and tangled a history as Mt McKinley, the highest peak on the North American continent. In one decade, shortly after the turn of the last century, a series of expeditions converged on the mountain and began an argument that continues to this day. The men who claimed to have been the first to stand on the summit included Dr Frederick Cook, America's most controversial explorer, a band of Alaskan gold prospectors who claimed to have carried a 14-foot tree trunk to the summit, and an eccentric English missionary who gave Latin lessons to his climbing team as they worked their way up the mountain.

K2 has never had a proper name but the epithets that have been attached to it over the years tell the story: the 'savage mountain,' the 'killer mountain,' the 'mountain of mountains.' The great Italian explorer, the Duke of Abruzzi, was the first person to make a thorough examination of its slopes, in 1909; he concluded that it would never be climbed in his lifetime, and he was right. Thirty years later, an extraordinary American climber, arguably the greatest of the twentieth century, led a party to within eight hundred feet of the summit. In the following days, Fritz Wiessner's expedition disintegrated and gave rise to the most bitter controversy in the history of American mountaineering.

We filmed on or around all three mountains. Our 'Victorian' climbing team scrambled to the summit of the Matterhorn in period costume. We filmed Stephen Venables from a helicopter as he inched his way along the narrow summit ridge in his tweeds and cap, a long wooden ice-axe in his hand, posing as Edward Whymper. With nothing beneath him but clouds and distant peaks, the scene could have been no different from 14 July 1865—and for a moment it was easy to see why Whymper had wanted to be there. But as the pilot moved around the peak we caught a glimpse of a vertical queue of brightly clad climbers, clinging head to toe to the rocks, apparently motionless, waiting for their chance to make the last few feet on to the summit.

While tens of thousands of men and women have followed Whymper's route to the summit of the Matterhorn, few attempt to repeat the gruelling journey of the pioneer climbers of Mt McKinley. The Muldrow Glacier route is now in the area of Denali National Park, protected from aeroplane and helicopter landings; if you want to climb as they did, you need a dog team, and a lot more time than the average adventurer can spare. From our helicopter, the vast glacier revealed no trace of visitors but for the single track of a wolf, weaving between the crevasses at 10,000 feet, apparently in the direction of the summit. Nearly a century ago, when Hudson Stuck, Archdeacon of the Yukon, led a team along the glacier, he reported that they were followed by a large rabbit that paused to gnaw the willow canes by which they marked their way, and at one point was seen to leap a crevasse. Sitting in an armchair with the Archdeacon's book, one wondered if the rabbit was a high-altitude mirage, having previously read that an English climber attempting Everest in the 1930s described an illusion of giant pulsating teapots in the sky above the summit. But the wolf's tracks seemed to vindicate the rabbit story.

Alaska was full of surprises. The Episcopal Archbishop gave us the use of a pilot and the church's light aircraft, the *Wings of the Spirit*, to fly out from Fairbanks to a remote Athabascan settlement where the 100-year-old Indian chief described meeting Hudson Stuck as he set out for the mountain in 1913. He held Stuck's communion set in his hands. At Stuck's old headquarters on the Arctic Circle at Fort Yukon, the beautiful wooden church is virtually unchanged and everyone talked about him as if he were a recent loss—but he has been dead for eighty years. His ghost is said to appear on the river.

K2 was the hardest mountain to get to. It took us almost ten days of trekking just to catch a glimpse of it. In Alaska and Switzerland we stayed in hotels and mountain huts, but in Pakistan, damp tents were the order of the day. All our supplies and equipment had to be carried by Balti porters whose skill and stamina never ceased to amaze. K2 also gave us our first, and fortunately our only, glimpse of death. On the same day that we filmed the shiny plaques on the memorial to Art Gilkey, an American climber killed in 1953, we took some shots from an icy glacier next to K2 base-camp. As we were heading home, someone spotted something. At first it was difficult to see but, as we drew closer, the outline of a human rib-cage emerged. It had probably tumbled down the mountain in a recent avalanche, having lain somewhere on the slopes above for an unknown period. There was nothing to identify it. It was a chilling moment, and we were reminded of the astonishing statistic that for every three people to reach the summit of K2, one will die on the mountain.

For both the television series and the book, we received a great deal of help from a large number of people. We would especially like to thank the following:

Alyson Jackson and Theresa Lydon were indefatigable production managers. The films were shot by Richard Adam and Keith Partridge, the sound recorded by Frank Bigg and Tony Burke. John McAvoy was the lucky editor who had to work with over a hundred hours of rushes. Brian Hall, our climbing safety consultant, was an invaluable member of the team at all stages, and our thanks are also due to Brian and Diane Okonek in Alaska for keeping us safe in the air and on the snow around Mt McKinley. Thanks also to his father Jim who twice flew us around the summit. Adventure Tours took us in and out of the Karakoram efficiently, and Cathy Beloe kept us clothed and fed in fine style.

We would particularly like to thank Margaret Ecclestone and Bob Lawford at the Alpine Club in London for all their help, Willi Hofstatter at the Alpine Museum in Zermatt, Fran Loft at the American Alpine Club, the Bishop of Alaska Mark MacDonald, Jennifer Peters at the archives of the Episcopal Church at Austin, Texas, Phil Cronenwett at Dartmouth College, Laura Kissell at the Byrd Polar Research Center, Ohio State University, Brad Washburn at the Museum of Science in Boston, Cynthia Seefahrt, Betty Cranmer, Stella Durrance, Paul Sibley, Michael Dolan, Ed Burlingame, Stella Bruzzi, Helen Conefrey, Ed Webster, Lodovico Sella and the staff of the Fondazione Sella, Mike Kemp at BBC Worldwide, Clare Paterson and Paul Hamann at BBC documentaries, Susan Winslow at TLC, and Katy Carrington at Boxtree.

During the series we talked to and interviewed almost 60 mountaineers and historians. Our special thanks are due to:

The Duke of Aosta, Robert Bates, Fred Beckey, George Bell, Luca Bich, Bob Bryce, Nadio Carrel, Achille Compagnoni, Terence Cole, Dermot Cole, Wally Cole, Bob Craig, David Dean, Alice Douglas, Ed Douglas, Norman Elliot, Fergus Fleming, Gus Gonnasson, Nigella Hall, Pen Hadow, Peter Hansen, Ted Heckathorn, Claudio Hosquet, Charles Houston, Lino Lacedelli, Darryl Lloyd, Ian McNaught Davies, De Moleenar, Bill Puttnam, David Roberts, Dudley Rochester, Galen Rowell, Pete Schoening, Lodovico Sella, Mike Sfraga, Tony Streather, Vern Tejas, Brad Washburn, Jonathan Waterman, Andy Weissner, Ed Webster, Jim Wickwire, Ken Wilson, Jed Williamson.

❈ CHAPTER I ❈

The Man Who Sold the Alps

Imagine a world without Imax or Gore-Tex, before Berghaus, North Face and Lowe Alpine, a world without mobile phones and high-altitude Internet links, carbon-fibre alloys and polyamide fleece. Imagine a time when the Alps were as remote as the Himalayas and the Himalayas were as remote as the moon, when television hadn't been invented and even photographs were a rarity, when audiences flocked to a London theatre, by their thousands, to hear one man talk about his ascent of Mont Blanc. Enter stage right: Albert Smith, the man who sold the Alps.

There's no one quite like Albert Smith. He wasn't one of the great climbers—there are no ferocious faces or precipitous peaks that still bear his name—but he was a uniquely gifted propagandist for the mountains. In March 1852, the curtain rose on 'Mr Albert Smith's Ascent of Mont Blanc.' In just two seasons almost 200,000 people flocked to Piccadilly to enjoy his lecture show. Popular composers were inspired to write music based on his show and Smith himself devised several lucrative sidelines, including a book, a board game and a range of fans for ladies. He did royal command performances and even took his show to Windsor Castle. When he died in 1860 his obituarist in the *Daily Telegraph* declared, 'Piccadilly and Mont Blanc became allied, as it were, in the public mind, and it was impossible to think of one without associating it with the other.' The story of Albert Smith's rise from the lowlands of England's Home Counties to the lofty heights of the Alps and West End fame is the story of the birth of a new sport: mountaineering.

Albert Smith was born in the small Surrey village of Chertsey in 1816, the son of a country doctor. At the age of ten he was given a small book, *The Peasants of Chamonix*, a vivid account of an Alpine tour. Within a couple of years he could be found scouring the libraries of local institutions for anything else to do with the Alps. He was the prototypical armchair mountaineer, falling in love with other people's literary versions of Mont Blanc long before he ever saw it for himself. In his own book, *The Story of Mont Blanc* (1853), Smith referred to three works that made a particular impact on him.

Horace-Benedict De Saussure's four-volume epic, *Voyages dans les Alpes*, was published between 1779–1796 and was very quickly seen as an essential part of any Alpine enthusiast's library. The young Albert Smith was so keen that he read it in French. Today, De Saussure is regarded as the founding father of Alpinism. An aristocratic professor from Geneva, he first went to the Alps in search of botanical specimens but his scientific curiosity grew quickly into a passion for the mountains themselves. In particular he was fascinated by Mont Blanc, which was just visible from the peaks around Geneva. In 1760 he travelled to the village of Chamonix at the foot of the mountain, looking for someone who could help him get to the top.

It's hard to conceive today that barely 200 years ago no one had ever trodden on the summit of Mont Blanc. At 4808 metres (nearly 15,750 feet), it is the tallest mountain in Europe—though dwarfed by the high peaks of the Himalayas. Today thousands of people climb Mont Blanc every year and it is not considered a difficult mountain. Modern Chamonix is full of Alpine guides and outdoor shops, but when De Saussure arrived there, he could find no one to take him mountaineering.

In the eighteenth century, even the word 'mountaineer' had a different meaning—it was someone who lived in the mountains, not someone who went there for sport. The peasants around Mont Blanc were desperately poor; they had no interest whatsoever in climbing. Most of them were subsistence farmers whose main priority was survival itself. Mountains were treated with superstitious awe; no one climbed them apart from intrepid men who went hunting for goats and searching for rock crystals (in those days a valuable commodity). Even these bold characters held to the widespread belief that it would be fatal to spend just one night on a peak. In desperation, De Saussure was forced to offer a reward to the first person who could stand on the summit of Mont Blanc, hoping that he could follow in their footsteps.

A full twenty-six years later the reward was claimed by Jacques Balmat and Michel Paccard. Balmat was a hunter from Chamonix, Paccard the local doctor. On 8 August 1786, they reached the summit. It was a glorious moment but one followed almost immediately by bitter arguments. Balmat wanted all the reward for himself and, in league with one of the doctor's rivals, a writer called Marc Theodore Bourrit, he tried to write Paccard out of the story. Bourrit wrote a widely circulated letter that was full of attacks on Paccard. The scandal raged on inconclusively for a whole year until De Saussure returned to Chamonix and climbed the mountain himself—with Balmat. After this, Paccard slipped into obscurity and De Saussure became even more famous. It was mountaineering's first controversy, but it would most definitely not be its last.

Smith's earliest encounter with Alpine literature, *The Peasants of Chamonix*, was published in 1824. It was literally a much lighter tome than De Saussure's multi-volume epic, but its impact on the young Smith was more profound. He was particularly impressed by its retelling of the infamous Hamel disaster, the first mountaineering accident. Hamel was a Russian scientist who, in 1820, put together an expedition to carry out an experiment on the 'rarefied air' at Mont Blanc's summit. His large party included two English students and twelve local guides. Initially they were held back by very bad weather, but about halfway up the mountain they unroped, thinking that the dangers were past. Suddenly a huge avalanche carried them all off, giving everyone the shock of their lives and depositing five of the guides in a gaping crevasse at the bottom. The others fought desperately to free their companions from the tons of snow that had engulfed them; they managed to pull two of them out but the others were never seen again. In the aftermath of the accident there was much criticism of Hamel and the English students: was it right for rich foreigners to persuade poor Chamonards to risk their lives in the mountains for the sake of a few francs? For two years there were no further climbs of Mont Blanc: Dr Hamel was turned into the local bogeyman and the students were despised for not giving enough compensation to the guides' families.

Albert Smith's favourite book on the Alps, however, was written seven years later: John Auldjo's *An Ascent of Mont Blanc.* By 1827, although Chamonix was still haunted by the Hamel incident, it was business as usual in the town. Six more British tourists had been guided to the summit and, after glimpsing Mont Blanc from afar, Auldjo decided that he was willing to pay to become the seventh. On 8 August he left the village with no fewer than six local guides. His account is a record of wonder and a diary of pain. In order to witness 'scenes of such dazzling brilliancy, too much almost for the eye to encounter,' he put up with headaches, palpitations, lassitude, knee pain, diminished respiration and an overwhelming desire to fall asleep. He had to be dragged up the final slope and collapsed for fifteen minutes when he reached the summit. When Auldjo's guides revived him, they drank the customary glass of champagne, but it only gave them all indigestion.

The return journey was even worse. The guides were unnerved by huge avalanches and the weather began to deteriorate. A storm chased them down the mountain and Auldjo collapsed again due to the combined effects of the exertion and the cold. In desperation his men formed a circle around him, gave him a huge hug and invited him to put his frozen hands on to their bare chests. He came back to life but soon the weaker of his guides started to lose heart and wail, *'Nous sommes perdus'*—'We're lost' . . . Somehow, the more experienced men managed to get everyone safely down to the bottom of the mountain where they were met by a maiden bearing a cauldron of hot milk. Though Auldjo declared that he had been thoroughly 'repaid' by the view from the top, he made no bones about how difficult it was to get there.

Then, as now, 'painography' was a key element of Alpine literature. Publishers love it, authors complain about it and readers lap it up. Frost-bitten extremities, near-death experiences, bruises, blood and broken bones—all have become the stock-in-trade of the climbing epic. And, strangely, the more harrowing the account of someone else's misery, the more people want to experience it for themselves. And so it was with the young Albert Smith: Auldjo's pain-filled travelogue and the story of the Hamel disaster only whetted his appetite for Mont Blanc. He even constructed his very own Alpine panorama based on Auldjo's tale: 'This I so painted up and exaggerated in my enthusiasm, that my little sister—who was my only audience—would become pale with fright.'

Smith's first encounter with a real mountain came in 1838, after he had enrolled in medical school in Paris. At the end of term, he and a friend took to the open road heading for the Alps and Italy. They set off with £12 each (now worth about £600), converted into numerous 5-franc coins that they stuffed into leather belts around their waists. It cost £2 for the seventy-eight-hour journey in a 'diligence' (a horse and carriage) from Paris to Geneva, but they saved money by sleeping under tarpaulins on the carriage roof and haggling for cheap food while their fellow passengers quaffed and slumbered in the finest restaurants and hotels. Smith's published diary reads like an early version of a *Rough Guide*. After declaring, 'If there is anything more delightful than travelling with plenty of money, it is certainly making a journey of pleasure with very little,' Smith proceeds to list in glorious detail all the bargains he made en route to Mont Blanc.

September 22:
...at Tonnerre we got plenty of grapes for nothing...

September 23:
…the landlord lent us a piece of soap and some towels and we washed at the fountain in the marketplace…

September 24:
…the *conducteur* told us, if we left him to pay he would get everything half price…

AT GENEVA THEY GOT THEIR FIRST SIGHT of Mont Blanc, illuminated by a glorious sunset. A day and a half later they arrived at Chamonix. At first Smith was a little underwhelmed by the mountain: up close, it wasn't quite as imposing as he had imagined. He was even more disappointed by Chamonix's famous glaciers: 'The story that the Mer de Glace resembles the sea suddenly frozen in a storm is all nonsense. From Montanvert it looks like a magnified white ploughed field.' They encountered travellers from all over the world who were similarly unimpressed: 'Each one told the rest that they could see something in his country quite as good. Of these comparing minds, the most daring were the Irish and the Americans.'

Smith's enthusiasm, however, quickly returned and by the end of his second day he had decided: 'Chamouni [sic] is the nicest place in Europe.' He couldn't separate the real Mont Blanc from the enchanted mountain of his imagination: 'I went to the window and the first view I had of the Mont Blanc range burst on me suddenly through the mist—that wondrous breath-checking *coup d'oeil*. Every step I took on the road that day was as on a journey to fairyland.' Smith and his friend didn't have enough money to hire guides and make their own attempt on the mountain and this time there was no way of getting a cheap deal. All they could do was daydream about being hired as porters by a rich traveller. Sadly, no one came forward and the penny-pinching pair left the Alps for Italy.

On completion of his training in Paris, Smith returned to Chertsey, where he joined his father's medical practice. He tried to settle down as a country doctor but his heart wasn't in it. Much more exciting were the occasional lectures that he was able to give about his journey to Mont Blanc. He put a new lick of paint on to his Alpine panorama and went on the road with his brother, aiming to enlighten the inhabitants of the local villages on the theory of glaciers and the dangers of Mont Blanc's Grand Plateau. Eventually, he got so bored with medicine that he upped stumps and moved to central London, changed his 'lancet into a steel pen' and began working as a full-time writer.

In a half-hearted attempt to keep his options open, Smith fixed a plate on to the front of his house informing passers-by that a 'surgeon–dentist' was in residence—but he spent most of his time living it up in theatres and literary taverns. He had become a successful hack, writing articles for the satirical magazine *Punch* and devising pantomimes and adapting plays for the London stage. In 1844 he met the great American showman P. T. Barnum, who was visiting England looking for new attractions for his circus. He and Smith hit it off straight away and they spent a day touring the sights of Shakespeare's Stratford. When they parted, Barnum delivered some enigmatic words of wisdom: 'If a man can't beat himself running he'll never go ahead; and if he can't go ahead, he's done.' What Smith made of this he never did reveal, but he did learn a vital lesson from Barnum that he would put into effect years later: whenever you put on a show, make sure that your name gets top billing.

Smith first gained fame with a series of short books and pamphlets, written in pseudo-scientific style, that satirized contemporary life. They included a series of 'Natural Histories'—such as *The Natural History of the Idler* and *The Ballet Girl* and *The Flirt*—and *The Physiology of Evening Parties*. Smith was most at home when discussing the pretensions of the upwardly mobile. In *The Natural History of the Gent* he poked fun at the vanity of the man about town, who anticipated today's taste for designer clothing: 'Gents usually speak of their get up as the ticket... the leaning of Gents towards distinguished associations is very evident. A great-coat must be a "Chesterfield," a "Taglioni" or a "Codrington."' In *The Natural History of*

Stuck-Up People Smith introduced the Spangle-Laquer family who have 'a pew in a very fashionable church, where religion is made a medium for the display of bonnets' and who love to travel abroad so that they can buy cartloads of souvenirs 'and feel great pleasure in paying twice as much as they ought for everything.'

The fashion for foreign travel that Smith poked fun at continued through the first half of the nineteenth century. This was the era of the Grand Tour, when well-bred young men, and occasionally women, were expected to finish their education by travelling to Europe, local wars permitting. There, they ticked off a selected list of cultural and natural must-sees, ranging from Roman ruins to the mighty Alps of Switzerland. In earlier centuries, mountains had been regarded as brutal and ugly, but by now they were at the top of the list of natural wonders. According to the poets and painters of the Romantic movement, the Alps were the epitome of what they termed 'the sublime.'

Like beauty, the 'sublime' was in the eye of the beholder. It referred to the strange sensation of simultaneous fear, awe and exhilaration that was provoked by striking landscapes. John Auldjo's narrative was full of references to sublime moments on his terror-filled trip up Mont Blanc. The Alps also appealed to devotees of the slightly less full-blooded cult of the 'picturesque.' Aficionados toured Europe searching for natural beauty: in extreme cases, they sat with their backs to the landscape and studied the world in a framed mirror. By the middle of the nineteenth century, Europe was covered with hotels called Bellevue, Bellavista and Belvedere, all promising rooms with a view, and even the humblest of villages were boasting unique panoramic lookouts. In *The Playground of Europe* (1871) Leslie Stephen, the great Victorian mountaineer and man of letters, eulogized Switzerland as a pre-industrial utopia:

> The mountains represent the indomitable force of nature to which we are forced to adapt ourselves, they speak to man of his little-ness and his ephemeral existence... they are the natural

retreat of men disgusted with the existing order of things...
soothing to minds out of harmony with the existing social
order... places of refuge where we may escape from ourselves
and from our neighbours. The love of mountains is intimately
connected with all that is noblest in human nature.

The writer and critic John Ruskin was one of the earliest and most influ-
ential propagandists for Alpine scenery. In *Modern Painters IV* he pro-
claimed: 'the mountains of the earth are its natural cathedrals' and speculated on their hidden role throughout history: 'Can we justly refuse to
attribute to their mountain scenery, some share in giving the Greeks and
Italians their intellectual lead among the nations of Europe?' Ruskin and
the Romantic poets gave the mountains a cultural legitimacy, but it is
important to realize that the early travellers came to look, not to climb.
Ruskin was quick to criticize those who promoted mountains 'chiefly as
places for gymnastic exercise.' It was permissible to indulge in a certain
amount of vigorous walking in order to arrive at a viewing point but,
according to Ruskin, mountains were best seen from the bottom. And like
all great snobs he wanted to keep the Alps unspoilt, by everyone except
himself. While extolling the wonders of Switzerland and recounting his
own travels, he warned, 'I believe that every franc now spent by travellers
among the Alps tends more or less to the undermining of whatever great-
ness there is in the Swiss character.' It was too late, though: Switzerland
had already changed for ever.

In 1838, the same year that Albert Smith visited Chamonix, John
Murray published the first edition of his famous *Handbook of Switzerland*.
Inside, prospective tourists were given advice on how to get there and what
to see. It noted that the British traveller had already made an impact on
the hotels of Switzerland and that 'the luxury of tea may always be had in
perfection,' but it also warned that, 'there are generally two sets of charges,
one for the natives, or Germans, and another for the English, on the prin-

ciple that the latter have both longer purses, more numerous wants and they are more difficult to serve.'

Travellers were also encouraged to take a map published by the Useful Knowledge Society and equip themselves with hobnail boots, walking sticks and tinted glasses. They were advised to always take a guide when crossing a glacier and warned not to carry more than a 20lb pack. Like Ruskin, Murray was adamant that the mountains were there to be seen, not climbed: 'The passion for climbing mountains so ardent in a young traveller, soon cools; they who have surmounted the Righi, the Faulhorn and the Dole, may fairly consider any further ascents a waste of time and labour.' Mont Blanc was acknowledged as the 'crowning glory' of any trip to the Alps, but anyone who was thinking of climbing it was warned off in no uncertain terms. Scientists had a reason to make ascents but 'those who are impelled by curiosity alone, are not justified in risking the lives of their guides. It is no excuse that the employer thinks his own life is worthless; here he ought to think of the safety of others.' And just in case the high moral tone wasn't discouraging enough, Murray's handbook added that those who had climbed Mont Blanc 'admit, however, when in safety, that the fatigue and the danger infinitely exceeded their gratification.'

But such warnings and admonishments fell on deaf ears. In the sixty years after Balmat and Paccard's first conquest of Mont Blanc, there were no fewer than thirty-five further ascents of Mont Blanc and more than half of these were by British tourists. In 1851, one more name was added to the growing list of those who had stood on the summit: Albert Smith.

During the previous year, Smith had starred in his own West End show, *The Overland Mail*, an illustrated lecture about a journey he had made following the postal route between Suez and Boulogne. Smith realized that there was a large audience out there who would pay for educational entertainment and decided to make a climb of Mont Blanc his next subject. On 1 August he headed for the Alps, accompanied by William

Beverley, a famous scenic artist. He booked into the Hotel de Londres in Chamonix, hired a guide and went shopping to procure a green veil, a pair of blue stockings and a new spike for his alpenstock.

Meanwhile another English party had arrived in Chamonix, also heading for Mont Blanc. They were three students from Oxford who had gone to Switzerland as part of a reading party: Francis Phillips, William Sackville-West and Charles Floyd. In a self-published book that appeared some months later, Phillips explained how the idea first came to them in a boat on Lake Geneva. They were floating quite happily when:

> I heard a sudden exclamation from Sackville-West and saw soaring above the intervening mountains the snow white summit of Mont Blanc. We gazed at it for some time, scarcely daring to draw our breath, till the exclamation, 'How awfully grand!' burst at the same moment from our lips. The words were scarcely uttered when the charm was broken, and I said to Floyd, 'I see no reason to prevent our being on the top before another month is over.' 'By all means,' replied Floyd. 'Will you join us, West? Let us make a jolly party of it.'

They immediately, and literally, cracked open a couple of bottles of champagne, breaking off the bottle necks with the tip of an oar. The very next day they went into training and, just to prove how serious they were, refused to eat any more croissants at breakfast and confined themselves to a maximum of two cigars per day. Shortly after they arrived in Chamonix, Phillips and his friends were informed that a certain Albert Smith and his guide wished to join forces with them on their forthcoming expedition. They declined his offer. When later they realized that it was *the* Albert Smith, 'the well-known comic author,' they had a swift change of heart and rushed over to shake his hand and plan their adventure.

Unfortunately at this point the weather changed abruptly for the worse and didn't improve for almost a week. Smith caught a cold and was on the point of returning to London when, just as suddenly, the clouds parted. While they were all having dinner at Smith's hotel on the night of 11 August, his landlady suddenly cried out from the top of the table: 'Good weather is coming; you will be able to make a beautiful ascent, my good Sirs; and tomorrow.' With that, they all rushed into a frenzy of packing and organizing. Smith's dream was about to come true: 'We walked about Chamouni that night with heads erect, and an imposing step. People pointed at us, and came from the hotels to see what we were like. For that evening, at least, we were evidently great persons.'

After a sleepless night, they set off on the morning of Tuesday, 12 August, in a huge party consisting of the four tourists, sixteen guides and eighteen porters. For provisions they carried thirty-five small fowls, eleven large fowls, one piece of beef, six pieces of veal, eight pieces of mutton, six lemons, four candles, ten small cheeses, twenty loaves of bread, sixty bottles of vin ordinaire, ten bottles of St George, fifteen bottles of St Jean, three bottles of brandy, one bottle of cassis, six bottles of lemonade and two bottles of champagne. Smith left his money and personal belongings in Chamonix with instructions on what to do if he didn't return.

He hired a mule for the first part of the journey, but it was more trouble than it was worth and he was glad to see the back of it. The next few hours were easy but, as they got closer to the glaciers, everything became much steeper and the tourists became more reliant on the guides. After Phillips made a slip, they roped up to cross that 'wild and awful tract,' the Glacier des Bossons. On several occasions, they needed ladders to cross particularly dangerous-looking crevasses. For Smith it was exhilarating and nerve-racking in equal measure: 'There is no great difficulty, to be sure, in doing this when the ladder lies upon the ground; but with a chasm of unknown depth below it, it is satisfactory to get to the other side as quickly as possible.' At four o'clock they stopped for dinner and had their first crisis: the guides hadn't brought any glasses for them to drink their champagne from! Ever resourceful, Smith grabbed a copper saucepan and pressed it into service as a communal tankard.

Down in Chamonix, other tourists and townsfolk had been scouring the mountain with telescopes, looking for any sign of Smith's party. When they were finally spotted at a group of rocks called the Grands Mulets, the Chamonards gave them a gunpowder salute, to which the brave mountaineers replied with an improvised flag, tying a handkerchief on to one of their alpenstocks. As the sun set and the wine bottles emptied, Smith grew lyrical: 'For two hours a scene of such wild and wondrous beauty burst upon me, that, spellbound, and almost trembling with the emotion that its magnificence called forth, I saw far more than the realization of the most gorgeous visions that opium or hashish could evoke.' Phillips grew melancholy: a friend of his father had been a member of the disastrous Hamel expeditions and now he began to wonder what had happened to the bodies. 'Might not a similar fate be ours?' he asked himself.

They started up again at midnight by torchlight. After circumventing a huge crevasse, the party arrived at the Grand Plateau, the scene of the Hamel disaster. This sent a frisson down Smith's back, amplified by the guide Tairraz, whose brother had been one of the victims. 'Are there still avalanches?' Smith asked. 'Yes, always,' Tairraz replied, 'night and day.' They carried on but their spirits were further depressed when they encountered another tourist, an Irishman, who was also attempting Mont Blanc. On the way up he had raced past them but now they found him in a much weakened state, 'lying on the snow, vomiting frightfully, with considerable haemorrhage of the nose.' Smith advised him to retreat.

Just when the going was getting really tough, dawn broke and Smith was transported back to Mont Blanc heaven:

When peak after peak rose from out of the gloomy world below, the spectacle was magnificent. In the dark, boundless space a small speck of light would suddenly appear, growing larger and larger, until it took the form of a mountain top. Whilst this was going on, other points would brighten, here and there, and increase in the same manner; then a silvery gleam would mark the position of a lake reflected in the sky until the grey hazy ocean, lighted up into hills, and valleys and the entire world below warmed into the glow of sunrise.

It was still tough climbing, though: for an hour and a half they battled their way up a ferocious ice slope only to find themselves on yet another glacier. At this point everyone started to suffer from the effects of the altitude. Both Smith and Phillips felt a terrible urge to fall asleep there and then but, not surprisingly, the guides wouldn't let them. Smith wandered along, hallucinating wildly: 'It is very difficult to explain the odd state in which I was entangled. A great many people I knew in London were accompanying me, and calling after me, as the stones did to Prince Pervis, in the *Arabian Nights*... a literary friend came up and told me he was sorry we could not pass over his ground on our way to the summit, but that the King of Prussia had forbidden it.' Finally, half-awake, half-asleep, scrambling on his hands and knees, Smith reached the summit of Mont Blanc—and passed out.

When he came to, emboldened by a glass of champagne, he paused to take in the view and found that, once again, he was a little disappointed by Mont Blanc. The sky was hazy and the vista was just so huge that nothing really stood out. Nevertheless, as they toasted and re-toasted each other, Smith's characteristic cheerfulness, and sense of the dramatic, returned:

> We had beheld all the wonders and horrors of the glacier world in their wildest features; we had gazed on scenery of such fantastic yet magnificent nature as we might not hope to see again; we had laboured with all the nerve and energy we could command to achieve a work of downright unceasing danger and difficulty, which not more than one half of those who try are able to accomplish, and the triumph of which is, even now, shared but by a comparative handful of travellers—and we had succeeded.

On the way down, one of the students, Floyd, fell into a crevasse but, luckily for him, the rope held. When they returned to town, they were cheered and serenaded by the locals, who gladly joined in when the champagne began to flow. It was an experience that none of them would ever forget. Francis Phillips ultimately admitted to himself that it was all much more perilous than he had ever thought. Before climbing Mont Blanc, he had assumed that the guides habitually exaggerated the dangers. Now he had come back humbled and full of praise for their efforts. In his account of the climb he concluded that Murray's handbook was right: it was immoral to risk the lives of guides for the sake of climbing a mountain even if they were quite willing to do it. For anyone wishing to make an ascent, he finished his book with these words of warning: 'In conclusion, I strongly recommend anyone who may feel ambitious of ascending Mont Blanc, to consider well before he attempts an expedition which cannot be productive of any good to himself or others, and which is attended with fearful risk, not only to himself, but of those persons who allured by the desire of gain, endanger their lives in his service.'

Albert Smith had no such qualms. It had all gone well: his fantasy had become reality and he spent another sleepless night back in Chamonix: 'When I was standing in the balcony of my chamber window, looking at the twinkling pine illuminations on the bridge, and watching the last glow of sunset once more disappear from the summit of the grand old mountain king, I could hardly persuade myself that the whole affair had not been a wonderful dream.' He returned to London and immediately began devising his new entertainment, which, following P.T. Barnum's advice, he billed as:

ALBERT SMITH'S
Ascent of Mont Blanc

IN MARCH 1853 THE SHOW OPENED in Piccadilly. The format was simple: Smith stood at a lectern recounting his journey to Chamonix and his heroic climb of the mountain. Behind him appeared William Beverley's illustrations of the Alps. Naturally, he talked up how dangerous everything was—but he also made it all sound like fun. Interspersed in his thrilling narrative were a series of comic vignettes, based around a set of characters who could have come from one of his earlier 'social anatomies.' They were woven into his story as fellow travellers who Smith had encountered en route to Mont Blanc and included a bumbling American traveller trying to follow in the footsteps of Byron and a 'literary lady' who was forever losing and finding a black travelling box. Smith further sugared the pill with the occasional song and tried to work in as many topical references as he could.

The critics were full of praise for Smith's skills as a raconteur and showman and the audiences loved it. In case anyone was in doubt of his mountaineering credentials, he prominently displayed a certificate given to him by his guides that confirmed he had reached the summit under his own steam and had not been carried in one of the food baskets as some of his rivals were suggesting.

His show was a huge success: in his first two seasons he made the huge sum of £17,000 after 471 performances. As time went on, there were detours in his narrative to keep the audiences coming. One season Smith got to the Alps via Holland; in another season he travelled via the Rhine. At one stage he even managed to work a trip to Naples and Pompeii into his itinerary. His stage set became more and more elaborate, eventually including St Bernard dogs, Swiss barmaids and a full-scale replica of an Alpine chalet. Sadly, his attempt to include two Chamois goats was not a great success: one broke its leg on the journey over to London and the other one pined away until it too died.

In 1855, when Smith celebrated his 1000th performance, British tourists were flocking to the Alps and climbing Mont Blanc in ever greater numbers. According to *The Times*, Britain was gripped with 'Mont Blanc mania.' Its letter pages were so clogged up with heroic accounts of yet more British ascents that eventually the editor decided that it was time to speak out. Mont Blanc was becoming boring, *The Times* declared, 'its majesty is stale, its diadem of snow, a mere theatrical gimcrack. Do not let us continue to treat the ascent of this well-trodden mountain as any extraordinary matter, for it will soon have become as ordinary an occurrence as a stroll up Regent Street on a fine afternoon in July.' The latest edition of Murray's handbook continued to pour scorn on anyone who climbed Mont Blanc: 'It is somewhat a remarkable fact that a large portion of those who have made the ascent have been persons of unsound mind.'

Neither *The Times* nor Murray could stop the growth of mountaineering, though; the Alps were booming. Whenever Albert Smith visited Chamonix he was treated like a hero and given a suite at the Hotel d'Angleterre with a gold name-plate on the door announcing his presence. Steamships and railways had made it much cheaper to get to Switzerland and every year there were more and more hotels opening up. Photographs of Alpine towns in the Victorian period are reminiscent of Spain's Costa del Sol in the 1970s: next to the huddles of traditional Swiss chalets and ancient churches there are enormous hotels that look very out of place against their mountainous background. Their names show how important the British travellers were—names such as the Hotel de Londres and the Hotel Bristol, as well as the Hotel d'Angleterre. And by now it wasn't just Chamonix and Mont Blanc that were prospering: tourists were climbing other mountains and frequenting the inns of Zermatt and Grindelwald and other Swiss villages.

In December 1857, seven months before he had given the final performance of his show—the 2000th—Smith received a letter inviting him to join a new club devoted to mountaineering: the Alpine Club. Its founders were a group of enthusiastic British climbers who had spent the last few years roaming the Alps looking for new peaks to conquer and new passes to cross. Unlike the aristocrats who had flocked to Europe for the Grand Tour, most of them had jobs and did their climbing in their summer holidays; they were businessmen, lawyers, vicars, men of the professional classes who were desperate to get out of their offices and into the fresh air. When the club started in 1857, there were barely a dozen founder members; a year later numbers had swelled to almost one hundred. The club's stated purpose was to 'facilitate association among those who, in their admiration of natural grandeur, possess similarity of taste,' a particular taste for mountaineering in this case.

Like the great Victorian gentlemen's clubs, they naturally included a clause in their rule book enabling members to blackball any prospective candidates to whom they were not partial. Letters preserved in the Alpine Club's archives reveal early controversies over how many annual dinners to have and how to sort out the real mountaineers from mere fellow travellers. Initially, it was suggested that to qualify for membership all candidates should have ascended a 13,000-feet (nearly 4000-metre) mountain, which in theory was no mean feat. However, it was quickly pointed out that this would make someone who had reached the easy summit of the Cima (13,500 feet) eligible, whereas someone who had made the much harder climb of the Wetterhorn (12,500 feet) would be excluded. Eventually they agreed on a compromise, replacing a specific height with the more general stipulation that their climbing records should be examined by the committee in order to decide if they made the grade. John Ball was selected as the Club's first president; he had been visiting the mountains for almost forty years compiling material for a series of Alpine handbooks. For men like Ball, a guided ascent of Mont Blanc was no great achievement. To get to the summit of the highest mountain in the Alps was 'an expedition involving no particular difficulties, nor when made in favourable weather any appreciable risk.'

When Smith received his invitation, he wrote back straight away agreeing to join 'with pleasure' and adding that he and his hero Auldjo had already had this idea several years previously. Smith was not universally approved of: one of the Club's founders, William Matthews, wrote to a fellow member on his inclusion, 'I cannot say that I see the introduction of Albert Smith's name with feelings of great satisfaction...' For some of the upper-middle-class members of the Alpine Club, nicknamed 'Cambridge University at Play,' someone like Smith would always be seen as a slightly vulgar 'Cockney.' There was also a fundamental difference in the approach of the new mountaineers from that of Albert Smith's generation. These men actually enjoyed climbing: it wasn't simply a means to an end.

Smith and his mentor Auldjo had climbed Mont Blanc because it was a challenge; their reward was the sublime view. The journey up and down was invariably full of exciting and dangerous moments, but these were seen as trials to be endured rather than experiences to be enjoyed. For the new generation who formed the Alpine Club, the act of climbing itself was definitely part of the pleasure. They were still reliant on guides but, if necessary, they were willing to go it alone; and when it came to choosing a route or deciding what to do next they had the final say. In 1854 five British climbers who soon became prominent members of the Alpine Club even went as far as pioneering a new route on Mont Blanc *without* guides.

The new generation didn't see a conflict between the physical pleasures of mountaineering and the aesthetic appreciation of mountains. In Leslie Stephen, the Alpine Club found an apologist for their new sport who was just as eloquent and just as passionate as John Ruskin. Without referring to Ruskin directly, he took on those who claimed that all the best views were from the bottom. Though he admitted that sometimes the summits might be wrapped in clouds, he argued that what you saw from the top was the 'crowning glory' of a mountain. In his account of his climb of the Schreckhorn in 1861, he compared the summit views to one of the poet De Quincey's celebrated opium dreams: 'You are in the centre of a whole district of desolation, suggesting a landscape from Greenland, or an imaginary picture of England in the glacial epoch... the charm of such views—little as they are appreciated by professed admirers of the picturesque—is to my taste unique, though not easily explained to unbelievers.' Ruskin had made derisory references to mountaineers as rock gymnasts who treated the Alps like greasy poles; Stephen was proud to declare that mountaineering was a sport and even admitted that he himself had occasionally suffered bouts of 'climbing fever.'

In the ten years after the foundation of the Alpine Club, British climbers stormed through the Alps. Getting to the top first was considered the greatest prize and the men of the Alpine Club celebrated it in their own publication, *Peaks, Passes and Glaciers*, soon to become the world-famous *Alpine Journal*. Within ten years there were national climbing clubs in Switzerland, Austria and Italy, but in the early years no one matched the success of the British climbers.

As for Smith, he returned to the London stage in December 1858 with *Albert Smith's Mont Blanc to China*. That summer he had made a tour of the Far East hunting for new material, but this show was never as successful as his Mont Blanc lecture and by now his health had begun to deteriorate. He died two years later in 1860 after a bout of pneumonia. His friends organized a small, quiet funeral. Eventually the Alpine Club raised money for a commemorative plaque to be placed on his gravestone in Brompton cemetery, but today he is largely forgotten. There is no 'Smith route' on Mont Blanc, there are no best-selling Smith ice-axes or Smith tents to commemorate his prowess as a climber; no one has even republished his book, *The Story of Mont Blanc*.

ALBERT SMITH WAS ABOVE ALL AN ENTHUSIAST and a great communicator. He was the first person who really understood that for every budding Alpinist who was willing to risk his skin on a treacherous slope, there were thousands of others who might never go near a mountain, but who would be willing to pay to hear about someone else's exploits. Perhaps he was so good at selling the Alps because he drew as much on his imagination as he did on his experience of the real thing. Tens of thousands of people were thrilled to hear his story of Mont Blanc and many of those did go on to become great climbers. On 4 June 1858 one happy customer left his show and headed home where he confided to his diary: 'People often go to these things with exorbitant expectations raised by previous descriptions which have been told to them; I however found myself quite satisfied and more.'

His name was Edward Whymper.

⊰ CHAPTER 2 ⊱

The Misfit and the Matterhorn

Few people have a good word to say about Edward Whymper. His biographer, Frank Smythe, revealed that even as a youth he had developed a habit of egoism that 'bred resentment, suspicion and parsimony towards others.' Sir Arnold Lunn, the famous ski-mountaineer, branded him 'a friendless and in many ways a pathetic man' and a more recent historian, Peter Hansen, described him to us as 'the kind of person who annoyed someone new every time he opened his mouth.' At one stage even Whymper himself joined in, confiding in a letter, 'I fear there must be something queer about me or some fault which sorely needs correction.' And yet there's no denying his achievements. In the Alps he made the first ascents of the Aiguille Verte, the Grandes Jorasses and the Barre des Ecrins. He held a world altitude record for climbing Chimborazo in the Andes, made two expeditions to Greenland and wrote probably the world's best-selling mountaineering book, *Scrambles in the Alps*. But all this matters little next to the events that occurred on 14 July 1865: the occasion of his ninth attempt to climb the Matterhorn—a defining moment in his life and a watershed in the history of mountaineering.

Seven years earlier, when the eighteen-year-old Edward Whymper was enjoying the fun at Albert Smith's lecture on Mont Blanc, he could have had no idea that one day his fame would eclipse that of the great entertainer or that he would ever even visit the Alps. He was born in London in 1840, the second of eleven children. His father, Josiah, was a well-known water-colourist and engraver. His was a devout family; in spite of all her own children, Whymper's mother still managed to spend a lot of time doing good works. According to his sister Annette, Edward was much more confident than his elder brother. Throughout his life, he was a great organizer, always collecting and organizing funds for everyone from sick relatives to former guides.

From an early age it was clear that Edward had potential as an artist, so much so that at fourteen he'd had to leave school and become an apprentice at his father's business. He was ambitious and talented and bored; his teenage diary is full of opinions on everything from the Crimean War to the latest photographic exhibitions. Like many Victorian boys, he was fascinated by the travelogues of Arctic explorers, but he knew that he stood very little chance of ever getting to the world of ice. His life consisted of monotonous days at the engraver's and weekends playing cricket and attending chapel. At the age of seventeen he confided to his diary that for a long time he had been frustrated with his 'fate': 'I had ideas floating in my head that I should one day turn out some great person, be *the* person of *my* day, perhaps Prime Minister or at least a millionaire. Who has not had them? They have not left *me* yet.'

Then, suddenly everything changed. In January 1860, Whymper was commissioned to go to Switzerland and bring back a series of sketches for the London publisher William Longman.

This was the first time that Whymper had travelled abroad and Switzerland was a revelation. Here were the Alps in their full glory and here was the young Edward Whymper surrounded by the elite of the Alpine Club. Leslie Stephen made admiring remarks about his drawings and Andrew Hinchcliffe offered to teach him the art of climbing, but Whymper was already a harsh critic, forever complaining about the inadequacies of Switzerland. He encountered 'cheese uncommonly like paste beginning to turn bad,' towns that looked worse 'by daylight than by moonlight' and people who were 'on the whole stupid and somewhat uncivil.' But something happened that year that would bring him back to the Alps time and again and set him on his way to become probably the greatest of the Victorian climbers.

That 'something' certainly wasn't his first encounter with the Matterhorn. Ruskin had called it 'the most precipitous and the strongest mass in the Alps' but young Whymper was disappointed. 'What precious stuff Ruskin has written about this... Grand it is, but beautiful it is not.' If he wasn't that impressed with its appearance, he knew a challenge when he saw one. The Matterhorn was the Everest of its day, the 'last great problem in the Alps,' its reputation unparalleled. According to Whymper, it remained unclimbed 'less on account of the difficulty of doing so, than from the terror inspired by its invincible appearance.' The 'father' of British mountaineering, J. D. Forbes, had described it as 'unscaled and unscaleable' and the president of the Alpine Club, John Ball, declared that 'alone among the great peaks of the Alps [it] will preserve the epithet "inaccessible".' Most of the local guides refused even to attempt it: 'Anything but the Matterhorn,' they pleaded. Whymper begged to differ: it may not have been love at first sight but for the next five years he kept on coming back to the Matterhorn, absolutely determined to become the first man to reach its summit.

It is easy to see why the Matterhorn had such a reputation and why today it is still considered in many ways *the* archetypal mountain. At 14,701 feet (4480 metres), it isn't the tallest peak in the Alps, but it is undoubtedly one of the most spectacular. It stands out on the horizon, straddling the Italian/Swiss border, dominating the other mountains around it and bearing down on the towns below. From Zermatt in particular it looks impregnable, the north and eastern faces seeming to be sheer cliffs rising towards a perfect spike. From the Italian side, however, the Cervino, as it is called, seems to be much more approachable. The southern face is broken up into a series of ridges and smaller pyramids that rise in stages towards the summit. In the 1860s most climbers agreed that if it was ever going to be climbed then it would have to be by the Italian route.

The Irish physicist John Tyndall made one of the first attempts on the Matterhorn from Italy in August 1860. Tyndall was a hugely ambitious mountaineer and a very cantankerous man who was continually falling in and out with other members of the Alpine Club while pursuing a distinguished career in science. At first he was one of those who saw the Alps as a vast laboratory for experiments on everything from what makes the sky blue to the movement of glaciers. He famously once spent twenty hours on the summit of Mont Blanc in order to conduct a particular series of tests. Then after his greatest achievement, the ascent of Weisshorn in 1861, he became a fully formed mountaineer: 'I opened my notebook to make a few observations but soon relinquished the attempt. There was something incongruous, if not profane, in allowing the scientific faculty to interfere.' He too had his sights on the Matterhorn, which he described as 'a black savage tattooed with streaks of snow' full of 'moral savagery, wild untamed ferocity.' He and Edward Whymper would soon become great rivals.

In August 1861 Whymper made his second trip to the Alps. After making a successful attempt on Mont Pelvoux in the Dauphine, he and a guide from Zermatt crossed the Theodule Pass to Breuil, the small town in Italy at the southern foot of the Matterhorn. Whymper had already heard that Tyndall had succeeded on the Weisshorn and was aghast at the idea that he might beat him to the Matterhorn. 'My interest in the Weisshorn abated, but it was raised to the highest pitch on hearing that Professor Tyndall was at Breuil and intending to try to crown his victory by another and still greater one.' Fortunately for Whymper, when he got to Breuil he discovered that Tyndall had been there a few days earlier but in the end he had not made an attempt and was already gone.

Whymper immediately went in search of a good local person to take him and the guide from Zermatt on to the Matterhorn but this was no easy task. In general, Whymper was cynical about the profession and reserved for the guides his most caustic wit: 'They represented for me pointers of paths and large consumers of meat and drink but little more… men whose faces expressed malice, pride, envy, hatred and roguery of every description, but who seemed to be destitute of all good qualities.' Many of the guides did aim to exploit their clients to the full. Today their descendants smile wryly as they tell you how English climbers were seen as 'cash cows' to be milked for all they were worth. The locals were poor and the travellers were rich: was this not the natural way of things?

But even Whymper admitted that there were some guides who were different and Whymper had come in search of one of them: Jean-Antoine Carrel, the 'Cock of Valtournache.' Carrel was known as a brilliant climber and one of the few men who thought that it was possible to climb the Matterhorn. He'd even gone to the unheard-of lengths of organizing his own expeditions. He was happy to take money from foreign clients and always tried to make sure that they also employed as many of his friends and family as possible, but if he went on the mountain he did so on his own terms. Whymper knew exactly where he stood: 'Carrel clearly considered the mountain a kind of *preserve*' and regarded all attempts on the mountain other than his own 'as an act of *poaching*.'

Whymper's first encounter with Carrel set the pattern for things to come. They haggled about fees and how many other men would be needed. Eventually 'negotiations dropped off,' Carrel announced that he was staying put and Whymper headed for the mountain accompanied by his reluctant Zermatt guide. A couple of hours later they were surprised to be overtaken by Carrel and his brother. Carrel informed Whymper that he had changed his mind and had decided to make his own attempt on the mountain.

They didn't get far, though, and in the evening the Carrels retreated; but Whymper persuaded his Swiss guide to spend the night on the mountain. He had brought a tent with him from England but it was so difficult to pitch that they ended up wearing it like a blanket instead. Huddled together in the freezing cold, they lay awake listening to huge avalanches rumbling down the mountain. On the following morning, Whymper persuaded his guide to carry on, but, when they reached a difficult passage, the Zermatter abruptly announced that he was turning back and no amount of abuse or cajoling could persuade him otherwise. Whymper returned to the bottom disappointed, but he had had his first taste of the Matterhorn and he was hooked. The next year he would return 'to lay siege to the mountain until one or the other was vanquished.'

In December he was elected to the Alpine Club and the following summer he returned to Switzerland with the English climber R. J. S. Macdonald. They hired two Zermatt guides and trekked over to Breuil where they took on Luc Meynet as a tent bearer and headed back up the mountain. Meynet was known as 'the hunchback of Breuil'; Whymper described his legs as 'more picturesque than symmetrical' but Meynet was always enthusiastic and Whymper clearly liked him.

Unfortunately, their expedition started badly when Whymper led them all down the wrong path. They retraced their steps but after that things only got worse: one of the guides had a terrifying and near-fatal fall and, finally, after enduring a ferocious storm, the Zermatt guides once again turned their backs on the Matterhorn. At this stage Carrel appeared and agreed to take over if they would also hire his friend Pession as a guide. The five men managed to go further, but eventually Pession, too, lost his nerve and Carrel refused to carry on without him. Whymper was disgusted: 'Want of men made the difficulty, not the mountain.' He crossed the border to Zermatt, hoping to hire new guides, but he found no one who was willing. So yet again he went back across the Theodule Pass to Breuil, where Carrel and Meynet now informed him that they too were otherwise engaged, in their respective jobs of hunting and cheese-making, leaving Whymper to head back up the mountain to retrieve his tent, alone.

Tempted by glorious weather and a newfound sense of freedom, Whymper managed to climb further than anyone else had ever done before. He found the experience exhilarating, but ultimately he was no fan of 'solitary scrambling': it was frustrating to be held back by obstacles that two men could easily overcome but were impossible for one. And, as he found out, it was dangerous.

Rounding a corner on his way down, Whymper slipped and fell. He flew from rock to rock, smashing his head repeatedly and narrowly avoiding an 800-feet drop on to the glacier below. When he finally managed to come to a halt, the only way that he could stop the blood spurting out of a wound on his head was to cover it with a large lump of snow. He lost consciousness for several hours, but was eventually able to drag himself back down the mountain. It was a strange and unsettling experience, but not quite what he had imagined:

> I was perfectly conscious of what was happening, and felt each blow; but, like a patient under chloroform, experienced no pain. Each blow was, naturally, more severe than that which preceded it, and I remember thinking, 'Well, if the next is harder still, that will be the end!'... I think that in a very great distance more, consciousness as well as sensation would have been lost, and upon that I base my belief, improbable as it seems, that death by a fall from a great height is as painless an end as can be experienced.

A few days later, after a brief but frustrating convalescence at a local inn, he returned to the mountain for yet another attempt. Carrel had deigned to accompany him for a second time but, again, to Whymper's great annoyance, after the weather deteriorated Carrel refused to carry on and the whole party trooped back to Breuil. In desperation, Whymper turned to Meynet as an assistant for his fifth and final attempt that year, but the hunchback's enthusiasm was not matched by his skill as a climber and this attempt also ended in failure. Then, to Whymper's horror, when he returned to Breuil he found that Carrel and his brother had been engaged by his rival Professor Tyndall and were just about to set out for an attempt on the summit.

Whymper could do nothing but wait: 'I could not bring myself to leave until the result was heard, and lingered about, as a foolish lover hovers around the object of his affections, even after he has been contemptuously rejected.' A flag was seen near the summit, but something compelled Whymper to stay. Finally Tyndall's party returned and revealed that they had in fact turned back, a few hundred feet from the summit. Tyndall headed off down the valley, warning Whymper that the Matterhorn would never be climbed and offering to leave his tent for anyone who wanted it—'more, I am afraid, out of irony than for generosity.' Whymper travelled back to England, only to spend another year dreaming of the Matterhorn and how to get to the top.

In 1863, the Golden Age of Alpinism was at its height. Since its inception in 1858, members of the Alpine Club had added eleven more peaks to the record of British successes. Whymper's reputation was growing as an Alpinist and as an engraver, but there was only one thing that would satisfy him: the summit of the Matterhorn. In July he boarded a ship at Dover armed with two ladders and several items of luggage 'highly suggestive of housebreaking.' He hoped that these would enable him to succeed where Tyndall had failed, but had to pretend to be a circus performer in order to get his climbing equipment past unsympathetic customs officers.

Once again he crossed the Swiss border to Breuil where he engaged Carrel as a guide, but once again he was held up by the weather. The Matterhorn was so covered in snow that they both agreed it was futile to try to climb it, so they made a long circumnavigation of the mountain to look for new routes. When Carrel saw the north face, its huge cliffs constantly battered by falling rocks, he was more convinced than ever that the only way to climb it was from the south side, in Italy. When they returned to Breuil, the weather seemed to have improved so they collected Meynet and Carrel's brother and set off up the mountain once again. The rocks were varnished with ice, familiar landmarks had been splintered by frost and avalanches and the going was painstakingly slow. Suddenly out of nowhere came a gust of freezing air and within minutes they were in the middle of a fierce snowstorm. Down in the valley the sun was shining, but all around their tent thunder and lightning raged. On the next day they tried to carry on, but they all knew it was useless and yet another attempt ended in failure.

As Whymper describes in *Scrambles in the Alps*, at this stage he transformed himself from an unrequited lover into a betting man but, whatever the metaphor, his passion remained undimmed: 'I arrived at Chatillon at midnight on the 11th, defeated and disconsolate; but, like a gambler who loses each throw, only the more eager to have another try, to see if the luck would change; and returned to London ready to devise fresh combinations, and to form new plans.'

In the previous three years, Whymper had made no fewer than seven attempts on the Matterhorn from the Italian side and all of them had ended in failure. He knew that he and Tyndall weren't the only members of the Alpine Club who were interested in bagging the summit. In 1860 and 1861 the three Parker brothers—Alfred, Charles and Sandbach—had made two unguided ascents on the Swiss east face and T. S. Kennedy had also made an attempt in 1862. None of them had got far, but eventually Whymper began to think that there might be a possible route from the Zermatt side. He contacted A. Adams-Reilly, another British climber who had impressed him. Adams-Reilly was attempting to survey the unmapped regions of the Mont Blanc range and Whymper agreed to assist him in 1864 if he would join him for another attempt on the Matterhorn.

The season began well: Whymper joined A. W. Moore and Horace Walker to make a famous first ascent of the Barre des Ecrins and then he left them to climb with Adams-Reilly. Together with the great Chamonix guide Michel Croz, they made first ascents of Mont Dolent, the Aiguille de Trélatête and the Aiguille d'Argentière. Their work done, in the middle of July they headed for the Matterhorn. Whymper had high hopes but once again he was thwarted; waiting at the post office was a letter requiring him to return to Britain immediately on family business. There was nothing he could do about it—the mountains and his new route would have to wait. Like most members of the Alpine Club, Whymper had to work for a living. They might have seen themselves as cut from the same block as Arctic explorers, but all their brave deeds had to be carried out in their summer holidays. A few were lucky enough to cite on their Club membership forms, 'Profession: None' but most needed a job to support their Alpine ambitions.

A year later Whymper returned to the Alps, full of confidence and determined to make his mark: 'The programme which was drawn up for this journey was rather ambitious, since it included almost all the great peaks which had not then been ascended.' This time there were no collaborators: Whymper alone would make the decisions and test his own judgement. He was particularly keen to try out his new route on the Matterhorn and wanted to make another significant change in his approach to climbing. Previously most of his experience had been on rock, but in 1864 he had been hugely impressed by Michel Croz's skill and ease climbing on snow and ice. He had noticed that on many mountains there were huge snow gullies that often stretched high up the rock faces and hoped that one such gully might provide a route to the summit of the Matterhorn.

He hired another renowned guide, Christian Almer, and tried to engage Michel Croz for the season, but found to his annoyance that he was available only for the first couple of weeks. Whymper and his men started quickly, making the first ascent of the Grand Cornier and the second ascent of the Dent Blanche in a matter of days, before heading over to the Matterhorn to try out his new route. Having passed the east face many times over the previous years, Whymper had come to realize that, close up, it was not nearly as intimidating as it appeared from a distance. He had noticed how snow clung to its upper reaches throughout the year and reasoned that this must indicate that its slope could not be that severe. The guides were still sceptical, but eventually everyone agreed that it might be possible to ascend the east face via a large snow gully that ran from Matterhorn Glacier to a point high up on the south-eastern ridge.

On 21 June they set off. At first everything proceeded according to plan, but as they climbed higher Whymper began to notice a growing number of boulders flying down the gully. He kept his observations to himself, so as not to 'alarm the men unnecessarily,' but when a huge rock avalanche suddenly roared past them, there was nothing he could do to stop them from turning back. When they regrouped at the bottom, Whymper tried to persuade them to make a new attack, but no one was willing. 'Why don't you try to go up a mountain which *can* be ascended?' asked Almer. Croz reminded him that he would shortly have to join his other client. Finally, after one more vain attempt, Whymper agreed to set off towards Mont Blanc to continue their programme.

The next two weeks were an incredible success. Whymper and his men barnstormed through the Alps, making first ascents of the Aiguille Verte, the Grandes Jorasses and the Ruinette. In eighteen days, he estimated that they ascended almost 100,000 feet (30,480 metres). Today, most climbers travel around the Alps in trains and cable cars, but Whymper thought nothing of walking fifty miles in a day. Like most of the other Alpine Club men, he was a confirmed 'pedestrian' and even in his late fifties managed to walk from London to Edinburgh in eight days. No modern climber would think of repeating his 1865 season, but for Whymper this still wasn't enough. There was one remaining prize that meant more to him than any other mountain: the summit of the Matterhorn.

Croz had already left him and Almer still thought that another attempt was useless, so once again Whymper headed for Breuil in search of Jean-Antoine Carrel. As always, nothing was easy. Carrel was even more evasive than usual, but finally he agreed to accompany Whymper on another attempt from the Swiss side, on condition that if they failed, Whymper would engage him for a further attempt from the Italian side. Whymper retired to the local inn to prepare for their climb.

And then Fate intervened.

Fate may seem a fantastical and vague notion, but it gives a sense of the strange series of unforeseen events and bizarre coincidences that now conspired to bring Whymper's final attempt on the Matterhorn to its final dramatic climax. It began with Whymper being informed that an English traveller had fallen ill and was laid up further down the valley. After his own fall three years previously and his miserable convalescence, Whymper had vowed to go to the aid of any English traveller in need of help. So he put off his climb and headed down to help him. En route, he bumped into Carrel carrying some barometers for a mysterious 'foreign gentleman' who appeared to have many bags and many mules. Whymper reminded him that when he returned they would have to set off straight away. Carrel replied that a letter had just arrived reminding him of a longstanding agreement to travel with 'a family of distinction.' He was no longer available to climb the Matterhorn with Whymper.

The mysterious foreigner was Felice Giordano, a geologist from Turin and right-hand man of Quintino Sella, a government minister and founder of the Italian Alpine Club. Sella was passionate about climbing and hoped that by capturing the summit of the Matterhorn for Italy he would inspire others to take up the sport. Months earlier he had contacted Carrel and offered him the chance to lead a well-equipped attempt on the mountain. He would make a route to the top and then Giordano would follow in his footsteps. Everything had to be kept secret, particularly from Whymper.

When Whymper returned from playing sick-nurse at Valtournache, he bumped into Carrel once again, but Carrel insisted that he couldn't break his agreement. They had a drink together before Whymper retired to his bed. The next morning he woke up to news that Carrel had left at the head of a large party on a mission to climb the Matterhorn for the glory and honour of Italy. Whymper was livid, but there was nothing he could do: he'd been 'bamboozled and humbugged.' In a letter to Quintino Sella, Giordano complained: 'I have tried to keep everything secret, but that fellow whose life seems to depend on the Matterhorn is here, suspiciously prying into everything. I have taken all the competent men away from him, and yet he is so enamoured of this mountain that he may go up with others and make a scene.'

Whymper had already parted company with Almer and the other guides and couldn't even find a porter to take his bags back to Zermatt. And then, for the second time, Fate intervened.

Striding over the Theodule Pass came Lord Francis Douglas, brother of the Marquis of Queensberry. His career as a climber had begun four years earlier when he had scaled the walls of Edinburgh Castle and he had just made a hair-raising ascent of the nearby Ober Gabelhorn. Douglas offered to help take Whymper's bags and equipment back over to Zermatt and, before long, had agreed to join Whymper in an attempt on the Matterhorn. They planned to engage the Zermatt guide Old Peter Taugwalder, whose son had accompanied Douglas across the pass and who had recently discovered a possible new route up the Matterhorn from the Zermatt side. They headed back over the Theodule Pass, encouraged by the sight of bad weather that, Whymper hoped, would hinder Carrel's progress. The two men booked into the Monte Rosa Hotel and over dinner made plans for an ascent on the following morning. And then… in walked Charles Hudson, the Vicar of Skillington in Lincolnshire, revealing that he too was going to 'have a shot at the Matterhorn,' along with his young companion Douglas Hadow and the famous Chamonix guide Michel Croz.

After a brief but fraught discussion, Whymper and Douglas invited Hudson to accompany them, arguing that this would be safer than having two separate expeditions on the mountain at the same time. The vicar agreed, but insisted that they also take Hadow who, he claimed, 'has done Mont Blanc in less time than most men.' Whymper wasn't keen, but Hudson was adamant. And so Whymper, who had always been so meticulous in his planning, now agreed to join three other English climbers, none of whom he'd met before, let alone climbed with, on a route that he had never tried before with a guide who had left him three weeks ago doubting that the Matterhorn could be climbed. Fate.

On the following morning they set off and were all surprised by how easy it was to get to the north-east ridge. Taugwalder had brought two of his sons along and it was agreed that one of them would stay with them for the remainder of the climb. While the others set up camp, the Taugwalders carried on upwards to reconnoitre the following day's route. They came back with amazing news: 'Not a difficulty, not a single difficulty! We could have gone to the summit and returned today easily.'

The next morning they set off before dawn. Just as the Taugwalders had said, it was much easier than anyone had imagined. At any moment Whymper expected to see an Italian flag on the summit but, until then, all he could do was push on. Carrel had by this time received news of Whymper's latest attempt, but he was confident that the Englishman would never be able to make an ascent from the Zermatt side. He was wrong. The climbing did get tougher: when they had to move on to the north face they had to totally rearrange the party, Croz muttering, 'Now for something altogether different.' But after about an hour and a half, they all passed safely over the difficult part and then suddenly Whymper and Croz found themselves on an easy slope. Whymper couldn't believe it: he and Croz unroped and dashed for the top.

The Matterhorn! He had dreamt about it for years and now it was beneath his feet. They looked for signs of Carrel but saw nothing. Finally Whymper spotted his party 1000 feet below. They waved, they shouted, but still no response, so Whymper and Croz sent a torrent of rocks down towards them. At last they took notice: 'There was no mistaking about it this time. The Italians turned and fled.' Croz took off his shirt, put it on to the end of a tent pole and waved it like a flag.

Down in Breuil figures were spotted on the summit and everyone began to celebrate what they were sure was an Italian victory. Giordano dashed off a telegram to Quintino Sella: 'At 2 P.M. today I saw Carrel and Co. on the top peak of the Matterhorn; many others saw them as well as I... Whymper has gone off to make an attempt from the other side but I think in vain.'

While the Italians caroused down below, up on the summit the English climbers were paying homage to the view. For Whymper it was an overwhelming experience:

> The day was one of those superlatively calm and clear ones which usually precede bad weather. The atmosphere was perfectly still, and free from all clouds or vapours. Mountains fifty—nay, a hundred—miles off, looked sharp and near… There were the most rugged forms, and the most graceful outlines; bold, perpendicular cliffs, and gentle undulating slopes; rocky mountains and snowy mountains, sombre and solemn, or glittering and white, with walls-turrets-pinnacles-pyramids-domes-cones-and spires! There was every combination that the world can give, and every contrast that the heart could desire.

Today, most climbers are lucky if they stay on the summit for longer than ten minutes; the weather is very unpredictable and guides, who in the high season ascend the Matterhorn several times a week, have no interest in hanging around on the top. Whymper managed a whole hour—'one crowded hour of glorious life.' He made a few sketches, then it was time to descend.

At the last minute, Whymper stayed back to write out a list of their names to leave in a bottle on the summit, while the others roped up and started down. Croz was in the lead, then came Hadow, then Hudson, then Douglas and then Old Peter Taugwalder. Hadow had found the going tough on the way up and now found the descent even harder. Douglas became worried that if anything happened, Old Peter wouldn't be able to hold them, so, when they caught up, he asked Whymper and Taugwalder's son to tie on to their rope. Whymper watched from behind as Croz painstakingly moved down the slope, literally placing Hadow's boots into every foothold. Suddenly he saw a movement of Hadow's shoulders and heard a scream from Croz and a moment later he watched as the two men went flying off into the abyss, followed closely by Hudson and Douglas. Whymper and the Taugwalders braced themselves, the rope went taut and snapped: 'For a few seconds we saw our unfortunate companions sliding downwards on their backs, and spreading out their hands, endeavouring to save themselves. They passed from our sight uninjured, disappeared one by one, and fell from precipice to precipice on the Matterhorn Glacier below.'

At this very moment, a boy ran into the Monte Rosa hotel in Zermatt, shouting that he had seen an avalanche on the Matterhorn. No one took any notice, but when a grim-faced and solitary Whymper returned the following day, everyone realized the worst. He told them how he and the Taugwalders had just spent a night on the mountain, after seeing their four companions fall to their almost certain deaths. A search party was quickly despatched; they came back reporting that they had seen the bodies on the glacier through their telescopes, but there was no hope that anyone had survived. On the following morning, Whymper, two visiting English climbers and the Reverend Joseph McCormick, a friend of Hudson's and the British chaplain in Zermatt that summer, set off for the Matterhorn Glacier with their respective guides. None of the Zermatt men came, threatened with excommunication by their local priest if they worked on a Sunday.

The men found an awful scene. The bodies were naked and dismembered and there was blood everywhere. Whymper spotted a bearded jawbone and realized it was Michel Croz's. A crucifix was embedded in his cheek. In the remains of Hudson's jacket they found a prayer-book, a letter to his wife and his watch—stopped at 3:45. In Hadow's pocket they found an unbroken pair of glasses. It was a scene that would haunt Whymper for the rest of his life. In 1911, forty-six years later, he wrote: 'I have seen nothing like it before or since, and do not wish to see such a sight again.'

The Italians were still celebrating when Carrel returned to Breuil 'more dead than alive' and revealed to Giordano that Whymper had beaten them to the top. Giordano immediately sent off another telegram to Sella announcing that the battle had been lost, but adding that they were going to make a second attempt on the mountain. News of the disaster on the Swiss side didn't reach Breuil until 15 July. It didn't make it any easier for Carrel to recruit new climbers, but three days later, he finally made it to the top. Giordano tried to claim a sort of victory: they had proved that there was a feasible route from Breuil whereas 'it does not seem likely that any ascent would be attempted in a hurry from Zermatt.'

Over the next few weeks confused news of the accident was slowly spread around the Alps. There were several reports in Continental newspapers but, as yet, there were no eyewitness accounts and strange rumours began to circulate. In Chamonix local guides accused Old Peter Taugwalder of cutting the rope in order to save his skin. A Viennese newspaper countered that it was Whymper himself who had wielded the knife. The author, Alfred Meissner, wondered if this could have any moral justification: 'The Englishman could say: "I had no choice. I behaved like a general. I sacrificed the ones who were already doomed and thereby saved my own life and that of two others."'

Whymper's old rival, Tyndall, was also in the Alps that summer. He heard the news of the disaster from a mountain guide who clearly had confused more than just a few details: 'On quitting Gadmen next morning I was accosted by a guide who asked me whether I knew Professor Tyndall. "He is killed, sir," said the man—"killed upon the Matterhorn." I then listened to a somewhat detailed account of my own destruction, and soon gathered that, though the details were erroneous, something serious if not shocking had occurred.' Tyndall rushed to Zermatt where he became involved in a well-intentioned, but slightly bizarre, plan to abseil down the north face of the Matterhorn in order to look for Lord Francis Douglas' body. He sent a man to Geneva to buy 3000 feet of rope and tools to hammer steel spikes in the rock face and vainly waited in Zermatt for the weather to clear. It never did and, twenty days later, Tyndall was forced to abandon his plan. Three years later he returned to the Matterhorn and completed the first traverse of the mountain, taking nineteen and a half hours to climb up the Italian route from Breuil and down the Whymper route to Zermatt.

There was something strange and supernatural about the events on the Matterhorn that would keep the public fascinated for years to come. The men had set off on Thursday 13 July and the accident had occurred on Friday the 14th. After the accident, when the survivors reached the bottom of the mountain, they saw two mysterious crosses emerging out of the fog (a rare atmospheric phenomenon called a fog-bow). On the night that he disappeared, Lord Francis Douglas' former maid was reported to have heard him call her name out several times at their house in London. Journalists were strangely fascinated by the revelation that all the dead climbers lost their boots on the fall down to the glacier. Hadow's received particular attention: it was reported that he had arrived in the Alps without proper climbing boots and pundits speculated as to whether it was his inexperience as a climber or the poor state of his footwear that had caused the tragedy. Nannies everywhere kept the story alive for years to come, warning their male charges of the dire consequences of wearing 'the wrong sort of shoes.'

On 22 July Reverend McCormick wrote to *The Times* from Zermatt outlining the details of the accident, but no one was satisfied with his brief account. As the days went by, the Alpine Club found itself at the centre of a very modern media storm. *The Times* led the charge in an article on Thursday 27 July:

Why is the best blood in England to waste itself in scaling hitherto inaccessible peaks, in staining the eternal snow, and reaching the unfathomable abyss never to return?... Is it life? Is it duty? Is it common sense? Is it allowable? Is it not wrong?... What is the use of scaling precipitous rocks, and being for half an hour at the top of the terrestrial globe?... In the few short moments a member of the Alpine Club has to survey his life when he finds himself slipping, he has but a sorry account to give of himself. What is he doing there, and what right has he to throw away the gift of life and ten thousand golden opportunities in an emulation which he only shares with the skylarks, apes, cats and squirrels?

THERE HAD BEEN ACCIDENTS BEFORE, but nothing on this scale and nothing involving a peer of the realm. For the last ten years, mountaineering had been growing in popularity; suddenly the future of the sport had become a public issue. And though the language may be archaic, the questions asked by *The Times* have a decidedly contemporary ring. Could it ever really be worth risking your life for the sake of sport and could an activity like mountaineering ever be risk-free? In 1865 the members of the Alpine Club responded with fundamentally the same answers that they would give today: yes, it was dangerous but so were many other sports and the risks of mountaineering could be much reduced by simple precautions. What was needed was a full account of what actually happened; only then could any conclusions be drawn.

Mountaineering was in crisis and the only person who could clear things up was a twenty-five-year-old engraver from Lambeth who didn't want to talk.

After the accident, Whymper had been required to remain in Zermatt for a public inquiry. A local judge heard his testimony and that of the Taugwalders and concluded that the inexperienced Hadow was to blame for the accident. Whymper found the whole process difficult; he resented what he saw as his detention and was frustrated by the refusal of the tribunal to allow him to hear the others give their evidence. On 25 July he sent a letter to the president of the Swiss Alpine Club, asking him to forward it to the editor of the main Geneva newspaper. Hoping to correct what he saw as the rumours and errors circulating in the Continental press, he went through the expedition stage by stage, explaining that, although at the final moment his view had been partly obscured by a rock, he believed that Hadow had fallen first and dragged the others after him: 'a single slip, or a single false step, has been the cause of all this misery.'

On his journey back to England he found himself continually pestered by what he saw as impertinent questioners. Whymper himself came in for some criticism and he was conscious that the press was looking for someone to blame for the accident. He wanted to clear everything up by having the Alpine Club hold its own inquiry, but no one else was keen. Finally, the pressure got too much and he wrote a long and detailed letter to *The Times* that laid out the events for everyone to see.

In the early press reports there had been a lot of confusion over names: *Douglas* Hadow was confused with Lord Francis *Douglas*, who was mistakenly identified as the climber who slipped. Whymper believed, and maintained for the rest of his life, that if anyone was to blame for the accident it was Charles Hudson, for insisting on bringing Hadow along. But he was very wary of offending either Hudson's widow or Hadow's parents and didn't want to attach undue responsibility to any one person for what was, after all, an accident. In his letter to *The Times*, he praised Hadow's courage and strength, but also made clear that his 'want of experience' was apparent when they reached the difficult sections on the mountain. For the next couple of weeks the arguments continued to reverberate through the letters page of *The Times* but gradually the hysteria died down. The Alpine Club continued to mount a vigorous defence of climbing as a sport, claiming that mountaineers were cut from the same block as imperial explorers of Africa and the Arctic and that climbing mountains was good for British manhood. *The Times* was grudgingly won over but, as many commentators have since noted, the Golden Age of Alpinism was over: ended—not crowned—by Edward Whymper.

At the time Whymper was praised by everyone for his cool head and lucid prose, but there was one issue he raised that has never been explained to everyone's satisfaction and fuels controversy to this day. Why had Old Peter Taugwalder used such a weak rope to connect himself to Lord Douglas? Whymper had brought several ropes along for the ascent: 200

feet of manila rope, which had been endorsed by the Alpine Club; 150 feet of even thicker rope; and 200 feet of rope that he described as 'stout sash-line.' The thick ropes were intended for use between the climbers; the other rope, which was older and visibly thinner, was intended to be fixed on to the rocks on the difficult sections and then abandoned. But for whatever reason, the climbers never put up any fixed rope and Taugwalder used the older, thinner rope to tie himself to Lord Douglas.

In his account in *Scrambles in the Alps*, Whymper noted that as soon as he saw the broken end of this thin rope he knew that something was very wrong: 'It was not brought, and should not have been employed, for the purpose it was used. It was old rope, and compared with the others, was feeble… I saw at once that a serious question was involved, and made him give me the end.' Later he expanded on this: 'This had a very ugly look for Taugwalder, for it was not possible to suppose that the others would have sanctioned the employment of a rope so greatly inferior in strength when there was more than two hundred and fifty feet of the better qualities still remaining out of use.' In a footnote he further explained why this was so suspicious: 'because if Taugwalder thought that an accident was likely to happen, it was to his interest to have the weaker rope where it was placed.'

Over all, Whymper's account of the Taugwalders' behaviour on the mountain was far from flattering. In *The Times* he referred to them as 'utterly unnerved' by the accident and told how, when they reached the bottom, Taugwalder junior 'was able to laugh, smoke, and eat as if nothing had happened.' In *Scrambles* he added that they had actually asked not to be paid any monies owed to them by Lord Douglas. Whymper was confused at this request, then appalled when they explained to him that they were hoping that such a gesture would impress next year's clients. In private, Whymper was even more critical: he referred to their 'heartlessness that was perfectly revolting' and 'most unmanly fear for their own lives.' In 1939, when Frank Smythe was researching his biography of Whymper, he discovered a memorandum signed by John Jermyn Cowell and his son that took the allegations one stage further. Cowell was a lawyer who had served as Secretary to the Alpine Club. In his memorandum he related a conversation between himself and Whymper, in which Whymper revealed that the Taugwalders' behaviour had been so 'suggestive of personal danger to himself' that he had spent the night on the mountain with his back to a rock, ice-axe in hand, 'prepared to defend himself.'

It is difficult to know quite what to make of this. Frank Smythe himself wasn't sure; he recognized that Whymper was unfailingly honest but wondered if he might have misunderstood the Taugwalders' behaviour, preferring 'the explanation of nerves' on behalf of everyone involved to Whymper's more sinister interpretation. Could Whymper have really understood the nuances of the Taugwalders' dialect? And wasn't everyone under huge pressure? Though he never admitted it in public, Whymper was clearly rattled by the accident. Adams-Reilly described him as 'terribly cut up' and a local newspaper described how, in the wake of the accident, he had made a solemn declaration that he would 'never set foot on a mountain again.' The great alpinist, Leslie Stephen, was full of praise for Whymper but criticized the suggestion that Taugwalder had deliberately used a weak rope. Other mountaineers and historians have been harsher and have increasingly shown more sympathy for the Taugwalders than for Whymper. His critics have accused him of passing the buck: after all, they say, the ropes were all provided by Whymper and he should have noticed that the weakest rope was being used when he tied on to Taugwalder. Hadn't Old Peter saved Whymper's life? And was the old guide really so devious as to deliberately choose a weak rope?

To the mountaineering establishment, Whymper had always been somewhat of an outsider: a self-made man who dropped his aitches and showed a rather ungentlemanly obsession with getting to the top of one particular mountain. Those who met him in his grumpy old age found it easier to criticize him than to praise him and gradually more and more of the responsibility for the accident has been moved on to Whymper's shoulders, the accident being portrayed as the inevitable result of his desperation to get to the top of the mountain. Fuel was added to the fires by the mischievous Bishop Browne of Stepney who went to his grave claiming that, after a brief meeting with Whymper in 1865, he had discovered the real truth of 'the day when the rope broke,' a truth so terrible that he would never reveal it. And he never did.

Today, when you visit the museum in Zermatt and see the thin, gnarled section of the actual rope that broke, it is amazing to think that this could have ever been used for climbing. But, then again, the samples of manila rope in the same display case don't look that impressive either. Modern nylon rope is designed to take a fall; it has a built-in elasticity; none of the Victorian ropes had this quality. In its first editorial after the Matterhorn accident, *The Times* thundered: 'Above all their ropes must not break'—but this was a completely unrealistic assessment. Even official Alpine Club rope, introduced in 1864, was designed to hold only 14 stone falling 8 feet. Whymper himself was quite sophisticated in his use of the rope, but these were early days for everyone, and for many guides ropes were seen as an irritation. In some respects, the whole issue seems like a red herring: even if they had all been tied together with one of Whymper's stronger ropes, it is unlikely that it would have held the weight of four men falling and, if it had, Whymper and the Taugwalders might have been dragged off too.

Whymper was equivocal about the key issue of whether or not Taugwalder deliberately chose to put a weak rope between himself and Douglas. In a letter from August 1865, he wrote to another climber, Woolmore Wigram, that he had 'no reason to suspect even that this was done intentionally,' but then six years later when he published *Scrambles in the Alps* he left readers in no doubt that there was still an 'ugly look' about the whole affair. Whymper was a hundred feet away, busy sketching the summit, while the others were roping up so he never saw exactly what happened. He actually wrote a whole page of questions for the inquiry held in Zermatt to put to Taugwalder that he hoped would clear the issue up once and for all, but he was never allowed to see the answers and the evidence

wasn't made public until the 1930s. In his testimony, Taugwalder said that
he had no reason to suppose that the third rope was any weaker than the
others and that there hadn't been enough of the strong rope available to
tie himself on to the others. He stated: 'If I had found the rope used
between Lord Douglas and myself was too weak, I would have taken good
care not to tie myself to Lord Douglas with it and I would not have
wished to endanger him any more than myself. If I had found the rope too
weak, I would have recognized it as such before the ascent of the Matterhorn and would have rejected it.' Whymper had no clear evidence that
Taugwalder had deliberately chosen the weak rope, but, in 1915, his friend
Henry Montaignier revealed that Whymper 'suspected to the end of his
life that the old guide used that rope intentionally, fearing that some of
the others might slip during the descent.'

Whatever ill feeling might have been generated by the Taugwalders'
behaviour or Whymper's comments, the effect of the accident on the
progress of mountaineering was contradictory. Writing in 1911, Captain
Farrar, the President of the Alpine Club, noted that the death of Croz and
Hudson 'held up the tide of mountaineering for fully half a generation of
man,' but it didn't stop mountaineers from coming to the Alps. Within
three years of the accident Tyndall had made the first traverse of the Matterhorn, ascending from Breuil and descending on the Swiss side. Other
Alpine Club members continued to bag whatever unclimbed summits
remained in the Alps. Zermatt's growth was unstoppable; today local
hoteliers are happy to tell you how, in the wake of the accident, there were
in fact more visitors than ever. The town received an even greater boost in
1871 when Whymper published *Scrambles in the Alps*, the epic account of his
adventures on the Matterhorn and in the Alps. It was an instant success
and has been hailed as the best mountaineering book ever written, trans-
lated into several languages, and, amazingly, is still in print.

IN 1866 WHYMPER RETURNED TO THE ALPS, as he would do
for many years to come, but his zest for climbing had gone. In August

1865 he wrote that the very name of the Matterhorn 'is hateful to me.' By the following year his hurt had abated, but he still had no appetite for climbing mountains. In 1870 he sent a letter to an Alpine Club friend, the Reverend J. Robertson, complimenting him on his first ascent of the Schreckhorn, adding: 'I have always been ambitious of ascending it but such luxuries are no longer for me.' Whymper was redrawing himself as a man of science. He was quite willing to spend money on travel and to climb mountains, but not for the sake of mountaineering itself. He financed his own expeditions to Greenland and South America, where he made the first ascent of Chimborazo in order to study the effects of altitude on the human body. His interests ranged from glaciology to the study and collection of flowers and insects.

He is referred to first and foremost as a scientist by both Coulson Kernahan, a writer and journalist who became his friend, and his nephew Robert Whymper, who knew him well in his later life. Whether or not this change of focus was partly a response to criticism after the Matterhorn accident that mountaineering served no useful purpose it's impossible to tell, but there's no doubting Whymper's industry. He was awarded a gold medal by the Royal Geographical Society for his work on the aneroid barometer and was nominated to become a fellow of the Royal Society. His curiosity led him to work with the Ilford company on producing photographic plates and even to contact Peek Freans with a new method he had devised for preserving meat.

Whymper eventually took over his father's engraving business, but he recognized that photography was the future and that he would need other sources of income. *Scrambles* was an unexpected and continuing success and Whymper was a sought-after and well-paid lecturer. He toured the Continent and the United States and in 1894 he gave 48 lectures to over 50,000 paying customers. He wrote lucrative guide books to Mont Blanc and Zermatt and personally oversaw their distribution. For all his outward success, there was a rootlessness that never went away. His sister Annette remembered that after the Matterhorn accident he suffered from terrible insomnia that lasted for the rest of his life. In an era without psychologists and trauma counsellors, it was easy for someone like Whymper to turn in on himself. He relived the accident again and again in his nightmares and, though he regularly lectured about the Matterhorn, and climbed it again in 1874, he was very sensitive to people asking questions about the accident and made this very clear to anyone who had the temerity to do so.

Perhaps the most interesting appraisal of Whymper comes from Coulson Kernahan, who struck up a friendship with Whymper when he was living in Southend. Then in his early sixties, Whymper was occupying the top of a large house, separated from his housekeeper by two empty, curtainless floors. His 'barracks bare' rooms had no carpets and little furniture, but he ate and drank lavishly, if at strange hours of the day and night. He refused to talk shop and rarely mentioned his mountaineering achievements, but he revealed that he still dreamt about the Matterhorn and was tormented particularly by his own inability to help his companions as they hurtled to certain death. Whymper was a difficult man to get to know, but he made a deep and contradictory impression on Kernahan who found him both 'the most remarkable man I have ever known' and 'A sad, gloomy, if not indeed a pathetic figure.' Then, at the age of sixty-six, Whymper surprised everyone by getting married.

Though most of his life he seemed to be the archetypal confirmed bachelor, Whymper could be quite charming to women and had a soft spot for children. In an affidavit to Frank Smythe, Robert Whymper made the surprising revelation that his uncle's sexual appetite was 'distinctly cave-man,' adding that he had learned this from 'at least one who should have known.' Edith Lewin was the niece of his housekeeper in Southend and forty-five years younger than her beloved 'Ted.' Whymper's sister, Annette, didn't approve of the marriage: 'Love of dress and extravagance were her outstanding features.' For a while though, at least, Whymper was smitten. In a letter to a climber friend he referred to his forthcoming marriage as his attempt to 'retire from civilization' and 'devote such time as remains to me to love and luxury and to digging (or to superintending the digging of) potatoes.' They had their first 'cub' a couple of years later and Whymper gleefully reported her walking, squawking and setting fire to her nursery. Four years later the marriage fell apart: Edith sued for separation on the grounds of cruelty and Whymper didn't oppose. He sent a cutting from the *Daily Telegraph* to a friend in Switzerland concerning the divorce, with a handwritten addition: 'Glad to get rid of her.' But though he later tried to cut her out of his will, he does seem to have been hurt by what he saw as her 'desertion.'

TODAY WHYMPER'S NAME IS REMEMBERED on plaques in Zermatt, street signs in Chamonix and café hoardings in Breuil. *Scrambles in the Alps* is still available and the Matterhorn attracts thousands of mountaineers from all over the world, most of whom make their attempts via the Hornli Ridge. According to the Alpine classification it is graded AD—Assez Difficile—and is still an exposed and dangerous ascent. As you walk up to the first set of fixed ropes at the beginning of the climb, you pass a large plaque put up by the friends and family of a young American who died on the Matterhorn, pleading with you to keep away unless you have the equipment and the experience to make an attempt. Just before the summit there is another set of fixed ropes, allowing you to avoid the dangerous traverse on to the north face of the mountain where the accident occurred. In a good year many people do make it to the top and nearly all get back alive, but the ever-expanding cemetery at Zermatt is a sombre reminder of the dangers of taking on the Matterhorn.

Whymper himself is buried at Chamonix, his simple grave topped by a large craggy stone recording the passing of 'Edward Whymper: Author, Explorer, Mountaineer.' He died, as in life, in solitude. On 9 September 1911, he arrived in Chamonix on one of his customary Alpine tours. He paid several visits to friends and acquaintances and then retired to his room. For years he had hated to see his own physical decline; he was gradually going blind and was continually worried about his heart. He had broken his heel, his collarbone and his head on a couple of occasions. In his last letters, you sense a winding-up of his affairs. On his last birthday, he donated a portrait of Michel Croz to the Alpine Club, writing that this year he had decided to give, not receive, presents. He added: 'Tears do not often come to my eyes but when I think of the miserable end of this grand guide they come out.' Now in a quiet hotel in the shadow of Mont Blanc, he locked the door behind him and died, as his nephew recorded, 'after keeping a record of his sensations as he felt death stealing on him.'

Whymper was undoubtedly a difficult man. He was prickly and arrogant, but he was also obviously much more sensitive than he cared to reveal. You can't imagine him asking for sympathy, but it's hard not to be struck by the deeply melancholy tone at the end of *Scrambles*. He had spent five years obsessed with getting to the top of the Matterhorn, only to see 'triumph turned into tragedy' within a matter of hours. The mountains gave him his greatest joys and deepest sorrows: 'and with these in mind I say, climb if you will, but remember that courage and strength are nought without prudence, and that a momentary negligence may destroy the happiness of a lifetime.'

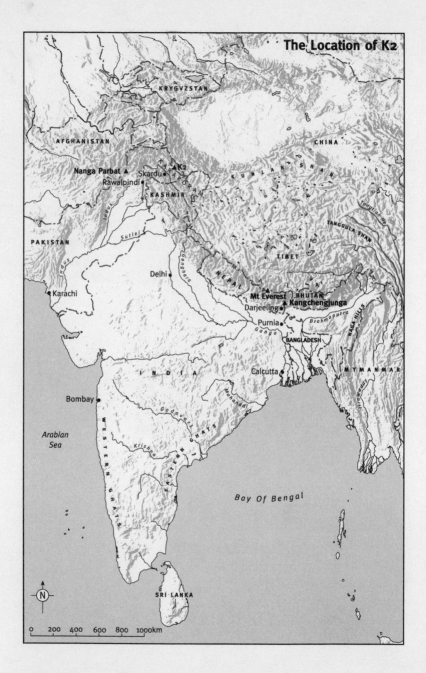

The Location of K2

≒ CHAPTER 3 ≒

High Society

Edward Whymper was not one to hand out praise lightly. He wrote a couple of articles eulogizing his favourite Alpine guides, but, other than these, all his books dealt with his own adventures and his own pet interests. All except one: a rather enigmatic pamphlet written in February 1909, towards the end of his life. Entitled *A Right Royal Mountaineer*, it celebrated a climber who was 'a master of the art of travel.' According to rumours that Whymper had heard, 'his career has been checked in the West... but it is reported that he has turned his attentions to the East... On "the Roof of the World," there is space enough for him to eclipse his conquest of the Mountains of the Moon.' It was all very mysterious stuff, but then again Whymper's subject was no ordinary man: he was Luigi di Savoia, the Duke of Abruzzi, heir to the throne of Italy and one of the world's greatest explorers, and he was about to set off for K2, the second highest mountain in the world.

He was born in 1873, the son of Prince Amedeo, a member of the Italian royal family who was briefly the King of Spain. In theory, Luigi was near the front of the queue for the throne of Italy, but in practice he had very little chance of getting there, so he turned his energies elsewhere. At the age of six he was enrolled in military school and ten years later he made his first round-the-world voyage as a midshipman. In 1890 he was given the honorary title 'The Duke of Abruzzi.' His aunt, Queen Margherita, encouraged him to learn how to climb and by the age of twenty-one he had made enough ascents in the Alps to be invited to join the Alpine Club in London.

For the next twenty years, he roamed the world looking for new peaks to climb. His first achievement came in 1897, when he and a party of Italians made the epic first ascent of Mount St Elias. Before McKinley was discovered, this was thought to be the highest peak in North America. It is a remote and inaccessible mountain and even today it is considered a real challenge for most climbers. Two years later, in 1899, Abruzzi joined the international 'race' to the North Pole, taking an Italian expedition to the Arctic for a year. It was a long, hard campaign: their ship got stuck in the ice, one man died and several members of his party were ravaged by frostbite. The Duke himself lost one of his fingers; his only consolation prize was a new world record for reaching the furthest north: latitude 86 degrees 34 minutes, 206 nautical miles from the pole. Six years later he headed for the remote Ruwenzori mountains of central Africa where he made several first ascents in the fabled 'Mountains of the Moon.' These expeditions turned him into one of the most famous explorers of his time, but today he is principally remembered for his expedition to K2 in 1909.

He was not the first climber to take on the second highest mountain in the world, nor was he the first traveller to explore this remote wilderness, but his expedition left an indelible mark on K2. One glance at a modern map shows that this is a part of Pakistan that will be forever Italian: the Negrotto Col, the Savoia Glacier, the Filippi Glacier, the Sella Pass—all features named after members of this expedition.

K2 is 28,267 feet (8616 metres) of snow, ice, rock and unremitting steepness. It is 700 feet (213 metres) shorter than Everest, but most mountaineers agree that it is the harder peak to climb. K2 was first measured in 1856 by Lieutenant T. G. Montgomerie, a surveyor for the Great Trigonometric Survey of India. While his assistant Henry Godwin-Austen took notes, Montgomerie measured a group of mountains 130 miles away with his theodolite. 'I have just seen a fine peak far away in the distance,' he said, with typical British understatement. It was K2. When Montgomerie enquired about it, he discovered that this mountain was so remote that the local people didn't seem to have a name for it, so it was logged as Karakoram 2, the second peak measured in the Karakoram range, or K2 for short. The name stuck, though over the years it has been known by a variety of epithets: the killer mountain, the mountaineer's mountain, the savage mountain.

The Duke chose K2 for one very simple reason: he wanted to break the world altitude record, which in 1907 had been set at 24,000 feet (7315 metres) by two Norwegian climbers, Carl Rubenson and Monrad Aas. In the official account of the Duke's K2 expedition, written by Filippo de Filippi, this was transformed into the slightly more noble motive of exploring the effects of altitude on the human physique, but in the Duke's own writing he made it clear that the simple desire to get to the top was paramount. Initially he had been interested in Everest, but in 1909 it was impossible for any foreign mountaineer to get permission to travel through the two closed kingdoms of Nepal and Tibet on either side of it. K2 also had the advantage of having several other mountains nearby which were also very high. If he couldn't get up K2, the Duke hoped that one of these might give him a second crack at the altitude record.

Abruzzi may have also had another motive for heading off on a long expedition. For two years he had been romancing a wealthy American heiress, Katherine Elkins, but their relationship broke down in the winter of 1908 when he had been refused permission to marry her ('his career in the West was checked' as Whymper noted obliquely in his pamphlet). Under royal custom, he could visit as many brothels and have as many affairs as he wanted, but when it came to marriage he couldn't simply choose a commoner. American newspapers were convinced that the Duke had gone off to Pakistan to hide a broken heart. The Duke said nothing.

He and his party left Italy in March 1909 with over 13,000 lbs of luggage. Over the years he had built up a strong team of climbers and explorers, who accompanied him on most of his travels. He took seven guides and porters from Courmayeur in the Alps, four of whom had already been to the Himalayas. His cartographer was Federico Negrotto, a lieutenant in the Italian Navy; Filippo de Filippi was the expedition doctor; and Vittorio Sella once again joined the Duke as his official photographer.

Sella was, and probably still is, the world's greatest mountain photographer. There were two key influences on his life: his father Guiseppe Venanzio, one of the earliest photographers in Italy, and his uncle Quintino, the founder of the Italian Alpine Club. Vittorio was encouraged to go climbing from an early age and by the age of twenty-three he was a strong enough climber to make the first winter ascent of the Matterhorn. 'This expedition is beyond doubt the most remarkable that has ever been made during the winter season,' congratulated the *Alpine Journal* in London. Sella spent the next ten years climbing and photographing in the Alps before making a series of expeditions to the Caucasus. His reputation continued to grow in spite of a bizarre accident he had on a trip to England in 1892. He had crossed the Channel and was on a train heading for London when he made the terrible mistake of poking his head out of the window as it was passing through a tunnel. Sella suffered severe head injuries and for two weeks he lay unconscious in a hospital in Folkestone. Then, to everyone's amazement, over the next six weeks he made a full recovery.

In 1897 he was invited to accompany the Duke of Abruzzi on his expedition to Mount St Elias, and nine years later he also went to the Ruwenzori, where he took some of his most remarkable photographs. When Sella was first approached by Abruzzi for K2 he wasn't keen at all, but eventually he was persuaded to take part; for someone who made his name photographing remote parts of the world, Sella was an uncertain traveller. He suffered from sea-sickness and had a very sensitive stomach, and the early pages of his K2 diary were full of references to how homesick he was feeling. He had tremendous respect for the Duke but he frequently bridled at having to follow his orders.

Today it is an eight-hour flight from Europe to Pakistan; it took Sella and the Duke almost two weeks in an ocean liner. En route they passed through the Suez Canal and dipped into the nude cabarets of Port Said. Sella didn't approve; he made a brief note in his diary: 'Miserable spectacle of semi-nude young women.' The ship finally docked at Bombay on 9 April and two days later they arrived at Rawalpindi. They parcelled out their equipment into numerous small loads and started their long journey north to K2, having chosen to go via Srinigar, the capital of Kashmir.

When they arrived a week later, the Duke spent several days organizing his supplies and equipment and enjoying the colonial hospitality of Sir Francis Younghusband, the local British 'Resident.' Kashmir was then one of the protectorates of the British Empire, ruled by a local maharajah. His territory was enormous: it extended from Afghanistan in the west to Tibet in the east, and from China in the north to India in the south. K2 and the Karakoram mountains lay in the far north of his territory in a province called Baltistan.

It took another two weeks for the Duke and his men to reach Skardu, the last city before K2. They travelled in a huge caravan that was frequently augmented by local dignitaries, come to pay their respects. This part of their trip was tough but luxurious: Abruzzi had his own 'tiffin-coolie' who ran after him with a large picnic basket, and at night the travellers slept on portable beds. The Italians were all intrigued with the racial characteristics of their Balti porters. Other explorers had been critical of the 'Baltis' but de Filippi was full of praise for their honesty and good humour. He was less impressed by their standards of hygiene: 'The smell of these natives is unbearable even in the open air, and if you get leeward of them it will simply take your breath away.' It was not recorded what they made of him.

Then, as now, all the Duke's travel arrangements in Pakistan were incredibly complex and constantly subject to bureaucratic scrutiny. He had to employ more than eight different officials to supervise his porters and 'incessantly interfere with, worry and keep them in a state of perpetual excitement.' Each porter was given a token that they could convert into rupees at the end of their particular leg of the journey. There were so many of them that the Duke had to bring almost half a ton of small change, requiring him to hire even more porters to carry the wages for the others.

When he finally arrived in Skardu, the Duke was greeted by an orchestra and yet more local dignitaries. Sella unpacked the cine camera that he had taken along for the first time on his travels, and filmed a polo match that was laid on in their honour. The Duke set up the first of a series of meteorological stations with which he wanted to make comparative measurements along their route to K2, and purchased more provisions. Then they continued on towards Askole, the last village before K2. Until the 1950s, the only way to get there was to cross the River Indus in a huge rickety barge, which was reputed to have been used by Alexander the Great. The Duke and his party all got across safely and Sella even managed to do some more filming on the way.

Then, as now, arrival at Askole meant taking on new porters. Abruzzi clearly enjoyed the complex logistical puzzles of setting up an expedition and was constantly rearranging all his supplies and equipment—he had a degree in mathematics and had spent most of his early life in the Italian Navy. On 16 May, they left with 260 porters. (This might seem like a lot, but he was travelling light when compared with a Japanese expedition from the mid 1970s, which left with a small army of 1500 men.)

After four days he and his men caught their first sight of the Baltoro Glacier, their 'highway' to K2. Outside the Arctic and Antarctic, the biggest glaciers in the world are found in the Karakoram. The Baltoro is 35 miles long—a huge body of compacted snow and ice, surrounded by mountains on either side, which slowly and imperceptibly moves downwards, carrying on its surface tonnes of rock and rubble from the adjoining peaks. It bears no resemblance to the transparent lozenge of popular imagination: from a distance it looks like a huge sand pit but, close up, the sand turns out to be a mass of rocks that range in size from coarse gravel to large boulders. It is a difficult surface to walk on and you have to always be on your guard.

In his expedition report, de Filippi described its snout as looking like 'a huge black monster, crouching with a flattened back in the bottom of the valley.' It was an amazing sight: 'No Alpine valley has the elements of anything even remotely similar to this vast roadway of ice between its precipitous walls. It is beyond all comparison.' For the Europeans, the glacier was an object of scientific curiosity, but for the porters it was something to be wary of: 'they kept looking at the glacier as if they had an obscure consciousness of the life animating the huge mass. It is so seemingly inert, yet so full of motion and ceaseless transformation, that one gets an impression as of something furtive and insidious.'

After four days, the Duke's party stopped at Urdukas, a group of rocks that face the spectacular Trango Towers. It is a stunning vantage point and the last real green patch before K2. It was designated as their base camp and the site of another meteorological station. Half the porters went back to Skardu and ten of the best remaining men were chosen to act as high-altitude porters and kitted out accordingly. For the first time, but not the last, the Duke was delayed by bad weather. It was a frustrating experience for everyone, but they tried to make the best of it. Sella took some photographs and then joined the others who were attempting to measure the flow of the glacier. They built a large cairn on the central moraine of the glacier and measured its position precisely with their surveying equipment. When they returned to the same spot two and a half months later, they discovered that it had moved 361 feet down the valley in 62 days—almost 6 feet a day.

This was also the first time that de Filippi noticed the effects of high altitude: 'When we stooped down to tie our shoes or twist our puttees, we would be caught by a slight sense of oppression on standing up again, and obliged to take four or five breaths.' Altitude is the hidden enemy of all mountaineers; its effects are complex, insidious and still far from understood. At high altitude, the air pressure is reduced so the amount of oxygen that a climber absorbs with each breath is diminished. In order to compensate for this, it is necessary to respire more deeply and more frequently. It is common to feel slightly short of breath at altitude, but it also has some other, more unpleasant, side-effects. Headaches, dehydration, loss of appetite and insomnia: all these are occupational hazards for anyone who wants to climb high mountains. Occasionally, these symptoms can develop into what is called acute mountain sickness (AMS); worse still, AMS can lead to two very unpleasant and life-threatening conditions: high-altitude cerebral oedema and high-altitude pulmonary oedema, an accumulation of liquid on the brain or on the lungs. Today there are drugs designed to prevent the onset of mountain sickness, but most experts agree that the traditional method of taking the walk into a mountain in slow gradual stages is still the most effective way of 'acclimatizing' to high altitudes.

After Urdukas, the Duke's party encountered fields of 'ice pyramids,' enormous jagged spikes of ice poking out of the moraine sometimes over 70 feet high. They were an extraordinary sight: 'like a graveyard with rows of tombstones, or a river dotted with fleets of white linen sails.' Nothing, though, could compare to their first sight of K2 three days later from Concordia. It is a large open space, where three glaciers terminate: the Baltoro, the Godwin-Austen and the Vigne glaciers. The view from the middle of Concordia was overwhelming: to the east soared the Gasherbrums; to the west the beautiful Mitre Peak and Crystal Peak flanking the Baltoro Glacier; to the south the fluted snow ridge of Chogolisa; and, standing proudly on its own, two miles to the north, K2 itself. Until this point, de Filippo's expedition book is very dry and scientific, but here he just can't stop the passion from coming through:

> Down at the end, alone, detached from all the other mountains, soared up K2, the indisputable sovereign of the region, gigantic and solitary, hidden from human sight by innumerable ranges, protected from invasion by miles and miles of glaciers. Even to

get within sight of it demands so much contrivance, so much marching, such a sum of labours. Its lines are ideally proportioned; the steepness of its sides, its ridges and its glaciers are appalling. For a whole hour we stood absorbed. We gazed, we minutely inspected, we examined with our field glasses the incredible rock wall. The atmosphere grew gradually thicker until even the last spectral image disappeared. The vision was gone.

In a speech that he gave on returning to Italy, the tight-lipped Duke was equally enthusiastic: 'Nothing could compare to this in terms of Alpine beauty, it was a world of glaciers and crags, an incredible view which could satisfy an artist just as well as a mountaineer.'

There are three other peaks close to K2 that are also over 8000 metres high—Broad Peak, Gasherbrum 2 and Hidden Peak—but none of them had anything like the impact of K2. The Duke's men immediately saw its resemblance to the Matterhorn and the similarity has been noted many times since then. Like the Matterhorn, from certain angles K2 looked as if it might be a perfect pyramid but, as they would discover, it was much more complicated than that.

Sella quickly set to photographing K2 and the surrounding peaks— or at least, he attempted to. As he discovered again and again, mountains are very frustrating subjects. In some senses, the best time to photograph mountains in the northern hemisphere is the winter, because the skies are usually clearer. The problem is that winter also means short days and very low temperatures so it's much harder, if not impossible, to travel in mountainous regions. In summer it is much easier to move around but the weather tends to be more unsettled and the skies are cloudier. To add to any photographer's woes, big mountains tend to generate their own peculiar weather patterns, and that usually means even more clouds—so you just can't win. Sella did come back with an amazing set of photographs from the Karakoram but his diary is a testament to just how frustrating the experience was.

Not only did he have to put up with unco-operative weather, but he felt that he had a group of companions who didn't share his aesthetic tendencies. Today Lodovico Sella is the director of the family archives at the Sella Foundation in Biella. He recalls one particular incident in Sella's diary when, on the way in to K2, he had gone to hunt for birds and came back to camp full of the wonders of everything he had seen:

> Vittorio tries to explain the beauty he has seen up there, but the others seem to be completely insensible. He grumbles and he wrote down: 'I don't know what I am doing here. I have never seen such dumb company. Instead of looking all around at the beauty of all this, they seem to do nothing else but think of climbing the mountain.' You know what I think—Vittorio was wrong. They were there to climb the mountain, not to be philosophical about it. Vittorio was like that, very poetic at moments. You can see it in his handwriting, it is the handwriting of an artist.

The Duke was so eager to get going that on the following day he left the others at Concordia and set off with a small advance party to explore the glaciers that surround K2. Everyone else followed a couple of days later, to set up an advance base camp on a strip of moraine at the foot of the southern wall of K2. The site is still used by most modern expeditions. The Duke had planned well and, though conditions in their camp could hardly be described as luxurious, it was well equipped and reasonably comfortable. Regular parties came up from Urdukas with supplies of fresh eggs and mutton and they even continued to receive post and newspapers from Europe. For the next six weeks they explored the area around K2, searching for a potential route to the summit.

One other expedition had attempted to climb K2, seven years earlier. It was led by Oscar Eckenstein, a British climber who today is remembered as the man who invented modern crampons and ice-axes; it was not a success. Eckenstein's problems began on the way in, when he was unexpectedly refused permission to enter Kashmir. While he stayed back to negotiate his way across the border, the rest of his team carried on. They were an ill-matched group: two Austrians, Heinrich Pfannl and Victor Wessely; a Swiss doctor, Guillarmod; and two other Englishmen, Guy Knowles and Aleister Crowley—the notorious Satanist. They all started arguing as soon as they arrived at the mountain. Crowley thought that he saw a route up the south-east ridge, which he claimed would get them to the top 'given one fine day.' When Eckenstein eventually rejoined them he overruled Crowley and decided that it would be better to attempt K2's north-east ridge. Crowley grudgingly agreed and promptly fell ill. The two Austrians were sent up to begin the attack on the north-east ridge but one of them, Pfannl, also developed severe pulmonary oedema and had to be evacuated back to Urdukas.

Things went from bad to worse: the weather was appalling and soon everyone was ill. Crowley had an attack of malaria and began waving his gun around and, whether out of madness or greed, the other Austrian, Wessely, ate all their reserve supplies. They finally admitted defeat and fled from the Karakoram. With his tongue in his cheek, Crowley claimed a world first for spending sixty-eight days on glaciers, but he wasn't sure that it was a record worth boasting about: 'I hope I may be allowed to die in peace with it. It would be a sorry ambition in anyone to grasp my laurels and I can assure him that to refrain will bring its own reward. Of these sixty-eight days, only eight were fine, and of these no three were consecutive.' By comparison, Abruzzi's expedition was a model of good teamwork but they didn't fare any better when it came to the weather. In the two months they stayed at K2 there were similarly never more than three consecutive days of good weather.

The Italians' most successful foray on to K2 was in fact their first. When they arrived at K2 the Duke's guides agreed that the south-east ridge looked the most promising. Abruzzi himself wasn't so sure, so he went off to look at the other side of the mountain while they made a preliminary reconnaissance. When both parties reconvened, the Duke was persuaded that if the guides could prepare a route for him up the south-east ridge, a small party might be able to make an attempt on the summit. On 30 May they all set off, accompanied by several huge black crows that had arrived out of nowhere to scavenge at their camp, and the ten Baltis they had chosen as high-altitude porters. The Italians had brought extra clothing and equipment along for them but none of these local men had any climbing experience and they were very nervous.

A new camp was established at the foot of the ridge and the porters and guides began to ferry loads up the mountain. Initially everyone was very optimistic: though they were 12,000 feet from the summit they thought that there was a chance of reaching their goal with just two further camps. Even if they couldn't make it to the top, the Duke believed that to reach the shoulder of K2 would be an achievement in itself. As he subsequently realized, K2 would not give in so easily. After barely climbing 1000 feet, the Balti porters flung down their packs and refused to carry on. From now on, the guides themselves had to carry all the equipment up and down the mountain.

Eventually even the tough men from the Alps became disheartened: 'The guides were unanimous in telling the story of the incredible optical illusions they suffered, all due to the deceptiveness of the terrain. Slabs of rock which at a few yards distant looked like gentle and easy inclines, turned out to be a little less than perpendicular. It was impossible to estimate the grade of the slopes or the distances between salient points of the ascent.'

Finally, after five days, the Duke decided that it was time to call a halt and they retreated back to camp. His men had reached 20,500 feet (6248 metres), but they realized that it was impossible to go on if they had to carry everything themselves, and they were doubtful that they would be able to find good places to erect a tent further up the mountain.

The Duke didn't lose heart, though. He still hoped that the north-west ridge might provide a route to the summit and quickly moved his camp around the corner to the glacier on the west of K2. This time they were, if anything, even less successful. Abruzzi thought it would be possible to get on to the ridge by climbing a saddle of rock and ice that ran from east to west along the glacier, but when they reached the top, they found their way blocked by huge overhanging ice cornices. As a fallback position, the Duke had hoped that, even if he couldn't get on to the north-west ridge, he might have been able to cross over this saddle and explore the northern, Chinese, face of K2. But again his optimism was short-lived: on the other side they were confronted by an almost vertical wall of ice. De Filippi was philosophical about their predicament: 'As a reward for all his labours the Duke had thus utterly destroyed the hopes with which he had begun the ascent.'

Abruzzi went back to the other side of the mountain, hoping to now try a third option, the north-east ridge. Once again, things didn't go well. The Balti porters began to fall ill with altitude sickness and, though they tried to maintain their good humour, they all clearly wanted to head back home. The Duke and his men persevered, making ascents of nearby Skyang Kangri and Windy Gap in order to get a better look at the north-east ridge, but it was all in vain. When in occasional breaks in the cloud the east face became visible it only depressed the Italians further: 'It looked like another mountain entirely; and of all the manifold aspects of the colossus, this is certainly the most imposing. Alas it is also such as to annihilate the last remnant of hope that might linger in the mind of the mountaineer.'

As the weeks rolled on, morale further declined. The Duke found the weather deeply frustrating: there might be blue skies in the morning but all too often, within a couple of hours, the cloud would roll in and they would spend 'long tedious hours in the tent learning off by heart the four pages of the newspaper.' Sella admired Abruzzi's tenacity, but from early on he thought that they would be better off setting their sights a little lower and aiming for one of the other mountains nearby. He was particularly enamoured with Chogolisa, a long elegant peak that they faced at the far end of the Vigne Glacier, and he tried to persuade the Duke to let

him take a party to explore it. In early June he broached the question with
Abruzzi, who agreed to consider it. '*Speriamo,*' Sella wrote in his diary: 'We
hope.' Another full month would pass before he got his wish.

In the time they spent in the Karakoram, there were no serious accidents but everyone was affected by the altitude. After falling into a crevasse, one of the guides, Alex Brocherel, developed a severe hacking cough
and his nephew Enrico spent a couple of days mysteriously coughing up
blood. He subsequently recovered but it was an unsettling experience.
Sella's assistant, Ernesto Botta, never felt right after Urdukas and was frequently ill. De Filippi, himself a doctor, noted that during idle periods
everyone tended to feel heavy-headed. They lost their appetites and found
it hard to sleep. He speculated that exercise was vital to promote 'the elim-
ination of noxious products.' They were all awed by the scenery, but they
also found it intimidating: 'Profound silence would brood over the valley,
even weighing down our spirits with indefinable heaviness. There can be
no other place in the world where man feels himself so alone, so isolated,
so completely ignored by Nature, so incapable of entering into communion with her.'

After six weeks, the Duke finally accepted that they weren't going to
be able to make an ascent of K2 and Sella got his wish. They all moved
several miles down the glacier and turned their attention to Chogolisa.
When they left, K2 was once again surrounded in cloud. By now it had
assumed a personality for the Duke—brutal yet coquettish, mocking his
efforts: 'The mountain which in our eyes had always stood out as the most
splendid in all this region perhaps to tempt us to try to reach the summit,
now that we were about to leave was hiding itself from us, as if it didn't
want to show itself to someone who couldn't climb it.'

From a distance, Chogolisa looked like an easy climb, but again
appearances proved deceptive. The weather continued to be awful and in
the end the Duke's attempt turned out to be an epic feat of endurance and
tenacity. It took them eighteen days to get from Concordia to a camp high
up near the summit. When the weather finally broke, the Duke and two

guides made a dash for it, but 200 feet from the top they were forced to turn back when they encountered impossibly dangerous cornices. Abruzzi's disappointment was tempered by the fact that in reaching 24,600 feet (7498 metres) on Chogolisa he had managed to set a new world altitude record.

Towards the end of July, after two months in the Karakoram, the Duke headed back to Italy. He was sure that they had explored all the possibilities when it came to K2, but doubtful that it could ever be climbed. When later he gave a lecture to the Italian Alpine Club in Milan, he summed up his frustrations: 'After having carefully examined all three sides, south, east and west, we realized that all our attempts to reach the summit were in vain and that we had to admit that we were beaten. If anyone else does succeed in getting to the top, it will be a pilot not a mountaineer.' De Filippi, in his expedition book, expanded on the Duke's feelings about K2. The problem wasn't a question of how high it was but rather how difficult it was to get there: 'The Duke was finally obliged to yield to the conviction that K2 is not to be climbed. This is not because of the mountain itself, but rather as a result of the remote situation of the giant, the impossibility of camping near its base for more than a few weeks and finally the unfavourable climatic conditions.'

TODAY K2 IS STILL A DIFFICULT MOUNTAIN TO REACH BUT, like most other remote corners of the world, it is fast succumbing to the inexorable demands of global tourism. In 1909 it took the Duke two weeks to get from Europe to Pakistan; in the summer of 2000 we made the journey in less than a day. If the availability of Coca-Cola can be taken as a modern-day index of accessibility, then even K2 base camp hardly counts as remote, the nearest vendor being just five days' walk away at the campsite of Paiju.

And now the issue of accessibility has taken on a slightly different twist. When the Duke went to K2 in 1909, it was part of the British protectorate of Kashmir and Jammu. Today Kashmir no longer exists as an independent state, and K2 and the Karakoram mountains have become a battlefield between Pakistan and India. The problems started at partition in 1949 when the Hindu Maharajah of Kashmir was given two choices: become the ruler of an independent state or join either Muslim Pakistan or Hindu India. While he was still making up his mind, his territory was invaded by Muslim tribesmen from Pakistan. The Maharajah turned to India for help and Indian troops have been stationed in Kashmir ever since. In 1949, after a brief war between Pakistan and India, the UN brokered a truce that gave two-thirds of Kashmir to India and the remainder, including K2, to Pakistan. Since then there have been two more full-scale wars between the two powers and the situation in Kashmir remains still far from resolved. In recent years it has become particularly bad: guerrillas from various Kashmiri independence movements have been sporadically at war with what they see as an army of occupation. Srinigar, the capital of Kashmir, used to be known as one of the world's most beautiful cities; today it has a reputation as one of the most dangerous.

When you get to Skardu you notice that the city is full of Pakistani soldiers and that there's a handpainted sign outside one of their barracks: 'Defenders of K2.' The conflict in Kashmir has spread into the mountains around it and now this whole area is part of the war zone. All along the route in to K2 you see military camps and mule trains bringing in supplies. Overhead helicopters clatter past, bringing up new troops or groups of journalists who are ferried in to see the latest Indian infringement of the Pakistani territory. Currently the main flashpoint is the 'line of control' that separated the two armies in the far north of Kashmir. Back in 1949, when the first wave of fighting ended, a ceasefire line was established between the advance positions of the Indian and Pakistani armies. Negotiators, however, didn't bother to redraw the new border line as far as the border with China and subsequent negotiations still left a 40-mile stretch of territory un-demarcated. No one ever thought that either side would be interested in fighting over the frozen wastes of the Siachen Glacier. Ironically, it was Western mountaineers' desire to make new 'conquests' that initiated the current fighting.

In the 1970s, the Pakistani government began allowing climbers to go beyond K2 into the Eastern Karakoram mountains, the area in which there was no recognized 'line of control.' When this was reported in Western climbing magazines and foreign maps started to include Siachen in Pakistan, the Indian government accused Pakistan of 'cartographic aggression,' claiming that this was in fact Indian territory. In 1984, they backed up their rhetoric with mountain troops and ever since then there has been sporadic fighting in one of the most remote and inhospitable corners of the world. At one stage in 1999, it was estimated that both sides were spending over a million pounds a day on lobbing artillery shells at each other over the disputed border. Climbers made their way up K2 and Broad Peak serenaded by intermittent bangs and explosions as an estimated 20,000 troops huddled together high in mountain camps.

It is difficult to know what the Duke of Abruzzi would have made of all this: he too was a military man and a great patriot, but there was always something rather detached and unworldly about him. Unlike most explorers and mountaineers of this period, there are very few photographs of the Duke. Whymper and Peary and Livingstone were always posing in front of the camera and their tough staring faces always left you in no doubt that these were men who meant business. The few images that there are of Abruzzi show him as a slightly world-weary character; when he is caught on camera he either assumes a stiffly formal pose or smiles cryptically. You sense that behind those eyes, there's someone who never took anything *too* seriously.

In many ways he was a rootless man, forever on the move and never really happy when at home in Italy. He was very modest about his own achievements and never sought to dramatize his adventures. His final days were spent in Somalia, where he built a huge model farm that he hoped would inspire the local people to take on Western farming methods.

When in 1933 he realized that he would soon die of prostate cancer, he visited Italy for the last time to say his goodbyes and then returned to Africa, to die. For sixty years he had roamed the world looking for new peaks to climb and new lands to discover; his final wish was that his burial place should be covered with a huge rock to keep the grave robbers away.

IN THE END, THOUGH ECKENSTEIN'S MEN actually got higher up K2, the Duke's expedition is still regarded as the foundation of the later climbs that finally reached the summit. Sella's superb photographs and Negrotto's maps were both inspiring and of huge practical value to generations of climbers to come. As his guides predicted, the south-east ridge was the best route to the top, and today it is universally known as the Abruzzi Ridge.

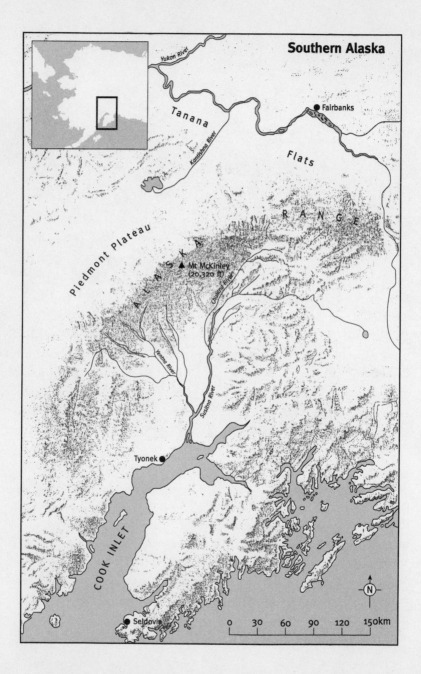

CHAPTER 4

The Shameless
Diary of an Explorer

Gold was discovered in the United States territory of Alaska in the 1870s. Prospectors reached the interior by following the westerly flow of the great Yukon River from Canada, close to the Arctic Circle. Steamers from Seattle brought them to the estuaries of the southern, Pacific, coast. Dividing north from south, visible for many hundreds of miles, was an apparently unbroken range of mountains, comprised of hundreds of sharp white peaks. For much of the time a curtain of cloud gathered along the roof of the barrier, but on clear days prospectors south and north saw a colossal dome rising from the centre, white and shining, far higher than anything around it.

Native Alaskans knew it simply as 'the big one.' The gold miners didn't care what it was called. For a few years, however, the men on the Yukon spoke of 'Densmore's Peak,' after a fellow prospector who ventured closer than most and returned with tales of its enormous size. But no descriptions of the mountain were published and it was unnamed on such maps as existed—until 1897. That year another prospector, exploring to the south of the range, wrote an account of his travels for the *New York Sun*. William Dickey told of dangerous river journeys, fierce timber wolves and monstrous bears that broke windows and climbed into cabins, scattering their occupants. But most of all he had been impressed by the sight of a stupendous mountain.

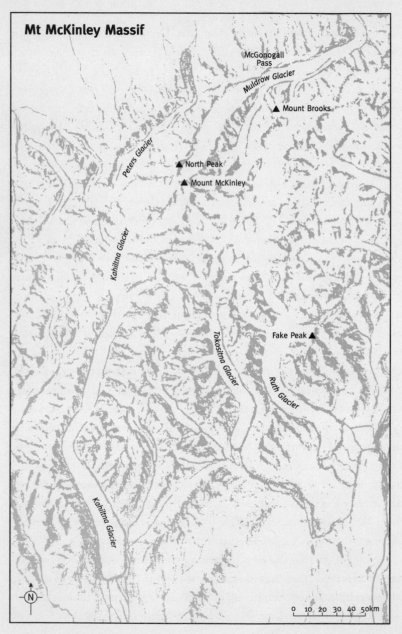

Mt McKinley Massif

McGonogall
Pass

Muldrow Glacier

▲ Mount Brooks

Peters Glacier

▲ North Peak

▲ Mount McKinley

Kahiltna Glacier

Tokositna Glacier

Fake Peak ▲

Ruth Glacier

Kahiltna Glacier

0 10 20 30 40 50km

For almost a week he had a clear view. Dickey estimated its height at over 20,000 feet (nearly 6096 metres), and claimed to have 'discovered' the highest point in North America. On an accompanying sketch map he named it 'Mt McKinley.' He later admitted that the idea occurred to him on a whim. After two miners on the trail had bored him with arguments about the economic virtues of silver, he decided to retaliate by naming the mountain after Senator William McKinley, leading advocate of the gold standard.

By the time anyone contested the name (and they did) it was too late. 'McKinley' was already appearing on the latest maps of the region—the demand for which had suddenly become urgent. When news spread of a gold strike in the Klondike, the steady trickle of northbound prospectors suddenly became a stampede. In 1898 alone, more than 50,000 people poured through Alaska. Many found that they were travelling through blank spaces on the official maps. The United States government now recognized the need for a systematic survey of the territory it had bought from Russia thirty years before, and commissioned a series of co-ordinated expeditions.

Between 1898 and 1902, in the course of a wider survey, four parties explored the limits of the 'Alaska Range,' producing an outline map. Dickey's guess proved a remarkably good one: surveyor Robert Muldrow calculated McKinley's height at 20,460 feet (6236 metres), confirming that it was indeed the highest peak on the continent. He gave his name to a great glacier on the north-east side of the mountain that was to become one of its most famous features. In 1902, Alfred Brooks' surveying expedition travelled from the Pacific coast to the Yukon on a route that took them within 10 miles of the foot of McKinley, thus becoming the first white men, as he put it, to 'approach the summit.'

News of Brooks' close encounter was widely reported in the newspapers and aroused great interest at the newly formed American Alpine Club, whose members urged him to suggest how the mountain might be climbed. A sober and scholarly man, Brooks was embarrassed by the attentions of the press, but he wanted to help the mountaineers: it seemed important to him that McKinley should be climbed by Americans. He believed he had already found the best, and perhaps the only, access to the mountain. The south and east sides were defended by a vast and tangled range of peaks. To the north lay the endless nothingness of the interior. But the plateau to the north-west, above the tree line, offered easy ground for travelling and was close to McKinley's base. From there he could only guess at a route, but if an experienced climber could find a way on to the mountain, the summit slopes did not seem to Brooks to present serious difficulties.

Before Brooks completed his official report for the Geological Survey, he wrote an article encouraging the organization of a climbing expedition, proposing three different courses of action. It concluded: 'The writer would strongly urge that if the expedition is undertaken that it be put under the direction of a man who is not only an experienced mountaineer but who has also had long training in frontier life and exploratory work, for the success of the expedition must depend in very large measure on its leadership...'

The January 1903 edition of the *National Geographic Magazine* found its way under the reading lamp of Dr Frederick Cook of Brooklyn, New York. After a series of pioneering expeditions to the Arctic and Antarctic, Cook had retired from polar exploration, married the widow of a colleague and was devoting his time to the success of his medical practice and to the well-being of his wife and stepdaughter. At the age of thirty-eight he had no intention of subjecting them to the long absences required by polar expeditions—or the financial anxieties. Business was good: patients trusted him, the practice was growing and his purchase of a Roentgen X-ray machine seemed to be paying dividends. However, he remained part of the establishment of American exploration: he was founder and president of the Arctic Club, a member of the American Geographical Society and the Explorers' Club of New York and was one of the forty men who launched the American Alpine Club in 1902. He was well known in the clubrooms as a charming and persuasive man, who could be pompous.

Brooks' 'Plan for Climbing Mt McKinley' was more than Cook could resist. Other than the conquest of the Poles, the first ascent of the highest mountain in North America was perhaps the greatest prize available to an explorer in 1903—since neither Nepal nor Tibet would allow foreign expeditions to approach Everest. What especially caught Cook's eye in Brooks' article was the suggestion that it could be accomplished in one season. He would not have to be away for long. He might even take his wife with him to Alaska; after all, the explorer Robert Peary had taken his wife on one of his Arctic expeditions.

In fact, of the three approaches suggested in his article, the one Brooks thought most likely to succeed involved spending a winter to the north of the mountain in order to take advantage of the snow. He suggested that dog sleds could be used to lay caches of supplies in advance of the climbing party. In the short Alaskan summers, the one-season alternatives were far more risky, requiring long journeys on tight schedules across difficult terrain—either from the Yukon river in the north or from the southern coast of Alaska, beginning at the Cook Inlet (named for Captain James Cook), following exactly in Brooks' footsteps. It meant crossing a land of swamps, rain and giant mosquitoes, but Cook decided that the southern approach, while not the best of the three, suited his personal agenda. Reaching the coast was easy from Seattle, it would be relatively cheap, and he could be back in Brooklyn before the end of the year.

Brooks warned that the journey would be an arduous one: 'Though Mt McKinley in an airline is only about 150 miles distant from tide water, yet to reach its north-west base from Cook Inlet necessitates a journey of at least 400 miles... the time required for the journey and the energy spent in overcoming obstacles, such as chopping trails, traversing swamps and crossing rivers, makes the reaching of the base of Mt McKinley a serious undertaking.'

Cook knew little about packhorses and trail-making, but he was no stranger to hardship. He had walked across the Greenland ice cap with Peary and spent a winter marooned in the Antarctic ice. As for Brooks' stipulation that the leader of an expedition should be an experienced mountaineer, it didn't worry Cook that he had never actually climbed a mountain. He set aside the element of technical skill involved in climbing, preferring to speak of courage and perseverance and make comparisons with polar travel. On his return from Antarctica two years earlier he claimed to have met Edward Whymper and discussed the common ground between them: 'The polar traveller walks over uniform snows, over moving seas of wind-driven ice; his siege is long and his main torment is the long winter darkness. The mountaineer reaches heavenward over the snows of cloudland. His task is shorter but more strenuous...'

Now that he was involved in a climbing expedition, Cook decided it was time to promote the status of mountaineering:

Among our British cousins there has long been an admirable spirit of mountain adventure which has developed into a well-defined sport. In America there has recently grown a similar appreciation of alpine ascents.

This is made clear by the vigorous growth of the Alpine, the Appalachian, the Mazama, the Sierra, and other mountain clubs. Mountaineering is too often put down as a kind of dare-devil sport, of risky feats on cloud-piercing pinnacles; but in climbing there is an inspiration expanding with the increase of vision which is capable of much development. In the records of high ascents there is not only the glory of the pioneer spirit of conquest, but also data for scientific research as well as fascinating studies in art...

Mountaineering as we assume it in this venture is a department of exploration, and as such it is worthy of a higher appreciation than that usually accorded it.

Brooks' article was more concerned with practicalities. If an expedition left the Cook Inlet in the second half of May then, with 'exceptionally good luck,' it might reach the base of the mountain by 1 July. This would leave no more than a month to find a climbing route and complete the ascent before the end of the summer. He suggested a party of ten men and a budget of $15,000.

As it was, Cook's party numbered six men, and they left Tyonek on the Cook Inlet on 25 June, a full month behind Brooks' schedule. None of them had mountaineering experience; one was a prospector they picked up in Alaska who wanted to try his luck in the creeks along the way. Their cash budget was a little over $3000—provided by Cook's wife and *Harper's Monthly Magazine.* Cook had made the tents himself, borrowed sleeping bags from Robert Peary, and bought horses from an Indian reservation en route from the East, untamed. Brooks had wished them luck, telling them they had 'a fighting chance of getting to the top,' but the party that set out from Tyonek was not the kind of expedition he had in mind.

While it never had a realistic chance of success, Cook's 1903 expedition was to prove remarkable for two reasons: first, as a feat of exploration; and second, for the presence in the party of a young journalist called Robert Dunn. He was recommended by Lincoln Steffens, editor of the *New York Commercial Advertiser* and the most distinguished member of Cook's Arctic Club. Steffens was making a name as a writer of political and business corruption exposés—as such, he belonged to a school of newspapermen and novelists that came to be called 'the muckrakers.' Like a great many Americans, Steffens was interested in exploration and liked to read expedition books, but he felt all of them concealed something: 'I had seen a good deal of Arctic explorers, read their books, and heard their gossip, which revealed to me that no book in that field had told it all; they all left out the worst of the wranglings and depressions which were an essential part of the truth about human nature in such tests.'

It was just the opportunity for his colourful protégé. Robert Dunn was a daring traveller, or so he liked to think. He had followed the gold trail to the Klondike, a vacation adventure financed by a doting aunt. In 1900 he had scrambled halfway up Alaska's great volcano, Mt Wrangell, discovered it was still active, and scrambled down again. On the *Advertiser* he had been a fluent and merciless critic, with a talent for annoying his fellow journalists. Steffens liked his confrontational style, attributing his unpopularity to the fact that he 'simply could not lie.' When Dunn resigned from the paper, implying that he was too good to write for it, Steffens was impressed.

He advised Dunn to keep a diary of the expedition: 'You must write exactly what happens. Whether you reach the top or not, be the first to tell the whole truth about exploring. The rows, the bickering –' Dunn replied that maybe there wouldn't be any rows; 'but Steffens looked knowing.'

The young man was unimpressed by his first meeting with Cook:

He was uninteresting, with a bovine face, straight pale hair and walrus moustache, milk-blue eyes, a set smile, and a slight lisp. There was a large-boned Mrs Cook who called him 'Doctor.' They lived in Brooklyn, in a large sloppy house where I dined with their friends and was taken as an honour into their 'Arctic Club,' a mutual, stay-at-home admiration society... Cook hoped that I had rich friends who would help to finance the trip.

In fact, Dunn's aunt gave him $1000, which he handed over to Cook at Tyonek on condition, according to Dunn, that Mrs Cook accompanied them no further. On the strength of his Alaskan experience, and in the absence of alternatives, Cook appointed Dunn as deputy leader of the expedition. Dunn hoped to hire a Swiss mountain guide, and while the party were en route to Alaska he made a detour to the Canadian Rockies in an attempt to find one, but was soon persuaded that he was wasting his time. 'You don't want no Swiss guides,' a man told him. 'They're handy high up on rocks and ice, but lose themselves in the woods. Six weeks across Alaska swamps? They'd die or quit you the first day.'

On Tyonek beach the men spent several days getting the fifteen horses used to their packs. One refused to be tamed and, after many hours chasing it up and down the sand, they left it behind. The six men who now set out for the Alaskan interior included Fred Printz, who had packed the horses on Brooks' expedition, Ralph Shainwald, a young friend of Cook's from New York, and Walter Miller, a photographer who had volunteered for the expedition in Seattle. The prospector who joined them was John Carroll. He had heard that Brooks' party had found a gold-bearing stream that yielded twelve and a half cents to the pan.

Cook placed Dunn in command of the pack train, while he and Miller moved some of the supplies northwards by river, rowing, pulling and pushing their boat as best they could against the current. Both parties made slow progress. Two days into the journey Dunn wrote in his diary:

> The real thing just hit us. The Indian winter trail we follow led straight out into tundra, through line after line of ratty spruces, where you sink ankle deep into sick yellow moss, and wobbly little ridges separate the small ponds. Suddenly every horse was down, kicking and grunting helplessly in the mud. They lost their heads. They seemed to like jumping off into the ponds. We tugged, hauled, kicked at the brutes, unpacked the heavy sacks, lugged them to the shore, pulled on tie ropes, neck ropes, tails; batted heads, poured water down nostrils till they hissed like serpents.

For man and beast, the greatest torments were the mosquitoes and horseflies. At the Cook Inlet, Dunn heard prospectors' stories about men venturing inland only to be 'tortured to death' by the insects. After two weeks on the trail he could almost believe it:

> *July 13.*
> Zzzzzzzz-Zzzzzzz—it makes you dizzy to look at them swarming over the kicking brutes. They are as big as bumblebees, with

striped yellow bellies. They blacken the sunny side of the birches... the swish of horsetails is incessant... the flies are driving them wild. Printz says they can't stand another day of this. Half the hair is eaten off their necks and haunches and you can grab the things off their faces in handfuls as the blood drips. The strain for any one with human feeling is fearful. A mosquito in my ear is driving me wild. Jack has blown smoke into it and Ralph has squirted in strong tea through a pipestem.

Dunn was already recording—and initiating—the kind of bickering that Steffens predicted. He admitted to a 'racial repugnance' for Shainwald, a Jew; it was soon compounded by contempt for his laziness. Shainwald did not enhance his reputation when he took aim at a mud hen and accidentally shot one of the horses through the head. Dunn called him names, the younger man sulked, and eventually the two of them scuffled in a stream—under the disapproving gaze of their leader. Carroll sided with Dunn, and one night discreetly placed Shainwald's mosquito-hat in the campfire. The prospector was given to brooding, punctuated by violent fits of temper in which he would lash out at the tents and kick the saucepans; twice Cook warned him that he was frightening the other men. He then became convinced that he was ill. 'You can never tell from a man's looks,' said Printz, 'how he'll stay it out up in this country.'

The doctor was proving inscrutable. 'He doesn't even smoke,' Dunn complained in his journal, 'and that makes me uncomfortable.' He would not take the men into his confidence. Dunn wondered if Cook had much of a plan to share; after all, he could never decide where to camp and seemed confused by a simple map. Dunn suspected that he didn't know how to use his scientific instruments, although he liked to unpack and admire them:

Our chief's down there by the river, praying over his junk, smiling at screws and nickel cases, lifting, stroking his old Abbey level. I no longer ask him to show quality; I wish he'd show something. He's too silent; hopeful without being cheerful; slow-witted...

It was funny to see the Doctor bucked off his horse fording a creek yesterday. Away he went after his mosquito hat, and didn't get it. Then he tied a red handkerchief over his ears, so he looked like a Bashibazuk... now he is telling about killing penguins in the Antarctic.

By mid-July the horses were close to exhaustion. The men blamed Cook for driving them too hard, and urged Dunn to confront him. 'If a man took horses on a trail like this in the Copper Valley,' said Carroll, 'they'd lynch him.' But Cook was determined to press on. Eventually, Dunn lost his temper. He ran ahead and shouted in Cook's face that he knew nothing about horses and needed 'some sense knocked into him.' Cook replied quietly, 'Dunn, it doesn't do any good to talk like that.'

A few minutes later Dunn apologized: 'I'm sorry if I put my feelings too strongly sometimes.' But Cook only answered, 'Dunn, you talk too much and too loud all the time.'

In forty-eight days on the trail, the mist and rain permitted only tantalizing glimpses of McKinley. It was not until they were crossing a pass to the west that the mountain revealed itself to Dunn:

It *was* McKinley. Falling mists defined a blur in mid air; a white feathery dome; tiny specks of rock and ridge lines developed, threw out the long curved summit in breathless and suppressed proportion—sheer on its broad face, buttressed by tremendous white haunches, to right and left, which quaked and quivered through the mist, mounting 20,300 feet to the very zenith. We crossed a low range of hills, and such a plain opened as you may not see beyond Siberia...

Dunn was gazing across the vast lowlands of central Alaska. It was past the middle of August when they finally reached their base camp, on a stream 14 miles to the north-west of McKinley. Brooks had camped on the same stream the summer before; they passed the skeleton of one of his horses. Facing them was the mountain's giant north-western wall, a cliff so imposing that it seemed to Dunn much closer, as if he could throw a stone against it. The end of summer was rapidly approaching: storms were beginning to pour down from the mountain, rain was frequent and the glacial streams were becoming dangerous—they had only days to attempt their ascent. Cook believed it was enough. Like Brooks, he saw nothing difficult about the slopes he scanned through his binoculars: 'Our position seemed so favourable and the mountain appeared so easy from our point of observation that we felt certain of reaching the summit within a few days.'

The south-westerly ridge seemed to Cook to provide the one possible route to the summit. Getting on to the ridge was another matter. Between base camp and the mountain was a rampart of smaller peaks, and behind them, according to Brooks' map, the frozen valley of the great Peters Glacier, beginning somewhere to the west of McKinley and extending across its north-western face. They needed to find a way on to the glacier. In the absence of a better idea, Cook decided to head in a direct line towards the summit and climb a slope on the rampart of intervening peaks. It was higher than it looked, and harder than they expected. Dunn wrote: 'Suddenly, what we believed the top of one slope stretched itself a full thousand feet higher into the sky; and steeper, steeper.' At 8000 feet (2438 metres) the slope came to an abrupt end. Dunn and Printz crawled forwards to see what was revealed beyond, and found they were peering down a vertical cliff of more than 2000 feet (610 metres). Below them was the vast, silent 'abandoned amphitheatre' of the Peters Glacier. The drop alarmed Dunn. He would not admit to vertigo or fear, but to thinking 'too fast, too much, and of acts which are not sane.'

Dunn made his way back in low spirits: 'This day, after our first defeat, dazing sunlight revealed each disheartening detail of our valley, and countless more walls all quite perpendicular, netted with converging paths of avalanches... They astounded me. All were as impossible as the ones abandoned.'

Cook announced that they would hit the trail again, head east, and look for the terminus of the Peters Glacier. Shainwald declared that their chances of reaching the summit were now brighter than ever. The other men's 'transparent bravado' exasperated Dunn, and he blamed Cook for it. The longer Dunn stared at McKinley, the more intimidating it seemed: its 'immensity grows into you, through you.' He was beginning to see that the task before them was impossible—and to suspect that the expedition was engaged in a kind of charade:

> I felt that the Doctor was not trying his best to climb the mountain; that recognizing it was beyond us, he was making half-hearted tries to escape our judging him a quitter... Every member of the party, except myself, had always spoken as if he thought that to reach the summit of Mt. McKinley would be little harder than scaling—Pike's Peak for instance... if such self-deception is customary, as it seems to be, in polar ventures, it is easy to understand their constant failure.

He confided this to Miller, who whispered agreement. 'When I read about you all in the papers,' Miller said, 'I thought you were experts at mountain climbing.'

Back on the trail, they proceeded in silence. Although the sight of Cook falling once more off his horse momentarily amused him, Dunn was determined to get some straight answers: were they really trying to climb the mountain?

> It took some effort to make him discuss our rebuffs and chances on McKinley. He expressed the same blind confidence we should reach the summit, now tinged with a melancholy ill concealed by

a smiling naivety, which made confidence ring even less sincere. The rasp in his throat, the precise phrasing, grated on my outworn nerves. At last, in a moment of real depression, he said: 'Yes, I'm afraid it will take two seasons to climb this mountain.'

With the little time remaining, Cook added, their priority was to explore the Peters Glacier. At the glacier's foot, they were astonished to find the remains of a camp, which they guessed had been left by surveyors. They were 'as thick as gamblers in Alaska,' according to Printz. Dunn wondered if the discovery meant a change of luck. They climbed the moraine, and for the next three days worked their way 15 miles up the glacier's twisting gorge, following it back across the mountain's north-west face, until, to Cook's delight—and apparently his surprise—they arrived at a spur of the south-western ridge. It was the ridge he had picked out from their original base camp as the route to the summit.

Suddenly the expedition was back on course. Looking up at the ridge, Dunn could see steep rock above the spur, but Cook was sure the angle would relax on the far side, where it was hidden from view. Having discovered the way on to the ridge, it seemed to Cook that the most difficult part was over, and he told the men that, unless they had very bad luck, they would be on the summit in five days. And that was not all: 'August 26th... The Doctor has just said over the pea soup, "We shall spend a night on top of McKinley. I don't think that has ever been done on so high a mountain in such a latitude—why I don't understand."'

Dunn winced. But when he woke the next morning to find Cook was already up and preparing breakfast for the first time on the trip, he was touched and conceded that his leader was 'showing real head lately—he's so sure of success...' Their camp was at 8000 feet (2438 metres). On 29 August they began climbing the spur, a gentle slope at first, increasing to between forty and seventy degrees. There weren't enough ice-axes to go round, and Dunn had drawn the short straw: a willow tent-pole. The others took turns to cut steps. 'As the steps changed from a stairway to a stepladder,' Dunn was annoyed that none of the others looked uneasy. He was scared. He pictured himself falling, wondered how long it would last, and what the moment of impact would be like. It was not vertigo, he insisted, but simply the force of his imagination. The only reason Cook is not afraid, he told himself as they panted upwards, is because he is an explorer and explorers do not have imagination; that is why their books are so dry.

In his diary that night, Dunn cursed himself for joining the expedition in the first place: 'Climbing Mt McKinley with a tent pole. Sometimes I boiled in those dizzy, anxious places that I had put myself in such a position with such men. My blind neglect of the Doctor's silence on alpining now reproaches in another way. It is not bringing out his lack of staying power, as I thought, but his foolhardiness. Yet I must reap my own sowing.'

At one point Dunn asked if it wasn't customary to rope up on such steep slopes and Printz replied, 'Y'ain't goin' ketch me roped up to no one.' They dug a camp out of the slope at 9800 feet (2987 metres). It was a long, dark night of the soul for Dunn. An eerie twilight glowed around the tent, and he wondered where his adventurous spirit had gone.

Dunn noticed that for the first time on the expedition the mood between the men had changed to one of mutual tolerance. The strangeness of their position, alone on a high mountain, seemed to infect them with an edgy humour. Having despised each other, they were now mutually dependent. Dunn no longer felt superior. After his fright on the slope, he had even lost the confidence of his habitual antipathy towards Cook. In its place there was a grudging respect: 'The Doctor has been a real companion the last two days. Probably he realizes this is the final effort and is making a grand play to come up to scratch. At any rate, tonight I'm convinced he's really trying for all he's worth to get up McKinley... Even if we fail, the worst suffering will be over... Oh! How I shall feel for him, perhaps an undeserved pity, but it will turn all the tables of my regard.'

The next day, the slopes were steeper, Dunn's terror greater, and in his diary he gave up trying to rationalize his vertigo: each time he turned his face from the slope, the ground below reared up towards him. At 11,000 feet (3353 metres), they approached the steep rock Dunn had seen from the Peters Glacier: scale had deceived them. They were near the foot of a yellow granite cliff that rose above them almost vertically for 4000 feet. Here they camped, and the next day Cook and Printz advanced a little further, but there was no way past. Dunn knew they were 'checkmated.'

'It ain't we can't find a way that's possible, takin' chances,' said Printz. 'There ain't no way.' The doctor was solemn and withdrawn. Dunn wondered if an experienced climber might succeed on the yellow cliff: 'I should like to see one there, but not a Swiss or Dago one.' The end of their attempt to climb McKinley was of less concern to Dunn than the immediate prospect of an even more terrifying descent. He had spent the night worrying about it, and, imagining his death was imminent, apologized tearfully to Shainwald for being unpleasant to him on the trail. As they began, he stuck close to Cook and talked incessantly to him about the various kinds of courage that men possess until, halfway down, Cook turned to him, relieved him of the tent pole and let him have his ice-axe.

The end of the climbing attempt was the beginning of a remarkable journey. Winter was approaching, and they had only two weeks' worth of provisions, but now Cook decided to take a chance. Rather than retrace their approach route to the west, he gambled on finding a way through the mountains on the unexplored eastern side of the range where, according to the government report they carried with them, it was 'extremely doubtful' that any pass existed. Should they fail, the entire party might starve or freeze to death on the high ground, but in Cook's opinion it was worth the risk—the reconnaissance of new territory would atone in some measure for their failure to climb McKinley.

The gamble paid off: there was a pass, and it led to a south-flowing river. Here they abandoned the horses, in what Dunn called a 'guilty conspiracy of silence.' He could not bring himself to shoot them: 'I could not stand by and see a horse that has served and suffered for you dumbly, on such a grind in such a land, shot in warm blood. It would be too much like murder; better to kill some humans.'

A hair-raising river journey on a makeshift raft, through 200 miles of uncharted country, brought them back to the prospectors' camps on the Cook Inlet. The 'bearded dreamers of gold' didn't ask them if they had climbed the great mountain; they wanted to see the maps they had drawn, and the rock samples Dunn had collected.

During the last days of the expedition, Dunn was in reflective mood. Since the climb he had been more tolerant of Cook, but he was not the younger man's idea of what an expedition leader ought to be like. He imagined someone imperious, passionate, even brutal; Cook was passive, inscrutable, a 'bourgeois' and a 'crank.' When they talked about the continuing quest for the North Pole, Dunn spoke his mind:

> 'Don't you think,' I asked, 'that the leader who rouses personal devotion and enthusiasm in his men, though he be sometimes unfair and his temper quick, would reach the Pole before the easy-going, colourless sort?'
>
>   'Dunn, your sort of leader would have to be an angel too,' said the Doctor. Well, then, only an angel will reach the Pole— and climb Mt McKinley.

Some time later Cook discovered that his expedition had not been the first to climb on McKinley's slopes. Judge James Wickersham, whose court was based at the new gold rush town of Fairbanks, 150 miles north of the mountain, had led a party of men on to the Peters Glacier two months before him. The campsite Cook stumbled upon and assumed had been used by government surveyors had been Wickersham's. The judge had not climbed quite as high as Cook, nor had he ventured so far along the glacier.

In January 1904, Cook published an uncharacteristically subdued account of their journey in *Harper's Monthly Magazine.* By agreement, Dunn was now free to have his say. His narrative was spread across five issues of *Outing Magazine* and used extracts from his diary, verbatim. Readers had never seen anything quite like it; at the Arctic Club there was outrage and an immediate move to expel Dunn. 'His conduct,' wrote the president, 'has been so at variance with what is popularly supposed to be the ethics of social clubs' that action had to be taken. Lincoln Steffens defended him, believing there was an important principle at stake: 'I am in conflict every day with what I call the criminal instinct for privacy... the Arctic Club did not object to dry, scientific observations made in a dull, scientific way. The moment the style becomes interesting, literary and full of what I call the science of humanity, then it does object.'

Cook also spoke in Dunn's favour. But when the Club's committee proposed a motion to reconsider his expulsion, Dunn decided that he was rather bored by the whole affair and voted against it. The committee duly asked him to leave and Steffens' resignation soon followed.

While Cook was embarrassed, many of his peers were sympathetic. He had been made to look foolish by a journalist, but had supported Dunn's right to say what he liked; his own account of the expedition had been simple and dignified. The ascent of Mt McKinley had proved impossible on this occasion, but with scant resources—and clearly a rather motley team—he had climbed higher on the mountain than Wickersham, led the first circumnavigation of the McKinley massif, discovered a new pass, and added much to the maps of the region.

Dunn's articles were eventually published in book form as *The Shame-less Diary of an Explorer*, with Cook's identity thinly disguised as 'the Professor.' But long before the title appeared in America's bookshops, the story of Dr Cook and Mt McKinley had moved on. Over the next decade, it would assume the various forms of an epic, a comedy and a detective story.

CHAPTER 5

The Fingerprints of
Dr. Cook

In his lectures and magazine articles, Cook talked up the difficulty of ascending Mt McKinley. It was 'the steepest mountain in the world,' 'the most Arctic,' 'a more prodigious task than Alpine enthusiasts are likely to realize.' The mountain is climbable, he said, but the man who does it 'must be prepared to withstand the tortures of the torrids, the discomfort of the North Pole seeker, combined with the hardships of the Matterhorn ascents multiplied many times.' In private, his optimism was less cautious. He told a friend it was a wonderful prize 'almost to be had for the asking.'

As Cook hoped, the lectures aroused serious interest from a few wealthy adventurers. One of them inspired a Columbia academic to pledge $2000 towards the cost of a new expedition if he could join it. Professor Herschel Parker was an accomplished alpinist who had climbed the Matterhorn and made several first ascents in the Rockies and Selkirks. A big-game hunter offered $10,000 if, when the climbing was over, Cook would meet him on the Alaskan coast and take him into the wilderness in search of moose and bear.

The money was in place by early 1906. Between them, Cook and Parker assembled a larger and more experienced party than that of 1903. Parker invited his friend Belmore Browne, well known as a wilderness enthusiast, climber and artist, while Cook recruited Russell Porter, a topographer who had been on several Arctic expeditions—including one with the doctor. Walter Miller, who took many of the excellent photographs that illustrated Cook's lectures and articles, agreed to return in the same capacity. To look after the packhorses there was no man better qualified than Fred Printz. If he recalled Cook's harsh treatment of the animals last time around, he may have signed up to protect them. This time he would have an assistant, 'Big Ed' Barrill, a laconic Montana blacksmith as tall as Printz was short and destined for an unlikely starring role.

When the expedition reached Seattle, they found a city on the verge of another gold stampede. The word on the street was that gold had been found in the Yentna and Kantishna foothills of Mt McKinley, and the steamer that took the climbers onwards was crammed with miners' horses and apparatus. At the Cook Inlet the climbers found many more white men than three years before. Belmore Browne wrote: 'We saw quantities of prospectors heading for the great unknown interior, and dreaming of creeks with golden sands. Stories of gold filled their conversation—of men made rich in a day, but the gold was always "behind the ranges" on "some other river"...'

Cook was as optimistic as the gold-seekers. He had a new plan for approaching the mountain. From the headwaters of the Yentna River they would seek a pass to the north side of the range—Cook was certain they would find one—and attack the mountain's north-eastern flank. Of the faces of McKinley he had seen during his circumnavigation, this had seemed the least intimidating. This time they would not rely solely on the strength of men and horses to move supplies inland: the expedition was equipped with a 40-foot motor launch constructed in Seattle to Cook's specifications.

He was depending on guesswork and the plan became vaguer the closer it got to the mountain, but it had the approval of one of the few men to have studied the south side of the range: Alfred Brooks. The surveyor had been greatly impressed by Cook's work in 1903 and was flattered that he had followed his trail. Although he believed an approach from the north more likely to succeed, he was willing to make a bet, if only a very small one, that Cook would climb McKinley. The man betting he wouldn't was Brooks' friend Hudson Stuck, the Episcopal Archdeacon of the Yukon, whose diocese included most of interior Alaska. He had read Robert Dunn's articles in *Outing Magazine*. He liked an argument, and had made up his mind that he didn't like Cook: 'I shall bet you a dollar that he doesn't get above 10,000 feet, $1.50 that he doesn't get above 15,000 and no less than $2.50 that he doesn't reach the summit. It is going to take a better man than he to reach the top of that mountain.'

The expedition started from Tyonek on 3 June, divided as before into a pack train and boat party. They made frequent rendezvous along the course of the Susitna and Yentna rivers. In the launch, Cook was soon setting local records for distances covered in a day. Fred Printz did not have to wait long to be reminded of the miseries of horse packing in Alaska. During his first camp, six of the fourteen horses wandered on to a coal vein that, for reasons nobody could understand, had caught fire and was burning beneath the surface. To Printz's horror, the terrified animals made no attempt to escape; they merely crouched down and trembled, and by the time he rescued them, four were so badly burned that they had to be shot.

After a month on the trail the expedition gathered at the head of the Yentna River and began searching for a pass across the range—but each stream they followed led into an impassable canyon. They had travelled into a cul-de-sac. Cook's plan was in ruins, but he dismissed the matter cheerily: 'We returned to our camp to devise some other line of attack. The pass-seeking adventure was a hopeless failure, but the many discoveries of glaciers, mountains, and rivers were sufficient reward for hard experiences.'

Browne wrote later that he was baffled by Cook's decision to try to cross the range by an unknown route when they could have followed the trail he used in 1903. It had been an unnecessary risk and seemed to place a greater emphasis on exploration than on climbing the mountain. Like

Robert Dunn before him, Browne wondered about the depth of Cook's commitment to the stated purpose of the expedition.

The new 'line of attack,' Cook decided, would be to head east, across unmapped lowlands, towards the great glaciers on the southern side of the McKinley massif. The going was as hard as it had been three years before. Mosquitoes hung in dense clouds, the horses were frequently mired, and on one day they could make only three miles, but this time there was no turning on the leader. Porter wrote in his diary that Cook was 'always in good spirits and ready for more than his share of drudgery, resourceful, and considerate of others.' They passed a bleak prospectors' camp and met an Indian by the name of Susitna Pete, who was keen to warn them of the presence of a dangerous fish in a nearby lake. He said a friend of his had seen it: it was enormous, swallowed caribou whole and hissed when it did so. Pete travelled with them for a while and his strange behaviour was a source of great interest to the men, as was theirs to him. Browne wrote:

> During all our wanderings Susitna Pete had been consumed with curiosity about our reasons for entering this country. To our answers that we wanted to climb [McKinley] he shrugged his shoulders with an air of amused tolerance. White men always wanted gold, and Pete decided that the search for gold must be our mission. He therefore told us of creeks where we might find the precious metal, and retired in outraged dignity when we showed no enthusiasm. Porter's topographical instruments mystified him greatly and he finally decided that in some way those mysterious instruments were connected with the thing we sought. One day Porter set up his theodolite... and took some angles. On leaving the theodolite for a minute we were amused to see Susitna Pete eagerly place his eye on the telescope. In an instant his body stiffened with excitement—he had seen a bear; the theodolite must therefore be a new and marvellous instrument for the find-

ing of big game! Porter at once rose in Susitna Pete's estimation, and we were no longer bothered with questions.

Reaching the western side of the Tokositna Glacier, Cook, Parker and Browne climbed a 500-foot peak for an unobstructed view of the southern face of McKinley, some 25 miles distant. Browne recorded the moment in his diary: 'We reached the top to find McKinley and all its tremendous foothills directly in front of us and at the first look we all said "unclimbable." The Professor came up for a short time and also saw how impossible it was. To climb Mt McKinley from the southern side, we would have to scale 18,000 feet of as difficult rock cliff as the world can produce.'

Between their vantage point and those cliffs lay a bewildering labyrinth of sharp black ridges and twisting glaciers. How they connected to the lower part of McKinley was impossible to see. It would take the whole summer, Browne thought, to climb the mountain just from where they stood—if a practicable route existed. It was already late in July, the frosts were not far away and when they came it would mean the end for the horses.

The next day Browne wrote, 'The Dr has I think given up all hope for making the top this year and I sympathize with him in his great disappointment.' They completed their reconnaissance without enthusiasm. Ten miles further up the Tokositna Glacier the southern approaches to McKinley looked no less daunting. Climbing a ridge on the Tokositna's eastern flank revealed an even larger parallel glacier, apparently several miles wide, that, Cook supposed, was the one he had seen in 1903 and named for his daughter Ruth. But where either of them flowed from he could not tell. In a general meeting of the expedition they agreed it was time to give up; they had seen enough to conclude that Mt McKinley could not be climbed by any approach from the south.

The expedition was back at Tyonek by mid-August. Parker now returned to New York. Cook was expecting to meet the sportsman who had sponsored the expedition. When news arrived that the arrangement was cancelled, he decided to send the men out in several small parties to collect specimens of big game, which he hoped to sell to an eastern museum. Cook himself was not quite finished with exploring: he wanted to find out if the motor launch could reach the head of the river that drains the Ruth Glacier; Ed Barrill was to help him. Browne did not want to be left out: 'I told him that if he contemplated exploring the southern foothills of Mount McKinley I would prefer going with him. He answered that he would do no exploring outside of seeing whether the water route was practicable and he again urged me to aid him with his game collection.'

Three weeks later Browne was biding his time at Seldovia on the Cook Inlet when he heard a rumour that Cook had reached the top of Mt McKinley. He didn't pay too much attention: rumours were 'as thick as the mosquitoes' among the prospectors and, anyway, Cook had not been away long enough even to reach the mountain. Browne knew it was impossible 'in the same way that any New Yorker would know that no man could walk from the Brooklyn Bridge to Grant's tomb in ten minutes.' It was therefore an unpleasant surprise for Browne when Cook and Barrill arrived at Seldovia and told him they had just returned from the summit of Mt McKinley.

They had got lucky, Cook said. They hadn't intended to try for the summit, but they had chanced upon a route and the weather had held. Browne listened to him in dismay. He knew that it was a lie. He took Barrill aside and walked him along the beach:

Barrill and I had been through some hard times together. I liked Barrill and I knew that he was fond of me for we were tied by the strong bond of having suffered together. As soon as we were alone I turned to him and asked him what he knew about Mount McKinley, and after a moment's hesitation he answered: 'I can tell you about the big peaks just south of the mountain, but if you want to know about Mount McKinley go and ask Cook.' I had felt all along that Barrill would tell me the truth, and after his statement I kept the knowledge to myself.

Browne did not quite do that. He immediately contacted Parker, who agreed that what Cook claimed to have done was impossible. While they made no public statements accusing Cook, as soon as Browne returned to the east coast of America they made their opinion plain to members of the Explorers' Club and the American Geographical Society. Many were friends of Cook and preferred to believe him. What was so implausible about climbing a 20,000-feet (6096-metre) peak in eight days? The Matterhorn—more than two-thirds as high—was often climbed in a single day. Their advice to Browne was that he should wait for Cook to publish an account of his ascent. If it contained evidence of a deception, Browne should make his accusations formally at that time. They reminded him that until then it was the convention to accept a fellow mountaineer's word as the truth.

When it came to writing his own account of the expedition for *Outing Magazine*, Browne observed the convention and only a few insiders would have detected evasion and ambiguity in his words: 'You have all heard of the Doctor's ascent. As I have seen the great mountain I can say that anyone who goes through the cold and exhaustion that he and Barrill must have suffered on the gleaming sweeps of ice and snow must indeed be of the stuff men are made of.'

By then Cook was enjoying the limelight. The *New York Times* had announced the first ascent of North America's highest mountain on 3 October 1906. For the first time the name of Dr Frederick Cook was brought to the attention of the American public. In the exploring fraternity on the east coast, where Cook was already well known for his role in pioneering expeditions to the Arctic and Antarctic, the dramatic news from Alaska turned him into a star. The Explorers' Club elected him president. The National Geographic Society chose him as guest of honour for their prestigious annual dinner. Even Robert Peary—whose latest attempt to reach the North Pole had broken the Duke of Abruzzi's record for 'farthest north'—had to wait his turn to speak. No doubt he was irritated to hear the guest of honour compare the ascent of Mt McKinley to reaching the North Pole.

The speech Cook made that evening gave a brief, thrilling and vague account of the ascent. The mountain he described was 'inconceivably high,' a place of biblical storms, alive with noise and movement: the cracking of glaciers, the hissing of avalanches, the trembling of the ground beneath their feet. While black clouds swirled and boulders crashed past, two men struggled upwards through the chaos, 'from crevasse to crevasse,' through 'cloud after cloud,' for 'hour after hour.' Cook enjoyed public speaking and knew how to engage his audience. 'Would we push on to the summit or return?' he offered the question, and paused. 'We agreed to push to the summit...'

He offered no information about the route they had followed. For this, and the photographs Cook said he had taken, Belmore Browne would have to wait for Cook to go to print. In the meantime a rumour made its way around the clubs and societies on the east coast: it said that as far as McKinley was concerned, all was not quite as it seemed.

In Alaska, there was more widespread scepticism, particularly among the miners and hunters—and missionaries—working close to the mountain. When Archdeacon Stuck received a letter from Alfred Brooks in Washington, reminding him that he had lost their bet and owed him five dollars, Stuck refused to pay. He told Brooks that he had been 'taken in' by a fake. Cook was an 'ass' and a 'prig,' he said, whose only hope of reaching the top of McKinley was to wait for the day they built a railroad to the summit. Brooks was not impressed. He had talked to Cook and had even seen some of his photographs. So certain was he that Cook was telling the truth that he agreed to contribute a chapter on the geology of the McKinley area to the doctor's forthcoming book, *To the Top of the Continent*.

Cook's first published account of the expedition appeared in the May 1907 issue of *Harper's Monthly Magazine*. Just as he knew how to thrill a lecture audience, Cook was sensitive to what the *Harper's* readership wanted to hear: a tale of hardship, danger and, above all, suffering. He assured them it was his 'worst experience' to date:

> We were not days or weeks, but months, in desperate positions, fording icy glacial streams, pushing through thick underbrush, crossing life-sapping marshes and tundras, enduring the tortures of mosquitoes, camping on the top of windswept peaks, and being drenched from above and below with frigid waters; in snow-storms, on ice, in gloomy canyons and gulches; on ice cornices and precipices, always with torment and death before us... For hellish conditions and physical discomforts the North Pole chase is, compared with Mount McKinley, tame adventure.

The article included detailed information about clothing and the preparation of rations. The reader might have been able to follow his recipe for biscuits ('we mixed the dough in the usual way, but omitted shortening'), but it was not so easy to follow Cook's route. He was as colourful and as vague as he had been in his lectures. However, of far greater interest to Browne were the photographs and map accompanying the article. Cook's summit picture showed Barrill holding a flag on a sharp rocky pinnacle, against a blanked-out sky. It didn't look like the summit of McKinley as Browne remembered it—it had looked like a snow dome through his binoculars. The rudimentary map confirmed to Browne that he was looking at a fraud. A dotted line took Cook across the east side of McKinley all the way to a point some 20 miles north-east of the mountain, before doubling back to the summit. To claim such a journey in only eight days was preposterous to Browne, but could he prove anything?

In fact, he could not. At the Geographical Society and the Explorers' Club, those who doubted Cook now doubted him further. Others who wanted to believe him were disappointed by the lack of a firm sense of the mountain's topography under Cook's florid, gasping prose. But to convict him of fakery, something more specific was needed, and it duly arrived in 1908 with the publication of Cook's official expedition book, *To the Top of the Continent.*

Browne noticed immediately that there was something different about the summit photograph in the book, and compared it to the version published in *Harper's Monthly Magazine* the year before. The picture in *Harper's* had evidently been retouched along the right-hand edge to hide what Browne could now see: the slope of a second rocky peak rising from the skyline to the side of the 'summit.' Since the camera was pointing upwards, the photograph implied that the second peak was of comparable height, and anyone who had seen Mt McKinley knew there was no such peak close to the summit. Studying the other pictures in the book, Browne noticed something else. In a view of the Ruth Glacier, one of the peaks looked remarkably similar to the slope erased from the *Harper's* photograph. He could not be certain, but he was willing to bet that the two pictures were taken from positions close to each other—somewhere in the vicinity of the Ruth Glacier. The true location of Cook's 'summit' photograph, his 'fake peak,' would be found there, at least 15 miles from the top of McKinley. At last Browne had his evidence.

But the suspect was already far away. In August 1907, Cook had sailed to the Arctic to hunt walrus and polar bear with his latest wealthy sponsor. Or so he said at the time. A few weeks later Belmore Browne was at the Explorers' Club when a telegram arrived from Cook, by now in Greenland, announcing that he had found he had 'a good opportunity to try for the North Pole' and hoped to return with the prize a year later. The sequence of events was unmistakably similar to the McKinley expedition, and Browne recalled that 'no applause or signs of enthusiasm followed the reading of the message.' One man who was positively furious when he heard the news was Robert Peary. The indomitable explorer was planning a final attempt at the Pole, after nearly twenty years of trying. The idea of *any* rival was bad enough for Peary, but one who departed in secret, followed the route *he* had established, used *his* Eskimos—it was intolerable, ungentlemanly, and Peary went to the trouble of writing to the *New York Times* to say so.

Members of the Explorers' Club advised Browne and his friends to refrain from publishing anything damaging to Cook while he was absent and unable to defend himself. It was a question of fair play—and concern that it might provoke a lawsuit. In the meantime Cook's claim to the first ascent of McKinley gained acceptance in Britain when *To the Top of the Continent* was reviewed by the august *Alpine Journal* in London. His prose was not to the journal's liking: 'It is obviously written to suit the taste of an American public... his style is exuberant, and words are put to what may seem, to European ears, strange uses.' Although the reviewer found 'the details of the great feat... somewhat difficult to follow' he did not question their authenticity. It may have amused Browne to read that he was particularly impressed by the photographs.

It became a standing joke at the Explorers' Club that Cook would return to New York claiming to have reached the North Pole. Whatever happened, an uncomfortable reception from his fellow members awaited the Doctor: he had some explaining to do since the publication of his book. It was agreed the matter was best dealt with behind closed doors— and so it would have been, had events not taken an unexpected turn on the other side of the Atlantic.

On 1 September a Danish steamer en route from Greenland to Denmark sent the following telegram to government offices in Copenhagen: 'We have on board the American traveller, Dr Cook, who reached the North Pole April 21, 1908. Dr Cook arrived at Upernavik in May of 1909 from Cape York. The Eskimos of Cape York confirm to Knud Rasmussen Dr Cook's story of his journey.'

Knud Rasmussen, an explorer and scientist, was the world's leading authority on Eskimo culture. The American ambassador to Denmark recalled that 'nobody questioned the truth of the story, for Knud Rasmussen's name is a talisman, and the officers in Greenland do not take travellers' tales seriously unless the travellers have serious claims. The whole city of Copenhagen was in an ecstasy of expectation.' A newsreel recorded the scenes as Cook's ship reached the Danish capital some days later. It shows a vast crowd pressing forward at the quayside, top-hatted royalty waiting to shake his hand, while on the steamer's deck there is a glimpse of Cook, a sheepish figure in a borrowed suit, shifting from one foot to the other. Later he is on a balcony, a conquering hero waving his cap to the crowd beneath, smiling broadly. Scores of correspondents had made their way to Copenhagen. Most of them were charmed by the doctor—the discoverer of the North Pole seemed to be a modest man, ordinary and pleasant, who answered their questions simply and directly. But at least one of them thought he saw something else in Cook's expression at the moment he was greeted by the Crown Prince of Denmark: guilt, fear and a struggle to remain composed. He had clearly not expected a reception on this scale.

But he held his nerve. On 6 September, Cook was guest of honour at a dinner given for the visiting correspondents when a telegram arrived with news of Robert Peary's expedition: it was announced that Peary had reached the North Pole in April of that year. Cook rose to his feet and calmly declared that he was pleased to hear of the success of his fellow American: 'There is glory enough for us all.' If some of those present were suspicious of Cook, they also admired him. The most outspoken of the journalists wrote for the *London Daily Chronicle*: 'If he is an impostor he is also a very brave man—a man with such iron nerve, such miraculous self-control, and such magnificent courage in playing his game, that he will count for ever among the greatest impostors of the world. That and not the discovery of the North Pole shall be his claim to immortality.'

Peary took a different view from Cook about glory. The discovery of the North Pole had occupied half his life. When he learned what had been happening in Copenhagen during the past week, he was apoplectic. He had heard about the rumours at the Explorers' Club and knew now that they must be true. He knew that the journey Cook was claiming to have made across the Arctic Ocean, with just two Eskimo companions, was impossible. Cook was a faker and, worse than that in Peary's eyes, he was a thief—the North Pole belonged to him. It was time to end the ridiculous charade in Denmark. He sent a telegram to the New York newspapers calling Cook a liar: 'I am the only white man who has ever reached the Pole,' he said. 'Cook has simply handed the public a gold brick.'

The 'Great Polar Controversy' had begun. Behind the doors of the Explorers' Club there was little doubt about where the truth lay, but soon the whole affair was spiralling out of control. Peary's comments were a public relations disaster. Many American newspapers portrayed him as a bad loser, and a bully. If Europe was satisfied with the truth of Cook's claim, what reason was there to doubt him?

Answers to this question were beginning to appear in the press. Parker now stated publicly that Cook had no evidence that he had reached the summit of McKinley. Fred Printz was quoted as saying that none of them had set a foot on the mountain, while Cook's climbing partner, Ed Barrill, interviewed in Montana, said that he was preparing a statement—with the help of Robert Peary. He added that Cook was 'the greatest hot air artist I ever met.' Both the hired men complained that Cook still owed them money.

However, the reports made little impact on the general swell of support for Cook. When he sailed into New York harbour on 21 September, the city organized a reception to match the one he had received in Copenhagen. Dignitaries greeted him, a band played, children chanted his name, and 100,000 people lined the street as Cook was paraded in a motor car beneath huge banners exclaiming 'We Believe in You.' A few days later it was announced that Cook was to become the first American to receive the 'freedom of the city' of New York.

Behind the scenes, friends of Robert Peary were plotting the doctor's fall from grace. In mid-October, the *New York Times* published an affidavit signed by the two Eskimos who accompanied Cook on his journey across the Arctic Ocean: it stated that they had never been out of sight of land.

Supporters of Cook argued that Eskimos tended to tell white men whatever they wanted to hear; after all, they had said something quite different
to Rasmussen.

But the next day the Peary Arctic Club played its trump card: they
published a second affidavit in New York's *Globe and Commercial Advertiser*. It
was signed by Ed Barrill.

'Guide Who Went on Alaskan Expedition Swears Alleged Discoverer
of the North Pole Was Never Nearer Than Fourteen Miles of the Summit of the North American Continent's Tallest Peak' ran the sub-headline.
In a lengthy statement, Barrill admitted that the ascent of Mt McKinley
had been a deliberate and elaborate fake. Cook had dictated parts of his
diary, he said. They had continued up the Ruth Glacier for several miles
so that Cook could study the mountain's north-east ridge, 'as this was the
side where he proposed to claim that he had climbed it.' The position
Cook chose for the 'summit' photograph was at least 20 miles from the
top of the mountain. He had warned Cook that the peaks behind might
give him away, but Cook had insisted that they would not show.

Three days later Cook finally sat before a committee of his fellow
members of the Explorers' Club investigating the 'ascent' of McKinley.
Browne and Parker had already appeared as witnesses. Cook was told that
he should not see it as an inquisition, but as an opportunity to clear himself of suspicion. They wanted to see his expedition diary. Cook, however, had no intention of answering their questions and had brought his
lawyer with him—a Mr H. Wellington Wack, who began by reading a
statement to the committee. Since the controversy about McKinley had
arisen so unexpectedly, Wack said, his client needed time to gather his
records. 'If there is really anything about the book,' Cook added, 'that you
would want to have cleared up, I should like to have that put in writing
as a request...'

After the publication of Barrill's affidavit, many of the newspapers
that had supported Cook now quietly dropped the subject from their
front pages, but some commentators continued to argue his case. Barrill

had no doubt been well paid for his testimony, and whether he had lied in 1906 or was lying now, his word was unreliable. Powerful forces were clearly trying to destroy Cook. It was a view that reflected public opinion: a great many readers would not be shaken from the belief that the unassuming doctor from Brooklyn was the victim of a conspiracy.

A few weeks later, Cook disappeared. On 21 December, the University of Copenhagen announced that the records Cook submitted of his polar journey contained no proof that he had reached the North Pole. And no proof that he had *not*. While his supporters argued tenaciously that his records were just as good as Peary's, the dispute was contracting into a simple question of trust—of whether Cook was the kind of man who ought to be believed. In the next six months, three separate expeditions closed in on Mt McKinley hoping to settle the matter one way or the other.

IN FAIRBANKS, ALASKA, ONLY ONE MAN bought a copy of *To the Top of the Continent*: Archdeacon Stuck. It was soon in great demand from the prospectors who worked close to the northern base of the mountain. Stuck recalled 'the eagerness with which my copy was perused by man after man from the Kantishna diggings, and the acute way in which they detected the place where vague "fine writing" began to be substituted for definite description.' Among them was Thomas Lloyd, a Welshman who came north during the Klondike gold rush of 1896. For the last few years, he had been working claims on Bear Paw River, only 20 miles north of McKinley; he hunted mountain sheep in the foothills and with his fellow pioneers explored the area in search of the shortest passes through the range. No one knew the place better.

One evening in October 1909, when the local newspapers were full of the Polar Controversy and the latest revelations of Ed Barrill, Lloyd was drinking in a Fairbanks saloon when the conversation turned, inevitably, to Dr Cook. Lloyd liked to boast. He said he had 'frequently partly ascended to the top' of McKinley, and it didn't look anything like the photograph in the book Stuck had showed him. From what he knew of the mountain, climbing it would be easy; easier, at any rate, than faking an ascent. The owner of the saloon, Billy McPhee, told Lloyd that he was too old and too fat to climb a mountain. This got a rise out of the Welshman: for two cents, he said, he would 'show' McPhee. Forget the two cents, McPhee replied—if Lloyd would climb McKinley and prove to the 'outsiders' that no man had set foot there before, he would give $500 from his own pocket.

Soon there was a further $1000 on the table from two local merchants, and on 1 November the expedition was announced in the *Fairbanks Daily News-Miner*. Lloyd recruited three men from the Kantishna mines: Billy Taylor, Charley McGonogall and Pete Anderson, a Swede. E. C. Davidson, a professional surveyor, and two of his friends completed the party. A farewell ceremony was held at the Pioneer Hotel in Fairbanks on 21 December— the very day the University of Copenhagen delivered its verdict on Cook's claim to the North Pole. The *Fairbanks Daily Times* declared, 'Our boys will succeed, they've got the route figured out, and they'll show up Dr Cook and the other "Outside" doctors and expeditions.'

There was good reason for the paper's confidence. Reaching the mountain from the north, using dog-sleds on hardened winter snow, over familiar trails, was far less demanding than the journey Cook had twice made from the south, in summer. Alfred Brooks had recommended a northern approach eight years before, but Cook had not had the means— or perhaps the will—to spend the winter in Alaska. Crucially, both he and Brooks had failed to realize something when they travelled across the northern face of the mountain: passing the snout of the Muldrow Glacier, they assumed it began somewhere among the peaks on the east side of McKinley. In fact, the glacier turned abruptly towards the top of the mountain and the great ridges that formed its walls led directly to the north and south summits. From vantage points in the foothills Lloyd and his men had figured out that a route on to the summit ridges would be found somewhere along the glacier. Up to that point, the climbing of McKinley was simply a long 'mush.'

Before they had even reached the Muldrow, however, there was trouble: Davidson discovered that he could not stand the company of Lloyd, and after an altercation—perhaps even a fistfight—the surveyor left the expedition, taking his two friends with him. Without Davidson and his instruments they were barely an expedition at all: just four miners climbing the mountain for a bet. They had a five-dollar Kodak camera which none of them was sure how to use, and a pocket barometer—until they dropped it in the snow and lost it. But what they *did* have was a 14-foot spruce pole and a 12- by 6-foot American flag. It was big enough, they reckoned, to be seen from Kantishna, perhaps even from the tall buildings in Fairbanks, 150 miles away.

They spent some time exploring the foothills for a way on to the Muldrow Glacier before finding a low and easy pass at the head of Cache Creek, which they named for Billy McPhee. Lloyd called the Muldrow the 'Wall Street Glacier' because of the huge cliffs on each side. By 25 March they had moved their camp by dog sled to the glacier's head, at about 11,000 feet (3353 metres)—although Lloyd believed it was much higher, and the summit much closer. Above them, rising almost vertically for 3000 feet from the floor of the glacier, was a giant icefall. To its left, the southerly wall of the Muldrow continued as a steep, exposed snow ridge: the only way past. If the ridge could be climbed, it seemed to give access to the wide, shallow basin between McKinley's two summits. This, then, was their route, and the men set to work cutting steps in the slope that led on to the ridge—with a coal shovel, since they had brought no ice-axes.

As McPhee had predicted, Lloyd discovered he was too old and too fat to do this sort of climbing, and remained on the glacier. At two o'clock in the morning of 3 April 1910, Taylor, McGonogall, and Anderson strapped enormous home-made climbing irons to their moccasins and set out for the summit, taking turns to drag the flagpole behind them on a cord. They did not see any need to be roped together, or to take a tent with them, since the north summit looked close enough to reach in a day.

Flasks of hot chocolate and a bag each of doughnuts kept them going. They climbed the ridge, crossed the high basin, and began to make their way up a steep gully on the north peak. About 500 feet from the summit, McGonogall decided he had had enough. There was no point in going further, it seemed to him, since it was not his turn to carry the flag-pole, and the other two men were already some distance ahead. A short time later, Taylor and Anderson stood on the north summit of McKinley. Perhaps it was only at this moment that they realized that the south peak, some two miles distant, was many hundreds of feet higher.

The three men were back at their glacier camp by about eight o'clock the same evening, having climbed and descended some 8000 vertical feet (2438 metres) in eighteen hours. Lloyd was waiting for them in the foothills and, as soon as he heard that his flag was flying on McKinley's summit, he set out alone for Fairbanks, with a tale to tell. The others pre-ferred to return to their claims in Kantishna.

The last Fairbanks had heard of the expedition was in February. A miner who met the climbers close to the mountain told the *Fairbanks Daily News-Miner* that all was going well and that Tom Lloyd had 'taken off about twenty pounds of excess weight and is ready for a dash to the top.' Now, as Lloyd made his way back to the city and contemplated the recep-tion awaiting him, he considered the matter of the two peaks and their misfortune in choosing the lower one. The prospect of admitting this part of the story did not appeal to him, nor did the prospect of conceding to McPhee that he had not been fit enough to climb with the other men. Since the expedition had been his idea in the first place and since it had succeeded, more or less, Lloyd felt entitled to dress up the story a little. In fact he could not resist it.

On 12th April the *Fairbanks Daily Times* used its largest font to pro-claim 'Mt McKinley is Conquered.' Tom Lloyd, it reported, had returned from the mountain the previous afternoon with sensational news—that he and his three companions had climbed both the north and south peaks of McKinley and had placed a flag 'higher than the Stars and Stripes were ever planted by mortal hands before.' Lloyd was said to have photographs taken at various heights and rock samples collected near the summit, which he intended to send to Alfred Brooks in Washington. As for Cook, 'Lloyd asserts that he has positive proof that Dr Cook never climbed the mountain and that he will be able to demonstrate this to all.' However, he was 'reticent as to the details.'

The detailed account of the expedition was valuable property, to be sold to the highest-bidding newspaper in America, and Lloyd had already found a man who would not only sell the story for him, but write it. W. F. Thompson was a fellow Klondiker. As editor of the *Fairbanks Daily News-Miner* he had a reputation for vigorously promoting all things Alaskan, for mocking 'Outsiders' at every opportunity and for writing atrocious—though eye-catching—headlines: the story of a local execution was entitled 'Jerked to Jesus.'

According to Thompson, Lloyd told him the whole story in the course of an evening at the paper's office. Lloyd read out his expedition diary while a court stenographer recorded it verbatim. Thompson now worked on the raw material and kept the world in suspense. He wanted the people of Fairbanks to think of the story as Alaskan property. In the *News-Miner* he told them how his offices had received dozens of telegrams 'from the magazines and newspapers of the Outside asking for cheap looks at the pictures and notes of the explorers'—but that he would not be releasing anything until they paid what it was worth. Lloyd's backers were entitled to be reimbursed, he argued, and his men to 'obtain a grub-stake as a result of their trip.'

By 20 April he had found a buyer: the *New York Times*, which outbid *Harper's Monthly Magazine* and the *San Francisco Examiner*. The story was already on its way east, the *News-Miner* announced, sealed in a specially made metal tube. The report identified the maker of the tube (Billy Gilcher), its exact dimensions (12 inches by 3), and the method used to seal it (Gilcher's soldering iron). Thompson knew that it contained the biggest scoop of his life.

Published on 5 June, his *New York Times* article presented Lloyd as a kind of legendary 'Sourdough,' who routinely performed superhuman feats of endurance and never wanted to talk about them. The story had to be 'dragged' from him, according to Thompson, and when he finished telling it Lloyd had declared, 'I never talked so much in my life—my mouth is all puckered up.' Thompson wrote:

> These four men have performed a feat that has set the world talking… They have stood upon the highest peak of the American continent, have seen sights that thousands of people would give much of their time and money to see, and have passed those sights up without particular interest or attention…
>
> They started out from Chena outfitted as no McKinley expedition was ever before outfitted, and with less junk with them than an Eastern excursion party would take along for a one-day outing in the hills…
>
> They wanted no publicity and they cared not if the world never heard of their trip… Their only desire was to prove to their three backers and to the pioneers of the North that they personally were just as husky as they ever were and could still reach any place they started for—that and the desire to give to the Outsiders 'the laugh' by proving that what the Easterner brags about and writes about in the magazines and which to the Easterner is impossible, the sourdough Alaskan performs as part of the day's work.

The article included the transcription of Lloyd's 'expedition diary,' which described the climb the way he had told it to McPhee and the others on the day he returned from the mountain: all four of them had made it; both peaks had been climbed. Four days before the article appeared, a newspaper in the Yukon town of Dawson warned: 'It would be anything but wisdom for any party at this stage of the game to lay claim to having reached the summit of McKinley unless it had done so. Just now McKinley is watched by the eyes of the world... while those who know Tom Lloyd and his party accept the Yukoners as honest, the world is far from Missouri. *It must be shown.*'

But it wasn't. There was Tom Lloyd's word and nothing else. The few photographs reprinted in the *New York Times* were of the lower levels of the mountain. The flag was proving invisible from Fairbanks. The 'positive proof' in the case against Cook, which Lloyd had promised, turned out to be rather less than that: he had simply found no trace of him on the summit. Within a short time, Lloyd's story was challenged by several prominent McKinley veterans. Ed Barrill told a newspaper in Montana that he didn't believe it; it was impossible, he said, to climb McKinley in the spring. Under the headline 'This Climber Claims To Be From Missouri' the *Fairbanks Daily News-Miner* reported that Herschel Parker would not believe it until he was shown that it was true. On 16 April, even the *New York Times* conceded that the 'McKinley Ascent Is Now Questioned' and called for corroborative evidence from the other members of Lloyd's party who had remained at their mines in Kantishna. From Fairbanks, it emerged that Lloyd's reputation for honesty was not quite as secure as the local newspapers claimed. The distinguished mountaineer Claude Rusk, writing to the *Pacific Monthly* in Oregon, explained:

> Alaskans are divided in opinion as to whether Tom Lloyd climbed the mountain. I know Tom Lloyd well, said a friend of mine... if he said he climbed Mount McKinley, I am satisfied he did it. I think there is no doubt he got to the top. But—I know Tom Lloyd, said another man to me. I wouldn't believe him under oath. He can't travel ten miles a day on level ground, why, he can't even kill his own moose meat.

Scepticism now spread quickly. At the end of June, when McGonogall, Taylor and Anderson returned from Kantishna with a rather different account of the expedition, they could find few men in Fairbanks willing to believe that any part of the story was true.

One man who heard their story and believed it was Archdeacon Stuck. He blamed Lloyd and Thompson for arousing the incredulity of their fellow Alaskans. Writing some years later, he was still astonished by their stupidity:

> It was most unfortunate that any mystery was made about the details, most unfortunate that in the newspaper accounts false claims were set up. Surely the merest common sense should have dictated that in the account of an ascent undertaken with the prime purpose of proving that Doctor Cook had not made the ascent, and had falsified his narrative, everything should be frank and above board; but it was not so.

In the *Fairbanks Daily News-Miner* Thompson stuck doggedly to the story as he had written it. Each time a prospector travelled in from the Kantishna area he was interviewed about the visibility—or otherwise—of the flag on the north summit. At least one claimed to have seen it, while a report that another had not is followed by the sub-headline 'Did Not Look Closely.' The paper sponsored an attempt to settle the matter with a long telescope positioned on a tall Fairbanks building—without success. Thompson blamed the scepticism on the eastern media:

> You couldn't get the price of a meal ticket from any newspaper or magazine on earth for carrying a grand piano to the summit of McKinley and then telling the story of the feat. The impression in Eastern newspaper and magazine shops is that there is something in the climate of the McKinley district which makes liars of all men who breathe the air thereof.

In newspapers across the nation, McKinley had become 'America's mountain of mystery.' The dubious story of the Sourdough expedition enhanced its reputation and added a new level of confusion, but the focus of interest remained firmly on the claims of Dr Cook. Neither Barrill's affidavit nor the verdict of the University of Copenhagen on his polar records had convinced everyone that Cook was a fraud. Large quantities of hate mail had been arriving at the houses of Belmore Browne and Herschel Parker ever since the press identified them as witnesses against the doctor. Browne wrote:

> In the face of this blind public partisanship, we realized that we would need more than documentary and circumstantial evidence to convict Dr Cook irrevocably. The Polar Controversy had put an entirely new light on our claims against Cook. Originally our claims against him were really more or less private and personal. While Mount McKinley was a splendid mountaineering prize, our attempt to climb it had been in the nature of a sporting proposition. We did it for the love of adventure and our attack on Cook was simply a question of mountaineering ethics. But the North Pole was an international prize, that had claimed the heroic efforts, and lives, of the explorers of many nationalities for many years. There was no sport here—it was a question of international importance.

The conclusive evidence that Browne and Parker had in mind involved nothing less than retracing Cook's route on the Ruth Glacier, locating the 'fake peak' and duplicating the photograph he had passed off as the summit of McKinley in *To the Top of the Continent*. Their expedition left New York in late April, financed by the Explorers' Club—which had by now terminated Cook's membership. In Fairbanks, W. F. Thompson was preparing to publish the story of the Sourdoughs' conquest of McKinley and did not miss the opportunity to gloat:

Prof. Parker of New York, Cheechaco explorer, starts from New York with a party of bespectacled highbrows to make the ascent of McKinley. They will sail from Seattle for here as soon as they have laid in the necessary supplies of ropes, knee-britches, alpenstocks, dinky caps, hob-nailed shoes, pate de foigras [sic], soup capsulese [sic], thermos bottles, hot-water bags, baled hay, ice-cream freezers, mosquito netting, canvas boots, Merry Widow veils, pneumatic pillows, collapsible stoves, wading boots, fur-lined parkas, silk underwear, cold cream, snake cure and frostbite salve, without which they know McKinley cannot be successfully ascended...

They were already roped together when they stepped on to the boat in Seattle, according to Thompson. In fact, Browne claimed that it was indeed the best-equipped American mountaineering expedition to date.

En route to the Ruth Glacier, Browne and Parker met another expedition following in Cook's footsteps: Claude Rusk and his three companions from the Mazamas Mountain Club in Oregon hoped to prove that Cook *had* climbed the mountain and were backed to do so by the *Pacific Monthly*, the *Portland Oregonian* and the *New York Herald*. Browne described them as 'a pleasant party of men' and denied there was anything other than a friendly rivalry between the two expeditions. It was not until forty years later, long after Rusk's death, that a rather different picture emerged.

Rusk was an attorney with an impressive climbing record. He had climbed Mt Adams, the 'Matterhorn of America,' no fewer than eight times. The *Pacific Monthly* described him as 'one of the most expert and daring mountaineers in the West, yet so level-headed and cautious that he has never had a mishap... Tenacity of purpose is one of his most striking characteristics, yet this tenacity is tempered by good sense and consideration for the welfare of others.'

His companions on the long march up the Ruth Glacier did not agree with the assessment. Rusk's tenacity seemed to be leading them towards ever greater danger among the cliffs and crevasses. The silence of the Ruth's vast amphitheatres unnerved them and they tried to persuade him to turn back. Rusk awoke one night to find one of the men reaching into his sleeping bag in an attempt to steal the expedition's funds; eventually they tried to kill him. A. L. Cool, a well-known Oregon guide, egged on by the others, attacked Rusk with a snowshoe and tried to push him into a crevasse. Rusk was momentarily stunned, but rose to his feet and declared that the expedition must continue—at which point Cool collapsed in front of him and begged for forgiveness. Knowing that Mt McKinley could ill afford another scandal, Rusk kept the story to himself—confiding only in his wife. 'I have always greatly admired,' she said in 1950, 'the courage required to continue the trip with men who would act with such purpose.'

While Rusk followed the Ruth towards the southern face of McKinley, Parker and Browne were closing in on the location of Cook's fake peak. They knew that if they could find one of the scenes shown in his photographs they could trace him 'peak by peak, snowfield by snowfield, to within a foot of the spot where he had exposed his negatives.' On 22 June they recognized the first of the scenes pictured in *To the Top of the Continent* and moved to the position from which the photograph had been taken. This turned out to be on a tributary glacier, at least a day's march from the course Cook claimed to have travelled. 'The scent was growing warm,' for it confirmed everything that Barrill had said in his affidavit. On the tributary glacier they found a rock wall of 300 feet that Cook had photographed and captioned as 'a cliff of 8000 feet'; they were only 5300 feet (1615 metres) above sea level. 'After this discovery,' wrote Browne, 'we no longer expected to find that the Doctor had climbed a moderately high peak—climbing with printer's ink was far easier.' They were sure the fake peak was somewhere close to them.

Parker saw it first. He shouted, 'We've got it!' and soon both men were gazing at the strangely familiar profile of a little outcrop of rock, protruding from the saddle between two higher peaks. It was perhaps 200 feet (61 metres) high. For a while neither man spoke. The sound of avalanches sounded sinister to Browne, 'like the noise of a snake in dry grass.' They now gathered around Cook's photograph and compared the contours of the rock: 'As our eyes reached the right-hand sky-line there stood the rock-ribbed peak on which we had based our denial of Dr Cook's claim, and by which we had traced his footsteps through the wilderness of rock and ice.'

Taking turns with the flag to pose as Ed Barrill, they duplicated Cook's photograph and eventually went on their way. As far as Browne was concerned, it was the end of the controversy: he had the proof in his camera that Cook was a fake.

Two weeks later, camped beneath the Ruth's ferocious granite cliffs, still nine miles from the summit and 14,000 feet (4267 metres) below it, Claude Rusk came reluctantly to the same conclusion. He had traced the route on Cook's map until it departed from reality: now, where the glacier should have emerged from east of the mountain, his path was blocked by a maze of fantastic ridges. The idea of a man with a single pack making the entire ascent by that route in only eight days was to Rusk 'utterly impossible and absurd... the man does not live who can perform such a feat.' When he came to write the account of his expedition for the *Pacific Monthly*, Rusk was once more in forgiving mood:

> Dr Cook had many admirers who would have rejoiced to see his claims vindicated, and I too would have been glad to add my mite in clearing his name. But it could not be. Of his courage and his resolution there can be no doubt. He is described as absolutely fearless. He was also considered as always willing to do his share and as an all-round good fellow to be out with. Had he been content to rest his laurels upon the things he had actually accomplished—to say nothing of the possibilities of the future—his

fame would have been secure. His explorations around McKinley
were extensive. They were of interest and value to the world. He
discovered a practicable route to the great mountain from the
south-east side. Had he persevered, he doubtless would have
reached the summit on some future expedition. He was the first to
demonstrate the possibility of launch navigation up the Susitna
and the Chulitna. That one trip alone—when with a single companion he braved the awful solitude of Ruth Glacier and pene-
trated the wild, crag-guarded region near the foot of McKinley—
should have made him famous. But the Devil took him on to an
exceeding high mount and showed him the glories of the icy alpine
world and—the doctor fell. Let us draw the mantle of charity
around him and believe, if we can, that there is a thread of insan-
ity running through the woof of his brilliant mind... If he is men-
tally unbalanced, he is entitled to the pity of mankind. If he is not,
there is no corner of the earth where he can hide from his past.

Cook was doing his best; the newspapers had been unable to trace him
since he left New York in December. Rusk concluded his article by
addressing the question of whether or not Tom Lloyd's party had reached
the summit. He was not sure what to believe:

In many respects their story is as contradictory as Cook's, and in
some ways it has no truer ring. The pains they take to express
contempt for the 'cheechacos' (outsiders) will not tend to
increase the faith of thoughtful people in their tale... if they are
fakers, their sins will find them out as surely as did Dr Cook's.
The matter must be settled beyond cavil. The original ascent of
Mt McKinley is so great an event that the question of priority
cannot long remain disputed. If the men of Fairbanks were the
first to stand upon that snowy crest, the glory must be theirs,
undimmed by the shadow of a doubt.

In the view of Parker and Browne, there was more than a shadow of doubt over the Sourdoughs' expedition. Having seen Lloyd's photographs, they accepted that he had discovered the route by which the mountain *could* be climbed, but were not inclined to believe that they had actually done it. They regarded the mountain as unconquered and in 1912 began their third and final expedition: to climb McKinley by Lloyd's route from the Muldrow Glacier.

Following the Sourdoughs' example, they used dogs rather than horses, and set out in winter—but not from Fairbanks. Hoping to combine climbing with survey work on the little-known eastern side of the mountain, they chose their familiar approach from the southern Alaskan coast, travelling along the frozen Susitna and Chulitna rivers. It was five months before they reached the position of the Sourdoughs' final camp at the head of the Muldrow; crucially, they were some eight weeks behind their precursors' schedule and summer storms were beginning to blow.

The ridge from the glacier, past the icefall, into the summit basin was just as Lloyd had described: exposed, steep, but practicable. They relayed their supplies to a camp at 16,615 feet (5064 metres), and rested for a day. 'Only a storm can stop us now,' Browne wrote in his diary. On 29 June they began to climb the final 3500 feet towards the gentle slopes of the south summit. At 18,500 feet (5639 metres) they paused to congratulate each other on surpassing the North American altitude record set by the Duke of Abruzzi on Mt St Elias. Browne smoked a cigarette. To the south, they could see the Ruth Glacier and its surrounding peaks spread beneath them like a map. While the south summit appeared as innocent as a 'tilted snow-covered tennis court,' the lower north summit, framed against the sky, looked comparatively difficult. Through their binoculars, they could see no sign of a flagpole.

The day had started bright and clear, but now the sky to the south began to darken rapidly. As they passed 20,000 feet (6096 metres) the full force of the wind struck them. It drove the breath from Browne's body: 'I held to my axe with stooped shoulders to stand against the gale;

I couldn't go ahead. As I brushed the frost from my glasses and squinted upward through the stinging snow I saw a sight that will haunt me to my dying day. *The slope above me was no longer steep!'*

On a fine day, it would have taken them minutes to walk the final 300 feet to the summit, but in a gale that was turning into a blizzard—Browne estimated the wind speed at 55 mph and the temperature at minus 15 degrees—it would have been suicide to continue. They were overwhelmed. 'Only those who have experienced bad weather at great heights,' Hudson Stuck was to say later, 'can understand how impossible it is to proceed in the face of it.'

On 1 July they tried once more from their high camp, but were again driven back by a blizzard. They were now short of rations, for the canned pemmican they had hauled up the mountain had proved indigestible at high altitude. In fear of being trapped on the mountain with only a few bags of biscuits and raisins, they retreated, reaching their base camp on Cache Creek by 6 July. And then something extraordinary happened:

> It looked like 'dirty weather.' The words were scarcely out of my mouth before a deep rumbling came from the Alaska Range. I can only compare the sound to thunder, but it had a deep hollow quality that was unlike thunder, a sinister suggestion of overwhelming power that was terrifying. I remember that as I looked, the Alaska Range melted into mist and that the mountains were bellowing... and then the earth began to heave and roll, and I forgot everything but the desire to stay upright.

It was the first and most violent convulsion of an earthquake that was to rumble on for thirty-six hours. Their dogs scattered. A few minutes later the men's eyes were drawn to the beautiful 12,000-foot (3658 metres) peak to the east of McKinley, which they had decided to name in honour of Alfred Brooks: its entire western wall was falling away in a gigantic avalanche. For a moment they watched in awe as a white dust cloud rose thousands of feet above the range—and then realized it was coming towards them at the speed of a train. They rushed to secure the tent and dived inside.

Had their rations, or their digestion, allowed Parker and Browne to remain longer on the mountain, they *might* have climbed it, but they *would* have been killed in the earthquake. The blizzard on the summit slopes seemed to Browne like 'the memory of an evil dream,' but he knew now that they had received good fortune and bad in equal measure.

Browne admitted that they could not claim the first ascent of Mt McKinley: 'There is a technicality in mountaineering that draws a distinction between a mountain top and *the* top of a mountain—we had not stood on *the* top.' They had been only a short walk away. Nevertheless he decided that he was entitled to call his expedition book *The Conquest of Mt McKinley*. Thoroughly documented and comprehensively illustrated with photographs, there was to be no doubt about its authenticity. It seemed to be the last word in the arguments about the claims of Tom Lloyd and his Sourdoughs: there had been no sign of the flag on the north summit. When W. F. Thompson mocked Cheechaco mountaineers in the *Fairbanks Daily News-Miner*, he often singled out Parker for special ridicule—presumably on the grounds that he held a professorship and wore spectacles. Now Parker had an opportunity to get his own back. He gave an interview to a New York paper accusing the Alaskans of a hoax: 'Dr Cook didn't have anything on the Lloyd party when it comes to fabrications.' That it had all been a tall story became the generally accepted view.

Archdeacon Hudson Stuck had followed the progress of the Parker–Browne expedition, as those preceding it, with a combination of interest and anxiety. He longed to attempt the mountain himself. During his correspondence with Alfred Brooks over the matter of Dr Cook, he declared, 'I would rather climb Mount McKinley than own the richest gold mine in Alaska.'

In his native England he had climbed in the Lake District and later spent a summer in the Alps. When he accepted his posting to Alaska in

1904 he packed his climbing equipment and barometric instruments in the knowledge that the country contained 'an unclimbed mountain of the first class'; while en route in Seattle he climbed Mt Rainier. After eight years as Archdeacon of the Yukon, he was a hardened wilderness traveller and something of an expert on the literature of McKinley, but there had been few opportunities to indulge his love of high places. It was exceeded by his passion for missionary work. 'I am more interested in men than in mountains,' he once said, and none concerned him more than the Athabascan Indians of Alaska. His outspoken devotion to their welfare, in the face of white encroachment, made him unpopular in some quarters. W. F. Thompson was particularly irritated by Stuck. The Archdeacon had come to dislike the 'hungry, stupid little Fairbanks papers' and now refused to pass on any news from the remote settlements he visited on his travels. After meeting him in 1910 Thompson wrote:

> He had grown a beard which changed his personal appearance until he resembled none else so much as the Man the world has been pictorially led to believe was He who died on Calvary. His once smiling countenance was replaced by the saddest face we had ever gazed upon, and he looked as though the sins of the world rested upon his shoulders and he was forced to carry the burden as his Cross. His voice was kind and sweet, yet so sad, and while his words were words of optimism, they were few and far between. There was nothing doing in the 'copy' line with Archdeacon Stuck... he tells no stories unless they point a moral or voice an indignity put upon his people.

In 1912, after Parker and Browne's near miss, it seemed to Stuck as if the mountain was waiting for him and he persuaded his bishop to grant him leave to attempt it in the following year. He was forty-nine years old and needed a younger and stronger partner who could lead the climbing. Billy Taylor, from the Lloyd expedition, was prepared to go if Stuck paid him $5000, but this, it turned out, was five times more than the expedition's total budget. Eventually, another man who had worked at the Kantishna mines agreed, after much coaxing, to go for nothing. Harry Karstens was well known locally as the 'Seventy Mile Kid.' Now thirty-four, Karstens had been in Alaska since he was nineteen, picking up his sobriquet while panning for gold on the Seventy Mile River. Enormously strong and self-reliant, he was to prove a fortunate choice. The party was completed by Robert Tatum, in training for the priesthood, and Walter Harper, Stuck's 'half-breed boy' whom Stuck was tutoring and had virtually adopted. Both were twenty-one.

The party left Fairbanks for the Kantishna in mid March 1913. At the remains of 'Diamond City,' abandoned since the gold rush of 1906, they met Pete Anderson, who, legend had it, carried the flagpole with Taylor to the north summit. Stuck listened once more to his story and recorded in his diary: 'Karstens believes him and I do too, though the task of carrying a fourteen-foot pole up that mountain must have been enormous and the feat sounds incredible.'

What Stuck heard from Anderson confirmed what he had read of the Parker–Browne expedition: that McKinley did not present any technical mountaineering difficulties: 'Its difficulties lie in its remoteness, its size, the great distances of snow and ice its climbing must include the passage of, the burdens that must be carried over those distances... like nearly all Alaskan problems, it is essentially one of transportation.'

Stuck had no intention of risking a dash up the mountain in the style of the Sourdoughs or of being driven down by storms, like Parker and Browne. His solution was to have more high camps and lay siege to the summit if necessary. As for rations, bringing tinned pemmican to the mountain was 'like bringing coals to Newcastle': they were travelling across some of the best game country in the world. At their base camp at Cache Creek, close to the pass on to the Muldrow Glacier discovered by Lloyd's party, Stuck and his companions killed four caribou and a mountain goat, and boiled the meat down in a 50-pound lard can. By combining the reduced meat with butter, and moulding it in their hands, they produced 200 balls of food, which, according to Stuck, they 'never failed to enjoy.'

They now had unexpected visitors. Although Stuck had carefully prevented news of the expedition reaching the Fairbanks papers, it was common knowledge at the mission stations and among the Athabascan people. A young couple arrived with their baby, having walked 100 miles in the hope of finding the Archdeacon and having him baptize the child. The ceremony was duly performed, amid the heads and skins of the butchered animals. To Stuck's astonishment, it then transpired that the couple had never been married and a second ceremony was performed before they went happily on their way:

> I was rejoiced at one more of the many instances I could recount of the fidelity of the natives to the teachings of the Church. I wonder how far up the mountain they would have followed us had they found our base camp deserted? Our little party discussed that matter when they were gone. Walter thought they would have followed us to the glacier, but not beyond, but I think they would have gone on until they could go no further, or until their food was entirely consumed.

On 11 April they made their way on to the Muldrow, some 20 miles from the summit, and for the next three weeks they ferried supplies to their climbing base at the head of the glacier. The work was 'ceaseless grind' and Stuck was amazed by the heat of the sun. The first of May, the Feast of Ascension, was a day of particular 'toil and penance'; it seemed impossible that he was panting and sweating while surrounded entirely by ice and snow. Strange, too, was the solitary rabbit that followed them to 10,000 feet. It gnawed at the willow canes they left to mark their path, and at one point was seen to leap a crevasse.

Two days later they were camped below the long ridge leading to the summit basin, where both Lloyd's party and the Parker–Browne expedition had camped before. At 11,500 feet (3505 metres), they were more than halfway up the mountain.

Stuck carried with him Browne's magazine article, which described the ridge above them as 'a steep but practicable snow slope' and included a photograph. But his first sight of the ridge had given Stuck an unpleasant surprise:

> It offered no resemblance whatever to the description or the photograph. The upper one-third was indeed as described, but at that point there was a sudden sharp cleavage, and all below was a jumbled mass of blocks of ice and rock in all manner of positions, with here a pinnacle and there a great gap. Moreover, the floor of the glacier at its head was strewn with enormous icebergs that we could not understand at all. All at once the explanation came to us—'the earthquake'!

This ridge, some three miles long, which the Sourdoughs had climbed in a single march, and Parker and Browne in a few days, now occupied Stuck's party for three long weeks. In order to relay their supplies to higher camps, it was necessary to cut a staircase through the tangle of ice-blocks, 'over them, around them, on the sheer sides of them, under them, whatever seemed to our judgement the best way of circumventing each individual block.' Karstens led the way, assisted by Harper, while Stuck and Tatum ferried supplies behind them. They were frequently driven down by bad weather, astonished by how quickly it could change. While they waited in their tent on the glacier for storms to pass, sometimes for days, Tatum practised reciting the Thirty-Nine Articles. Stuck worked on a forthcoming book about his travels as a missionary, *Ten Thousand Miles with a Dog Sled*, and resumed his tutoring of Harper: 'An hour or two of writing from dictation, an hour or two of reading aloud, a little history and geography, gave the day variety and occupation. A pupil is a great resource.'

But time passed slowly. It was not until 27 May that Karstens reached the unbroken snow above the earthquake cleavage. Stuck no longer believed that climbing McKinley was entirely a matter of logistics and endurance: the shattered ridge 'adds all the spice of sensation and danger that any man could desire.' He was full of praise for his partner's judgement and daring. The four men now moved their camp up Karstens' precarious staircase, passing remnants from the Parker–Browne expedition—biscuit and raisin packages, and discoloured snow—to the edge of the 'Grand Basin' between the two summits. The worst was now behind them.

They camped at 15,000 feet (4572 metres), and again at 16,500 feet (5029 metres). Altogether they were to make no fewer than five camps in the Grand Basin, the highest at 18,000 feet (5486 metres), to which they relayed more than two weeks of supplies. Stuck explained:

> We were at the base of the final peak, prepared to besiege it. If the weather should prove bad we could wait. We could advance our parallels, could put another camp on the ridge at nineteen thousand feet, and yet another halfway up the dome. If we had to fight our way step by step and could advance but a couple of hundred feet a day, we were still confident that, barring accident or desperate misfortune, we could reach the top.

Stuck was resolute, but he was not enjoying himself. The summer he spent in Switzerland had been nothing like this: 'To roam over glaciers and scramble up peaks free and untrammelled is mountaineering in the Alps—to toil upward with a forty-pound pack on one's back and the knowledge that tomorrow one must go down for another is mountaineering in Alaska.'

The thin air was taking a heavy toll on him. Every twenty or thirty paces he was forced to stop by fits of panting that grew more violent the higher they climbed; several times he fell on to the snow, choking, as 'everything turned black' before his eyes. At 15,000 feet he had stopped smoking his pipe, but continued to fare worse than his companions, who gradually relieved him of any burden other than the large mercurial barometer. To this Stuck clung tenaciously, afraid that one of the others would break it.

On the way to the highest camp, they paused for a rest. Sitting on the snow, gazing across at the dark pinnacles of the north peak, they talked about the Sourdough climbers. Once they had reached the summit, Stuck wanted to cross the basin to the north peak and look for traces of the earlier expedition. At that moment Walter Harper cried out:

'I see the flagstaff!' eagerly pointing to the rocky prominence nearest the summit, for the summit itself is covered with snow. Karstens, looking where he pointed, saw it also, and, whipping out his field glasses, one by one we all looked and all saw it distinctly, standing out against the sky. Through the glasses it rose sturdy and strong, one side covered with crusted snow; and we were greatly rejoiced that we could carry down confirmation of the matter.

The Sourdoughs' flag, which the wind had long since ripped from the pole, had been 12 feet by 6, the largest they could find in Fairbanks. Stuck had forgotten to bring one at all and now set Tatum to work looking for red, white and blue material among their equipment. The result was a dainty miniature, made from two silk handkerchiefs and the cover of a needlework bag.

At four o'clock in the morning of 7 June 1913, they began to climb the final 2300 feet to the summit. The sky was entirely clear, but a keen north wind was blowing. Stuck wore six pairs of socks inside his moccasins, and still his feet felt 'like lumps of iron.' On winter trails in the Yukon he had endured lower temperatures, but he was colder now. After a little more than seven hours, they passed the point at which they supposed Parker and Browne had been overwhelmed by a blizzard. The north peak was already below them. Stuck's shortness of breath grew more distressing as they neared the summit and he wondered if he might be physically unable to do it. At Harper's insistence he finally 'surrendered' his mercurial barometer; all he had to do now was carry himself to the top.

> With keen excitement we pushed on. Walter, who had been in the lead all day, was the first to scramble up; a native Alaskan, he is the first human being to set foot upon the top of Alaska's greatest mountain, and he had well earned the lifelong distinction. Karstens and Tatum were hard upon his heels, but the last man on the rope, in his enthusiasm and excitement somewhat overpassing his narrow wind margin, had almost to be hauled up the last few feet, and fell unconscious for a moment upon the floor of the little snow basin that occupies the top of the mountain.

As soon as Stuck recovered, he said a brief prayer of thanksgiving. They now set up their scientific instruments—a procedure they had carefully rehearsed lower on the mountain. When the readings were taken, Tatum attached his tiny flag to a tent pole and waved it for a moment—then removed it and handed the pole to Stuck, who lashed on a crosspiece to form 'the sign of Our Redemption.' Around this the men gathered to say the Te Deum. After ninety minutes on the summit, they began their descent. Stuck wrote later:

> Only those who have for long years cherished a great and almost inordinate desire, and have had that desire gratified to the limit of their expectation, can enter into the deep thankfulness and content that filled the heart upon the descent of this mountain. There was no pride of conquest, no trace of that exultation of victory some enjoy upon the first ascent of a lofty peak, no gloating over good fortune that had hoisted us a few hundred feet higher than others who had struggled and been discomfited.

Rather was the feeling that a privileged communion with the high places of the earth had been granted.

Two weeks later, Stuck reached the town of Tanana, west of Fairbanks, and sent a telegram with news of his success to a Seattle newspaper. The same morning he received a reply asking for 'five hundred more words describing narrow escapes.'

HUDSON STUCK DIED IN 1920 and is buried at the remote Athabascan settlement of Fort Yukon, his mission headquarters, a few miles inside the Arctic Circle. The monument on his grave dominates the cemetery. His portrait looks down from the wall of the church. Close to it is a painting he dedicated to the memory of Walter Harper, drowned in a steamboat disaster in 1917. The 'lifelong distinction' that Stuck anticipated for the young man whom he regarded as his son was tragically short-lived and his death was said to be a blow from which the Archdeacon never recovered.

Although Stuck himself has been dead for eighty years, a few people still remember him—Peter John, Chief of the Athabascans, now aged one hundred, was at the mission in Nenana when Stuck passed through on his way to climb the mountain.

On today's map of Mt McKinley are Karstens' Ridge and the Harper Glacier—names suggested by Stuck that have passed into common usage along with Mt Barrill, the Browne Tower, Mt Brooks, the Sourdough Gully and McGonogall Pass. While the naming of features on the mountain was one thing, the naming of the mountain itself was quite another. Stuck believed it should never have been called Mt McKinley. He called the book of his expedition *The Ascent of Denali*, and it begins with 'a plea for the restoration to the greatest mountain in North America of its immemorial native name.' While McKinley has remained on the map, most Alaskans use the name Stuck preferred.

Cook never retracted his claim to have reached the summit. In 1915 he announced the departure of an expedition to climb Mt Everest. Europe was at war and Cook, born of German parents, seemed to arouse the suspicions of Britain's imperial police. He was arrested in Rangoon, detained in Calcutta and denied permission to approach the Himalayas.

Robert Dunn was to see him one more time:

One night, years later, I walked into the Waldorf's old square bar, deserted except for one man alone at a table sipping champagne. It was Cook. We must have talked for an hour, his stream of words repeating his published story about his reaching the Pole. Whether or not he believed what he said, I couldn't tell; but his justification of his claims soon grew pathetic. I never saw him again.

CHAPTER 6

The Misplaced Optimism of Maurice Wilson

The first thing he saw was a boot. A little further on was another, then a heap of dark fabric partly covered by snow, which he guessed was a tent. He turned and shouted that he had found the supply dump from the last expedition, and his companion, who had been resting on a stone, rose wearily to his feet and began trudging up the slope behind him.

The dark shape was only a few yards away and the first man didn't wait for the other to catch up. He was almost standing over it before he realized what it was, and for a moment he struggled to contain his shock. The body was frozen solid. Lying on its left side, the knees were drawn up to the chest and one hand reached out towards a stone, to which a guy-rope was tied. It trailed off into the snow and no doubt to the remains of a tent ripped off him by the wind. A mauve pullover, grey flannel trousers, long woollen underwear and bare feet, but no sign of a sleeping bag: why, then, had he removed his boots?

As a doctor, Charles Warren thought that he was used to the sight of the dead, but this was closer to home. After all, the man had died trying to do exactly what *he* was there to do: climb Mount Everest or at least part of it. He had known immediately whose body it was; it couldn't be anyone else. They had all read about him in the papers, first in 1933, when he had set off for the mountain—something of a comic figure then, larger than life—and again the next year, when he was reported missing. It was Maurice Wilson, the eccentric.

'I say!' Warren shouted down the slope. 'It's that fellow Wilson!' and soon the other members of the party were gathering around. Warren wondered if they ought to hide their discovery from the porters, but it was too late. They had already come to see what the sahibs were looking at. One of them backed swiftly away and vomited, but the rest, to the Englishmen's relief, seemed to accept the matter casually. Before disturbing the body they searched the snow around it. The guy-rope was indeed attached to the shreds of a tent. A small rucksack lay nearby, a Union Jack apparently signed by girlfriends, a gold pen and pencil, film canisters, a ring made of elephant hair—a lucky charm, perhaps—and at last, what they hoped most of all to find: a diary. His sleeping bag turned up almost 100 yards away. It was extraordinary that the wind had somehow stripped it from him.

The men agreed that if they buried him where he lay the movement of the glacier would soon undo their work. After some discussion they decided to wrap Wilson in the remains of his tent and carry him over to a crevasse. Having cut away the lip of a suitable one, they mumbled a prayer and, like a burial at sea, slid the shrouded body into the depths. 'We all raised our hats,' Warren wrote in his journal, 'and I think that everyone was rather upset over the business.'

Only a short distance up the slope they came to the food dump left by the last great Everest expedition two years earlier, which had clearly travelled in some style. As they helped themselves to jam and sweetmeats, cakes and Carlsbad plums from Fortnum and Mason, the men took it in turns to read out Wilson's diary. They knew something of his background, but the little notebook conveyed something altogether different from what they had imagined. It proved to be, in Warren's words, 'a most extraordinary revelation of monomania and determination of purpose.'

MAURICE WILSON WAS BORN IN BRADFORD in 1898, the third son of a manager at a woollens mill, but the true beginning of his story was the First World War. Aged sixteen when it started, he enlisted in a local infantry regiment on his eighteenth birthday and was soon selected for officer training. A portrait photograph of Wilson in uniform shows a burly youth with a strong jaw and large features; he looks into the camera with an open, expectant expression. Commissioned as a second lieutenant, he had been in France for only a few weeks when his regiment was thrust forward to defend the line at the fourth battle of Ypres. A ferocious German assault almost engulfed the machine-gun unit he commanded and, by the time it was driven back, every man around him was either dead or wounded. Wilson, however, had not received a scratch. He was awarded the Military Cross for conspicuous gallantry and mentioned by name in the newspapers.

A short time later the positions were reversed. In almost exactly the same location on the battlefield Wilson led a charge against an enemy machine-gun and was seriously wounded. Hit in the chest and arm, he was near death when a stretcher party retrieved him. His brief experience of the trenches was over. Evacuated to England, it took him a year to recover from his injuries, though his left arm was to give sudden bouts of pain for the rest of his life.

For that reason alone he was unable to forget the war. How it influenced his personality is impossible to know for certain, but two things were to shape his later life: an interest in the human body's mysterious powers of recuperation and a conviction that God had spared him for a purpose—if he could only discover it.

Like many of his generation, Wilson was unable to settle back into civilian life. After working briefly in his father's office, he moved to the brighter lights of London, but it only increased his restlessness and he began to take bolder steps. He emigrated to New York, grew impatient when he could find nothing there that he wanted to do and, after only a few months, crossed the continent to San Francisco, with the same result. It was only when he had travelled as far from home as any Englishman could—to New Zealand—that he decided to remain and make the best

Albert Smith,
The Great Showman

Jean Antoine Carrel,
The Cock of Valtournache

Edward Whymper,
a Lambeth Boy in the Alps

Frederick Cook,
The Great Pretender

The Top of the Continent
(according to Frederick Cook)

Robert Dunne,
a Muckraker

Browne and Parker,
Mountain Detectives

The Sourdoughs,
Thomas Lloyd
(center)

The Archdeacon
of Yukon

The Duke of Abruzzi

Dudley Wolfe

Fritz Wiessner

*The 1938
Wiessner Expedition*

*The 1953 American
K2 Expedition*

of it. A series of peculiar jobs followed. He took to the road as a sales-man of weighing scales, then as the purveyor of a unique restorative med-icine. He prepared and bottled it himself, but the recipe was the invention of another man—or so he told his customers. The scheme was a failure and his next job was more conventional. He bought a small farm, where his energy, pragmatism and eagerness to learn served him well, until he grew tired of the isolation. After eighteen months in the country he moved into Wellington and used the money from the sale of his farm to buy a women's dress shop.

After all, he had some background in the trade. The shop flourished and at last Wilson seemed to be blending into the local community as a successful independent businessman. He married twice and separated twice; without a wife or family to support, he saved a small fortune, but was beginning to realize that this kind of success did not make him happy. It only proved what he knew already: he was capable of succeeding in whatever he turned his hand to. A *driving purpose* in life was what he want-ed, and selling dresses to the women of Wellington was not it. He had run the shop for several years when he abruptly sold up and took a boat for England. He was both dropping out and returning home.

The long voyage via India and the Suez Canal completed his circum-navigation of the globe. His fellow passengers, it seemed to Wilson, pre-sented a transitory microcosm of humanity: rich and poor, purposeful and itinerant, ordinary and exotic. A party of Indian yogis joined the ship in Bombay and Wilson engaged them in conversation; he was curious about their beliefs. Quiet and reserved, the yogis responded politely to the expansive Englishman's persistent questions and, the more he listened, the more he wanted to learn. Wilson was no theologian, but he believed earnestly in the transcending power of faith. He liked what he heard about the purification of mind and body, concentration on a single object and the generation of supernatural powers. Where all this belonged in the yogis' philosophical system he soon forgot, but the fragments, a series of resonant phrases, stayed with him.

Wilson had been away for a decade. His father was dead, his mother an invalid and his brothers had become strangers. Life in Bradford had passed him by. While he was casting around for something to do in London, Wilson began to realize that he was not well. He had lost weight and was plagued by a persistent cough that seemed to be getting worse. Aimless, disorientated and now ill, he felt that his life was approaching a crisis. But everything was about to change.

When Wilson arrived in London he had tried to buy a second-hand car. He struck up a friendship with the dealer and eventually his wife. Leonard and Enid Evans became used to regular visits from the garrulous, opinionated, yet rather lonely Yorkshireman. They knew that he was ill, most probably from consumption, and that he would not see a doctor; it was typical of him to reject advice. Suddenly his visits stopped and they heard nothing. Several months passed before he called again and when he did, a very different man breezed into the house. There was no trace of the cough and his eyes were shining. He was utterly revitalized. He had important news for them, he said, but it could wait a little longer. They celebrated at a restaurant, continued to a nightclub and finally, in the small hours, Wilson told them the following story.

He had been not to a doctor, but a faith healer. The man lived in a Mayfair flat and had once suffered from a disease that his doctors diagnosed as terminal; they had given him three months to live. That was seventeen years ago, Wilson said, and the man was now in perfect health. He had discovered a means of curing himself and had been sharing the knowledge ever since with a succession of visitors to his home. More than a hundred people had been cured by his method and Wilson was now one of them. He had followed it to the letter and the result was nothing short of miraculous. It was simple: he had fasted for thirty-five days, drinking only small quantities of water. His bodily and spiritual maladies had drained away. Once purged, he had prayed to God to be born again.

Wilson would repeat the story many times, but he never named the man and there seems to be no evidence of his existence other than Wil-

son's word. In New Zealand, as a travelling salesman of a restorative medicine, he had claimed the recipe was the invention of another man; it may
have been, but it is equally plausible that Wilson invented him and repeated the strategy in his story of the mysterious faith healer of Mayfair.
He had learned about purgation from the yogis, but, whatever its prove-
nance, the treatment had worked for Wilson and he believed in it. He had
fasted and prayed and it had made him well.

But this was not the most important part of the news that he was
bursting to tell his friends. What had happened to him, he said, could
happen to others, if only they knew what faith could achieve. He realized
now what he wanted to do with the rest of his life: to tell the world about
his discovery. And he knew just how to do it: 'I believe that if a man has
sufficient faith he can accomplish *anything*. I haven't gone mad and I haven't
got religious mania. But I've got a theory to prove and I intend to try and
prove it. I'll show the world what faith can do! I'll perform some task so
hard and so exacting that it could only be carried out by someone aided
with Divine help. *I'll climb Mountain Everest alone.*'

It is not difficult to see where the idea came from: Wilson had been
reading the newspapers. It was towards the end of 1932 and Everest, after
a long absence, was back on the front pages. Eight years earlier, the first
serious attempt to climb the mountain ended in mystery and disaster
when George Mallory and Andrew Irvine disappeared close to the summit. Since then, the Dalai Lama had refused to give permission for
climbers to approach the mountain through Tibet, but in 1932 he was
persuaded to change his mind and preparations were under way for an
expedition the following summer. The party included many of Britain's
outstanding mountaineers and the nation's hopes were high.

A second Everest project aroused even greater interest: the Nepalese
government had granted permission for an expedition to attempt the
world's first *flight* over Everest. The brainchild of a committee of British
aristocrats and high-ranking military officers, it was financed by Lady
Houston and would be piloted, among others, by the Marquess of Doug-

las and Clydesdale. The project was undertaken not 'to perform a sensational feat,' the committee insisted, 'but for the most sober purposes.' There was 'much to learn about the down-draughts and up-currents caused by the deflection of the wind on the highest peaks.' Nevertheless, the Gaumont—British Picture Corporation was planning a film about the expedition for general cinema release. It was an age of aviation heroics, when papers reported the latest feats and records set on an almost daily basis. In spite of the committee's pious statements of intent, the proposed flight over the highest mountain in the world promised to be the most sensational yet and it made headlines everywhere.

Wilson knew that Everest commanded public attention and he selected his 'task' for no other reason. He had no mountaineering experience and had taken no interest in the subject until then; if he had, he might have preferred to try swimming the Channel or walking to Cape Town instead. But his mind was made up. Influenced no doubt by reports of the Lady Houston expedition, he told the Evanses that the best way to reach the mountain was in an aeroplane. It was simply a matter of crash-landing on the lower slopes and then walking to the summit.

Leonard and Enid listened patiently. Interviewed in the 1950s by Wilson's biographer, Dennis Roberts, they said that they were immediately sceptical about his story of a faith healer in Mayfair and yet moved by the account of his own recovery. It was miraculous. But when he began to talk about Everest, they were appalled. They pointed out to Wilson the two gigantic flaws in his plan: he wasn't a mountaineer and he certainly didn't know how to fly an aeroplane. 'I know,' he replied with a confident grin, 'but I can learn.'

It seemed to Roberts a positive measure of their friendship with Wilson that the couple did *not* try to talk him out of it. Leonard, in fact, was to become the manager of Wilson's affairs. According to him, Wilson toyed with the idea of approaching members of Lady Houston's team to ask if he might parachute on to Everest from the wing of one of their planes. He doubted, however, that they would agree to it and decided that his first idea was a far better one: he would fly himself to the mountain.

Within a short time Wilson had bought a two-year-old Gypsy Moth biplane and an impressive pilot's outfit of the kind he might have seen in the movies, including leather jacket, breeches, gaiters and improbably large boots. He moved to lodgings near the London Aero Club at Stag Lane and promptly enrolled on a course of flying lessons. The instructor's first impression of the new pupil striding towards him was of a large man with an eager grin and a glint in his eye, apparently dressed for horse riding.

He soon discovered that Wilson liked to handle the controls vigorously. Wildly enthusiastic and in a hurry to learn, he had to be tamed as much as taught and needed twice as many lessons as a typical pupil before his instructor considered him safe, or safe enough, to take to the skies alone. Meanwhile he became a well-known character around the aerodrome. The name 'Ever Wrest' was painted on the nose of his plane and he made no secret of his plans. All attempts at dissuasion were dismissed with the same theatrical bravado, as Wilson declared that he would fly to India or die in the attempt. When he was not in the air he was to be seen marching around the field's perimeter in pursuit of physical fitness. He was known to be on a peculiar diet and stayed away from the clubhouse bar. 'I don't need a drink,' he told his instructor, 'I'm an apple and nuts man!'

By now the Wilson story was beginning to appear in the newspapers. He was delighted, of course, to co-operate with journalists and to pose for photographs in front of 'Ever Wrest.' With goggles on his forehead, he would tilt his head to one side and look directly at the camera, his large, animated features presenting a study in thoughtful determination. He had already devised a system of wires for photographing himself on the summit of Mount Everest.

Up to a point, he was realistic about the equipment he needed. 'Ever Wrest' was refitted with strengthened undercarriage and extra fuel tanks. He bought a tent and sleeping bag of the kind specially designed for the

official Everest expedition, an altimeter, ice-axe and a selection of maps.
With his preparations already at an advanced stage, he took five weeks off
from flying practice in order to learn how to climb. If lessons in mountaineering were available at that time, he didn't bother to find a teacher,
preferring instead to go alone to the Lake District and roam across the
hills. Wilson had proved, and would prove further, that he was a practical
and adaptable man. The plans for his journey, as far as it extended to
India, were reasonably well thought-out. Great risks were involved in flying alone in a frail aircraft over vast tracts of ocean and desert and he
understood them. But he took a quite different attitude to Everest. He
made no serious attempt to learn about the environment. He might have
approached veterans of previous expeditions but chose not to. His 'training' in the Lake District was irrelevant to high-altitude mountaineering; he
didn't *try* to learn how to cut steps in ice or use crampons. None of this
mattered to Wilson. The mountain was simply part of an equation: if he
had sufficient faith, he would climb it.

As the date of departure neared, press interest increased and when he
met two reporters by chance at Piccadilly Circus, he took the opportunity
of stealing a headline by telling them how he had spent the afternoon:
making a parachute jump over central London. With affected nonchalance
he said that he had done it on impulse, to test his nerve for the adventure
ahead. The story may have been an invention, but the newspaper took it
at face value and within a few days a letter from the Air Ministry arrived
at Wilson's lodgings to remind him that the stunt was illegal. He was
rather proud of the letter and decided that irritating the authorities could
add a new string to his bow.

On 23 April 1933, the eve of his departure, he decided to fly to
Bradford and say goodbye to his mother. A couple of hours later, he was
hanging upside-down in his cockpit having crash-landed his plane in a
field outside the city. He had stalled the engine in mid air. Attempting to
glide on to a large field, he had missed it by a considerable distance, flown
through a hedge, spun on to a country lane and flipped over. Within min-

utes press photographers were at the scene and Wilson, having released his harness, clattered to the ground and dusted himself down, was assuming a familiar pose for the camera: thoughtful determination. But the aircraft behind him was a wreck and would take weeks to repair.

A new departure date was set: 21 May. Meanwhile the Air Ministry, responding to the stories in the press, wrote another letter to Wilson. The Deputy Director wanted to know if the reports of his intention to fly to Mount Everest had any foundation; if they did, Wilson was to understand that previous permission from the Nepalese government was required— and he was most unlikely to get it. Wilson responded by pointing out that the Houston expedition was at that moment making flights over Nepal; why, then, shouldn't he? The reply came very quickly. Wilson, it was clear to the Ministry, had 'completely misunderstood the position.' Permission for the Houston expedition had been obtained by long and elaborate negotiations, and was subject to many conditions. *His* case was quite different. The flight would not be allowed.

He was keen to tell reporters of this development, announcing that he would defy any attempt to stop him. When the day of departure came, he brought a telegram with him to Stag Lane airfield: it was a final message from the Air Ministry, forbidding any flight into Nepal. He tore it up in front of the press and strode purposefully towards his aircraft. A small crowd had gathered, most of them newspapermen and photographers. Leonard and Enid Evans signed Wilson's 'flag of friendship'—a small Union Jack—and he started the engine. As he taxied away, his instructor watched with his head in his hands: Wilson was aligning his plane with the wind *behind* him. A nervous moment followed, when it seemed to onlookers that the accelerating aircraft would never leave the ground, but at the last moment it lifted, avoiding a hedge at the end of the runway by a very small margin. And that was the last any of them saw of Wilson.

One of the newspaper reports of the event carried a short interview with Wilson's mother. He had left without saying goodbye. She had no doubt that he was afraid of upsetting her. 'I have one great fear,' she told them. 'His left arm is practically useless. I keep asking myself, can it stand the strain? He can't carry anything heavy with it.' When a reporter pressed her on whether she believed that her son could climb Mount Everest alone, she wouldn't answer directly: 'My son,' she said, 'is a very brave man.'

The press regarded Wilson as an accident waiting to happen and, when he did not appear along the route he had advertised, they reported him missing. In fact he had simply changed his mind. Rather than crossing the Alps, he had decided to skirt around them via Lake Geneva and was approaching Italy by way of Marseilles and the Côte d'Azur. Navigation was proving easier than he had expected and he was in high spirits. Four days into his journey he wrote to the Evanses from Rome: 'So far this trip is a piece of cake. I'm now able to keep the plane on course without constantly looking at the compass. Funny how it comes to you.'

Crossing the Mediterranean from Sicily, he made his way in stages along the featureless coastal deserts of North Africa. The newspapers reported his arrival at Tripoli and then Cairo, just as they reported the progress of several other remarkable flights in the spring of 1933. Departing at almost the same time as Wilson were pilots attempting the first non-stop flight from London to Darwin and the first from New York to Baghdad, while a third was aiming to set a new record time for London to the Cape. But these were experienced aviators who knew what they were doing; the special appeal of Wilson was that he did not. The spotlight of the press was trained on his solitary plane.

By reaching Cairo, Wilson had already exceeded expectations. It may have been for that reason that he began to find himself restrained by the long arm of the British Establishment. His permit for flying across Persia—which he had previously arranged to collect in Egypt—was now mysteriously unavailable. Delayed but undeterred, he flew as far as Baghdad before diverting south east to avoid Persia. From Basra he followed the Gulf as far as the British Protectorate of Bahrain. Here the authorities tried a little harder to block his onward journey. On the orders of the

British Consul, he was refused permission to refuel. An official at the consulate explained that as all easterly landing strips within range of his aircraft were in Persian territory, he could not be allowed to continue without a permit. It was suggested that he should fly to the nearby Persian town of Bushire and apply for a permit on landing—a sly proposition that infuriated Wilson as he knew that his aircraft would immediately be impounded. Agreeing instead to retrace his route to Basra, he was accompanied to the airstrip by the official and allowed to refuel. Once in the air, however, he turned his plane towards India.

The airstrip at Gwadar, the westernmost in India, was not *within* the range of his aircraft but almost precisely at its estimated limit. It was a reckless gamble, but Wilson was lucky: when he touched down, after more than nine hours in the air, darkness was only minutes away and his fuel gauge read zero. In spite of further attempts to deny him fuel, Wilson now made his way in a series of steps across India until he reached Purnea, the base used by the Houston expedition.

His arrival in India seems to have surprised everyone except Wilson himself. By any standards it was an unlikely achievement for a novice pilot, not least because he had outwitted a devious bureaucracy. Touching down in Karachi, Hyderabad and Jodhpur, he received a celebrity's welcome. Journalists were keener than ever to interview him; the quotable crank from Stag Lane was providing a far better story than any of them had hoped and it promised to run on. He was said to have challenged Gandhi to a fast; reports wired from India to the *Daily Express* looked forward to the next instalment:

> Maurice Wilson, the young Bradford airman and rock climber who has undertaken the amazing adventure of a combined aerial and foot climb of Everest, gave some remarkable details of his plans when he landed here after flying from England. 'Enough rice and dates to last fifty days will be in my rucksack when I begin to climb Everest after landing on the mountain some

14,000 feet up. One trained man can succeed where a large group has failed. For ten months I have trained, testing foods and special types of fasts until I have found that the best procedure is to take one meal a day; this will enable me to breathe deep down in my stomach, taking in a vastly increased supply of oxygen.' His ten months of training and experimenting have given him the utmost confidence. He considers his optimism fully justified, as he has read every known book and studied every known map of Everest in that period. 'There is no stunt about it,' Mr Wilson reiterated. 'Mine is a carefully planned expedition.'

He emphasized the point by displaying his specialist equipment:

Mr Wilson produced various warm garments made specially to order for him; all were of the lightest woollen material. His whole kit weighs only forty pounds, including the tent, sleeping bag, outer suit of warm light material lined with silk and made to resist wind, sun and water, and a series of woollen cardigans. The unique feature of his climbing outfit is his boots, made with insulated cork, running from toe to heel.

In spite of the Air Ministry's warnings Wilson believed that he would obtain a permit to fly over Nepal, if he were tenacious enough in applying for it. But he was wrong. For three weeks he tried by every means to win a sympathetic hearing from either the British or Nepalese authorities—and failed. Nor could he make the flight illegally: the police had impounded his plane on arrival in Purnea and were keeping it under surveillance, its fuel tanks empty. The monsoon was coming and Wilson knew that he was checkmated. He would have to find another way.

He decided to sell his aircraft and forget about Nepal. He would travel to Darjeeling and approach the mountain on foot by the route of previous expeditions, through Sikkim and Tibet. He had missed his chance to make the climb that year, but would be ready by the spring. With £500 in his pocket from the sale of 'Ever Wrest' to a tea planter, he set off from Purnea and drifted out of the news.

Arriving in Darjeeling by its famous twisting railway, Wilson was relieved to be away from the heat and frustration of Purnea. It was cool and misty and he was making a fresh start. The news that the official British expedition had narrowly failed to reach the summit delighted him. With the whole winter before him, there was time to fast and pray, get fit and make plans. When the authorities informed him that he would not be given a permit to enter Sikkim and Tibet on foot, he was not unduly worried, nor did it bother him that the police were clearly keeping tabs on his whereabouts. He was confident of giving them the slip in due course, if he had to. For the time being he resumed his physical training by taking long daily walks through the hills and embarked on a diet of porridge and vegetables. In the three weeks leading up to Christmas it became a total fast.

To reach the mountain Wilson needed an ally and for a while it seemed that Karma Paul, the interpreter who had served on each of the last three Everest expeditions, might help him. He was a well-known and respected figure among both British climbers and the local authorities and Wilson hoped to use his influence to secure permission for his journey— by a direct appeal to the Dalai Lama himself. Karma Paul was eager, at first, to help, but the more time he spent with Wilson the less he liked him. According to his biographer, drawing on information from the Evanses, Wilson was 'a difficult man to get on with,' but he does not elaborate and perhaps did not need to. He was an obsessive and a loner. Although he won many admirers for his courage and perseverance, he formed few friendships. No doubt Karma Paul discovered that he could be stubborn and manipulative, and at some point he must also have realized that the Englishman knew little of mountaineering. Wiser not to be involved, he decided.

The loss of Karma Paul was a setback, but Wilson was used to impediments by now and each new one seemed only to provoke his determination. Dismissing any chance of making his journey legally, he considered another plan. Priests, he had learned, were allowed to travel freely between Tibet and India. He was a good deal larger than the average Tibetan, but, if he could obtain the right costume and travelled only at night, he believed he had a good chance of getting away with it. Fortunately, he was able to find three Sherpa porters from the recent Everest expedition who were willing, if he paid them well enough, to go along with his scheme. They had even agreed to help him procure an elaborate disguise. He described it in a letter to the Evanses:

> Did I look sweet? Chinese brocaded waistcoat in gold, with golden buttons at the side. Slacks of cheap dark blue cotton. The worst of it is I have to hide the lovely waistcoat under a huge mantle, about six inches longer than a nightdress. Next come about four yards of bright red silk girdle. They showed me how to walk with one arm outside the mantle, disclosing the brilliant plumage of the waistcoat underneath. Then came the hat, furnished with large earflaps; dark glasses to hide my honest blue eyes. Then I had to spoil the 'I'm Jackie' feeling with a pair of oversized hobnail boots.

The final touch was an attractive rice-paper umbrella. He bought a small pony and put word around that he was joining a tiger hunt and would be away from his lodgings for a couple of weeks. Knowing the police would be suspicious, he paid six months' advance rent; by the time they discovered his subterfuge, he intended to be well out of their reach. 'It would just be too humorous,' he wrote, 'to be returned to Darjeeling under police escort.'

On the night of 21 March he packed his climbing gear, dressed up and slipped out into the back streets. The Sherpas Tsering, Rinzing and Tewang were waiting for him in the woods.

They had been walking for only a few hours when they encountered their first policeman. It was too late to take evasive action. Wilson positioned the umbrella in front of his face and bent his knees as they passed, hoping to reduce his height; he wondered if the policeman was staring at him but he didn't dare look back and a moment later was breathing a heavy sigh of relief. Wilson knew that they would have to be more cautious and when another uniform loomed suddenly in the moonlight he leapt off the road and lay face down in the bushes, emerging a few minutes later badly stung by nettles.

They camped at dawn. After a second night's travelling they found themselves within a mile of a small village. As they rested by the roadside, the inquisitive villagers gathered around. Wilson hid his face in his elbow and hoped no one would notice his unusual boots. Tsering explained that he was a priest, and not only a priest but deaf and dumb too. He was also feeling unwell and wanted to be left alone. The villagers wandered away disappointed, but Wilson realized that he would have to spend the daylight hours confined to his tent.

He had plenty of time for his diary. Dedicated to Enid Evans, addressing her sometimes as 'girlie,' its entries read more like a letter than a journal:

March 26th.
Quite interesting to estimate nearness of dawn by the many sounds of the jungle—the birdcalls are so pretty and I use one when wanting anything inside tent. The Tibetans we pass sleeping on the road at night are as black as the Ace of Spades and it is only by their dirty rags that we can recognize them. Been a bit upset with water. Just had wholewheat bread—that stuff will play no small part in success. Pity the chappie is keeping it so near his socks in his rucksack.

March 27th.

Am roasting in the sun in this heavy mantle. Beautiful cascade playing right ahead of me. Wish I had a zip on my pants. It's quite a business doing a job for myself as I must first take off my hat and shed all my little treasures from my pouch before undressing. Then Tsering comes and screws me into this damned waistband again. Feel a bit like a cross between the Prince of Wales and Santa Claus. I'm hiding off the road while the boys have a meal.

March 28th.

Overcame latrine difficulty by digging hole inside tent. Had lovely bath in a washbowl today, and needed it. Done a bit of darning. Pity mother never showed me how, though I'm improving.

Wilson was looking forward to a 'good nag.' The Sherpas spoke only a little English and the language barrier was causing a few misunderstandings. In one entry Wilson complains that Tsering is going off to a pony race and will probably come back drunk, only to realize the next day that the Sherpa had gone to a village merely to get food for their pony: pony *rice.* Generally, he was full of praise for his companions, saying that he 'couldn't wish for better.'

On 30 March they crossed the frontier into Tibet. It was an important moment for Wilson, who felt like sending a wire to the British government: 'Told you so.' Out of reach of the Raj, he could now dispense with his costume and travel by day. They had been climbing steadily and quickly from the lush valleys of Sikkim and were now at 15,600 feet (4755 metres), on the edge of the Tibetan plateau. Wilson had liked 'jungle life,' but a far bleaker environment lay ahead, a place of burning sun, loose sand and almost constant, freezing winds. In spite of the altitude, he pressed on at up to 30 miles a day, but was soon suffering from headaches and sleeplessness; much of the playfulness now vanishes from his diary. Attempting to observe his special diet, he wrote monotonously and sometimes guiltily about food. Eggs, rice, dried fruit and Quaker Oats seem to have been his staple; on 8 April, after drinking nothing throughout the day, he says that he is 'going off the rails with a pot of tea.' Food begins to seep into other areas of his diary: he described the sky as 'duck egg blue,' while one of the Sherpas looks like 'a couple of sacks of wheat' and another, burned by the sun, has 'a face like a dried apricot.' It reads like the journal of a very hungry man.

Three weeks after leaving Darjeeling, Wilson was rewarded with his first view of Everest: 'Saw Everest today. Looked magnificent. One half in snow plume. Two nights from now I shall be at Rongbuk where I hope to fast for a couple of days and get my system ready for the big event. *I must win.* Looking forward to getting back—what a time we'll have over tea...'

Sixteen miles from Everest and in full sight of it, the famous Rongbuk monastery was the final staging post for expeditions. It had become a tradition for the head lama to meet incoming climbers and bless them as they departed for the mountain. Wilson was uncertain about the kind of reception he would receive, but in hoping the lama would welcome him he had an ulterior motive: the previous year's party had left behind a quantity of supplies and he wanted to be able to help himself. He decided to pretend that he was a member of the official expedition, returning on reconnaissance duty: 'Shall tell the Lama I am one of the expedition if anything wanted from stores—bar of chocolate or anything like that. Tsering says there is plenty of meat. What a game: maybe in less than five weeks the world will be on fire.'

Wilson dressed for the meeting in his best flying shirt and white helmet. It seems unlikely that the lama believed his ruse and in the end it didn't matter: he liked the Englishman and was touched by his courage. 'Made a hit by all accounts,' Wilson wrote in his diary. Invited to rummage freely in the stores, he selected a new tent, boots and a collapsible lantern and was relieved to find no chocolate or other food: he was spared from temptation.

News of Wilson's 'escape' from Darjeeling had reached the British newspapers. While many reported the impending climax of the story with an open mind and a sense of romance, those that drew on expert opinion were more judgemental: 'While one cannot but admire the pluck of Maurice Wilson in attempting to climb Mount Everest alone, his whole project and his training methods in particular seem to have been ill judged. It is said that he has been fasting for five months and accustoming himself to a diet of figs, dates and cereals. This will be just about as useful to him in his present venture as it would be if he were intending to swim the Atlantic.'

The article warned of intense cold, frequent blizzards and of rarefied air producing feelings of depression and hopelessness that can be assuaged only by human companionship and proper food. Quite apart from this, the climbing of Everest presented many technical difficulties and Wilson was not qualified to deal with them.

Wilson would never read the reports, but he had heard it all before. As he looked towards Everest he felt confident and serene. Of course there would be cliffs and glaciers in the days ahead, but he was now more certain than ever that Divine Providence had brought him to the mountain and would lead him, in due course, to its summit. He had seen the optimism on the Sherpas' faces; the head lama had not expressed a word of doubt—he had smiled and laughed throughout their meeting. It was as if they all *knew* that he was going to succeed.

Now he just wanted to get it over with and return home. Telling the Sherpas that he would be away for six or seven days, Wilson set out in the early morning of 16 April. On the back of his rucksack he tied a shaving mirror, hoping that the sun would catch it and that the lamas, keeping a lookout from the walls of the monastery, would see a distant glinting signal rising slowly up the mountain.

But they didn't, and nine days later the head lama became concerned that Wilson had not returned. He asked one of the Sherpas to go and wait for him at the site of the previous expedition's Camp I, but almost immediately they saw a figure stumbling towards them from the direction of the mountain. His limbs were emaciated and his face horribly swollen—the man was barely recognizable as Wilson.

According to his diary Wilson had made good progress on the first day. As if God were already helping him, the sun was bright and the air almost perfectly still; the enormous rucksack seemed astonishingly easy to manage. From what he had read he knew the 'real climbing' started at Camp III and expected to reach it within a couple of days. By the next morning everything had changed. Having assumed that he would find a track to follow along the glacier, he could find no trace of one and within a few hours he was hopelessly lost. Wherever he tried to walk he found yawning crevasses. Strange ice pinnacles towered above him and he could not see the way. His eyes burned and his head spun. He had wandered into a labyrinth and it was, as he wrote in his diary, 'a *hell* of a day.'

It took him three days just to reach Camp II and by then he was exhausted. The thin air was hard to breathe and seemed to burn his throat: 'got hell of a thirst on this damned glacier, don't know why. Am eating snow and ice.' All he was eating apart from that—indeed all he had brought with him—was bread and Quaker Oats and it gave him little strength. On the fourth day he made only three-quarters of a mile before a blizzard forced him to pitch camp; by the end of the next he was still nearly three miles from Camp III, a steep glacier ahead of him. It was not as he had imagined. That evening he confessed to his diary that he should have brought crampons. He understood now what they were for and wondered if he would find a pair in the supply dump near Camp III. If he did not, he intended to improvise with tin cans and a length of rope. He concluded tersely: 'Think I shall have to take a bit more to eat and see if that will solve the lassitude business. Don't think anyone would undertake this job for sheer bravado. Think the climbers had it cushy with servants and porters.'

The next day was his birthday, which he had hoped to celebrate on the summit. All he wrote was: 'Many happy returns to myself. Overtaken by snowstorm and parked early.' In the morning he decided that he had had enough: 'No use going on. Eyes terrible and throat dry. Thought

because lack of water but have been keeping mouth open. Discretion better part of valour and with even Herculean effort could not make Camp
III in time. Weather bad.'

During the long trek back to the monastery Wilson suffered acute
pain in his left arm and his eyes swelled until he was nearly blind. In his
distress, he found that he was thinking about his mother. Having spent the
whole of his adult life away from Bradford, he suddenly wanted to be with
her and to revisit the places of his childhood. He drew a line around the
entry in his diary and may have intended to delete it; he wrote earlier that
he would 'clean up' his writing before setting out for the mountain, no
doubt with posterity in mind.

'Spent all day in bed and ATE,' Wilson wrote of his first day back at
the monastery. He did not get up for three days and it would take him
three weeks to recover from his ordeal, but there was no question of his
giving up. 'Faith,' he wrote, 'is not faith that wavers when its prayers remain
unanswered.' The diary of his convalescence dwells on his diet; he was
delighted that he could find no trace of fat on his body. Eating biscuits,
eggs and dates, he was occasionally disappointed with the standard of his
Sherpas' cooking, but, when he tried to make them a Yorkshire pudding,
it was a disaster. He was slowly 'thawing to normal,' his cheerfulness
returning. It was time to think of fasting again. 'Don't suppose an evening
goes by,' he wrote to Enid, 'but you and Len speculate as to where I am
and what I'm doing. Good to think that I shall be with you again in less
than a couple of months.'

On 12 May he set out from the monastery for the last time. He
would not risk losing his way on the glacier again. Rinzing and Tewang
were to accompany him as far as Camp III; from there, in the first fine
weather, Wilson intended to strike out alone.

With expert guides, the climb to Camp III was 'like a spring walk' and
they reached it in three days. If Wilson was breaking his bargain with God
by taking the Sherpas with him, he was also about to depart from his diet
in spectacular fashion. Close by was the supply dump abandoned by the

official expedition. It contained an extraordinary delicatessen: plum jam, butter, Bourneville chocolate, Fortnum and Mason's anchovy paste, sugar, Ovaltine, Nestlé's milk and, Wilson wrote, 'other treasures from heaven. Talk about a Santa Claus party outside my tent.'

The next evening Wilson continued: 'Eaten everything about the place today. Soup, Ovaltine, and heaven knows what, Rinzing went for another box of food and brought a greater variety including maple sugar, cake and a vegetable ration. Guess what I'm wallowing in as I write? A one pound box of King George chocolates!'

A blizzard had confined them to camp and it lasted several days. At more than 21,000 feet (6401 metres), the altitude was giving all the men painful headaches and Wilson seemed to be suffering more than the others. He was unable to sleep: 'Terrible when you can't put your head down for aching nerves.'

They had been at Camp III for a week when Wilson set out towards the steep slopes of Everest's famous North Col, Rinzing agreed to show him the route taken by the last expedition. In spite of the passage of time, wind and snow, Wilson expected to find intact a staircase of cut steps and a guiding rope, but there was nothing: the vast escarpment was blank. Any mountaineer could have warned him, but Wilson, of course, had never sought their advice. As the sun descended Rinzing made his way back to the camp, and Wilson, alone once more, turned to the slope.

For two days he struggled to ascend the North Col. He had made some progress when the slope suddenly rose ahead of him into a vertical wall of ice more than 40 feet high. However hard and however many times he tried, he could not master it. It drained the last reserves of his strength and, on the third day, he was too exhausted to get out of his sleeping bag: 'Had a terrible job yesterday and whoever selected that route ought to be pole axed. Am parked at an angle of 35 degrees but have shaped the snow to my carcass. Had five dry biscuits yesterday morning and nothing since, as there is nothing to have. Funny, but I feel all these stick ups I get have a reason.'

The pencil felt like a shard of ice in his hand and his writing was beginning to trail wildly across the page. The next morning he roused himself: 'Only one thing to do—no food, no water—get back. Did two sheer drop rolls down the face of the ice, but fortunately without any effect. Ribs sore but not much.'

At Camp III the Sherpas pleaded with him to return to the monastery. Wilson refused and merely lay in his bag for the next three days. He did not want to speak and wrote nothing in his diary. On 29 May he began to climb again: 'This will be the last effort and I feel successful. Have pulled out my flag of friendship and it feels quite cheering. Strange, but I feel there is someone with me in the tent all the time.' He walked only half a mile before pitching camp. He lay there for a further thirty-six hours and again wrote nothing. The next entry in his diary were the last words of Maurice Wilson: 'May 31st, Thursday. Off again. Gorgeous day.'

A YEAR LATER DR CHARLES WARREN held the small book in his hand. The next pages were blank. If Wilson had moved at all on that 'gorgeous' day, he had evidently not travelled far. His body was found only a short distance from Camp III and the food dump he described so vividly; he had died of exhaustion or from exposure. While his men took turns to read from the memoir, Warren had been eating sweetmeats from the dump and now wished that he hadn't. He felt suddenly queasy.

Why did Wilson not return to his Sherpas? It was a matter of record that Rinzing and Tewang remained at their post for ten days before giving up hope and retreating to the monastery to report him missing. Like many who have read the diary since, Warren wondered what thoughts had passed through his mind in those last days and hours when he wrote nothing.

Wilson must have realized by then that, for all his determination, he could not climb Mount Everest alone. For all his faith, God had not answered his prayers. He might yet have saved himself, but he decided to carry on, if it was only for a few yards. Perhaps he believed it was better to die there than admit, after all, that he was a fool. But if those were his last thoughts, he never expressed them. He wanted others to read his diary and had already written his own epitaph: *Faith is not the faith that wavers when its prayers remain unanswered.*

Curiously, it was not quite the end of Maurice Wilson's story. From time to time the glacier has cast up his body on to the surface and from time to time subsequent expeditions have reburied it. It continues to appear, in increasingly small fragments. A short time after the publication of Dennis Roberts' biography in 1957, a strange rumour emerged. Its origin is unclear, but it rapidly gained currency. Roberts, according to the rumour, had not told the whole truth about Wilson. He had chosen to omit an important detail: the burly Yorkshireman had climbed Everest in women's clothing—or had at least carried some articles on to the mountain. Charles Warren was said to have discovered a lady's shoe among his effects. Those who promoted the rumour spoke of certain clues and evasions in the biography and newspaper reports of the time. Wilson once owned a ladies' dress shop. His marriages ended abruptly. He liked needlework. He clearly liked dressing up in the girdles and robes of a Tibetan priest. 'I'm Jackie!' he said in one of his letters to Enid Evans, but was he joking? According to some versions of the rumour, when Wilson's body was discovered it was festooned in women's handkerchiefs.

The rumour circulated so widely and for so long that when Charles Warren's obituary appeared in the *Guardian*, it confidently referred to his discovery of the mysterious shoe. In fact, the event never happened. In an interview he gave in 1992 Warren said: 'There was one rumour that he had a lady's slipper with him, and another that he was wearing women's clothes, but I think I can refute both those ideas. After all, I was there when the body was found and he certainly wasn't wearing women's clothes, and I, for one, didn't see any sign of a slipper.'

Warren offered an epitaph for Wilson: 'I think that we must admire him for being a very brave man, but not a very *wise* man.'

CHAPTER 7

The Rise and Fall of Fritz Wiessner

An elderly man was sitting in the top of a tree. The neighbours were used to seeing him up there among the branches. He would sometimes call out in his strong German accent, inviting them to join him and admire the view. He was astonishingly agile for a man in his eighties.

His accent and rather stern demeanour had made him formidable at first, but they had got to know him. He had lived in Stowe, Vermont, for many years, although he had been born in Germany. A retired chemist, he had run a successful business and raised two children; this was one side of him. Over time his neighbours learned that he used to be a famous mountaineer, one of the best in the world, it was said. Now he just climbed the tree in his garden; always the same one. His house was full of books about climbing and decorated with photographs of peaks and cliffs he had conquered. Younger mountaineers often visited and seemed to regard him as something of a guru, but he had not always been so popular, it transpired. To his surviving contemporaries he was still, at best, a controversial figure. There had been a terrible tragedy on one of his expeditions to the Himalayas. It had happened almost half a century before, but old men have long memories.

When Fritz Wiessner came to the United States in 1929 he had intended to return to Germany permanently at some point. He meant to study for a while in New York, make some friends, explore business interests and, in the meantime, climb. Alpinism was a relatively new sport in America: the principal clubs were less than thirty years old and, although his achievement seemed to belong to a different era, only sixteen years had passed since Hudson Stuck, Archdeacon of the Yukon, had struggled to the top of the highest peak on the continent. Few American climbers had reached the level of technical skill on display in the Alps, where Austrians, Italians and Germans were seeking ever more difficult routes up mountains that had long since been conquered. Aged twenty-nine when he left Germany, Wiessner had been considered one of the brightest talents in Europe; in America, there was nobody better.

Diminutive, short-limbed and barrel-chested, he looked like a circus acrobat. On the rock faces that he loved he showed immense strength, superb balance and certain judgement, and was soon leading climbs where no American had previously dared to go.

He was ambitious. In 1932 he was accepted into the American Alpine Club and helped to organize a bold attempt on Nanga Parbat in the Himalayas with a German–American team; he was in the party that reached a high point of 23,000 feet (7010 metres). In 1936 his ascent of Mt Waddington in British Columbia, with the American Bill House, brought his name to public attention for the first time. Regarded as the most difficult summit in North America, the mountain had resisted no fewer than sixteen previous attempts and had cost the life of one man.

'Fritz Wiessner is bald, thirty-six years old, and only five feet five inches high,' a newspaper reported. 'He doesn't look like a mountain climber, but he is—one of the greatest.' There were more headlines the next year when he and House made the first free ascent of one of America's national landmarks, the spectacular Devil's Tower in Wyoming; the only other men to climb it had needed ladders.

Seeking greater challenges, he looked once more to the giant peaks of the Himalayas. By tacit agreement, Everest was reserved for the British and Nanga Parbat for the Germans, but the second highest mountain in the world, and by reputation its most difficult, had not been attempted since the Duke of Abruzzi's expedition nearly thirty years before. It was therefore a 'free' summit. In the spring of 1937, with the support of the American Alpine Club, Wiessner applied to the British authorities for permission to enter Northern Kashmir the following year and attempt K2. The application made slow progress through the State Department, the American Embassy in London, the India Office, the Indian government, and finally the government of Kashmir. By the time the permit had made the same bureaucratic journey in reverse, it was almost winter, too late for Wiessner to free himself of his business commitments. Permission, however, had been granted for two consecutive years and the American Alpine Club decided to send a reconnaissance party to the mountain in 1938; Wiessner would follow the next year with a larger expedition and capitalize on their groundwork.

The reconnaissance was entrusted to Charlie Houston, a young doctor with impressive expeditionary credentials. Though still in his twenties, he had made the first ascent of McKinley's forbidding neighbour, Mt Foraker, and had organized the Anglo-American party that reached the summit of Nanda Devi, at that time the highest mountain ever climbed. Preferring small expeditions, he had earned a reputation for leading them efficiently and harmoniously. He was the perfect choice and had soon recruited a powerful team that included some of the best young climbers in America. Among them was Bill House, Wiessner's former climbing partner.

Houston's expedition was a resounding success and might have been a triumph. After a thorough reconnaissance around the base of the mountain, he concluded, like Abruzzi before him, that the south-east ridge presented the only realistic route and promptly began to climb it. In three weeks on the ridge, his party reached a high point of 26,000 feet (7925 metres) and discovered a series of cramped but workable locations for a line of camps, establishing a route that a later party could follow. One of the most difficult obstacles was a cliff of 80 feet, rising vertically—and unavoidably—above the site of Camp IV. House had inched his way up a chimney in the rock and, once ropes were fixed in place, the whole party had been able safely to proceed. From their high point, they could see no reason why a future expedition would not go all the way—no reason, that is, except the weather. It changed quickly and could be murderous, anywhere on the ridge. Houston might have pressed on and made a bid for the summit himself, but clouds were gathering, supplies were low and he was not the kind of man to gamble, least of all on K2.

Wiessner was sanguine and perhaps relieved. Like Archdeacon Stuck, he believed his mountain was waiting for him, but when he began to recruit for his own expedition, he ran into problems. Bill House turned him down; then two or three other prospective candidates did the same. They told him that they didn't have the money or the time, but what they lacked more than anything was the inclination to spend six months under his leadership.

Cultivated and sociable, with a certain courtly charm, Wiessner had made many friends in America and House counted himself among them. He did not, however, want to test their friendship on another expedition. On Mt Waddington and the Devil's Tower, Wiessner's intensity of purpose had become oppressive. He had little sense of humour. He wanted—he *insisted*—*on* doing things his way. If Houston's style was democratic, Wiessner's was dictatorial. At a time when everyone was conscious of a German national stereotype, it was impossible to miss how well Wiessner seemed to conform to it.

In fact the issue of his nationality caused Wiessner much anxiety throughout the 1930s. Changing citizenship, he said, was not like changing a shirt. But after six years in the United States he decided that he preferred the 'free life and free ways' to the prospect of returning to his much-changed homeland and applied to become an American citizen. By the time his papers arrived, only a few weeks before he left for K2, he knew it meant that one day he might have to fight against Germany.

Eventually, Wiessner enlisted eight men in the expedition. Despite the absence of his first choices, the list included a few big names—until bad luck and second thoughts gradually deleted them. One of the strongest climbers broke his leg skiing. Another withdrew when his wife suffered a miscarriage and a third pulled out almost on the eve of departure. Of the five who remained, only one had any expeditionary experience at all and it was limited to Canada. None was in Wiessner's class. But final preparations were under way and it was too late now to call it off.

Wiessner appointed Oliver Eaton Cromwell as his deputy. He was wealthy enough to have spent each of the last twenty summers in the mountains and was well known at the American Alpine Club for the sheer number of ascents he had made in the Alps and in Canada—at least 200. He had climbed both the Matterhorn and Mont Blanc three times. No American could claim more peaks, but he had usually climbed with guides and, at the age of forty-seven, believed he was too old to work at extreme altitude. He joined the party on the understanding that he was not to be counted on to go higher than Camp IV. Jack Durrance was a twenty-seven-year-old guide, a brilliant rock climber and skier. Chappell Cranmer and George Sheldon, classmates from Dartmouth College in New Hampshire, were promising twenty-year-olds. The sixth member of the party, and the odd one out, was Dudley Francis Wolfe.

Wolfe was a multi-millionaire. Now forty-three, he had inherited a share of his father's fortune—one of the largest in America—while still young and owned an estate on the coast of Maine that his nephew has described as being like something from *The Great Gatsby*. He owned a racing yacht and travelled in a chauffeur-driven Rolls-Royce, but behind the trappings of a playboy lifestyle, Wolfe was a serious, introspective and unhappy man.

'Quiet and rather dull' was the first impression he made on his sister-in-law, and it may have been a verdict that he dreaded. He was not as clever as his brother or as witty as his friends and had spent most of his life trying to find something at which he excelled, to achieve *something* remarkable. When the United States entered the First World War he immediately abandoned his studies to enlist in the American Army—and was rejected because of his poor eyesight. Determined to find some kind of role, he made his own way to France, joined a reserve transport unit, and then travelled to Italy to serve with the American Red Cross. He drove an ambulance for the Italian Army and won its equivalent of the Croix de Guerre. But the medal was not enough and at the time of the armistice he was in training with the French Foreign Legion. He had discovered that he had no shortage of physical courage and although he was large, clumsy and bespectacled, he sought new challenges in increasingly dangerous sports: first big-game hunting, then transatlantic yacht racing, competitive skiing, and finally mountaineering.

In 1934 he married Alice Damrosch, an American socialite and champion skier, daughter of the composer Walter Damrosch. Lively and ambitious, she dominated her husband and, despite their shared interest in the mountains, the marriage drifted towards failure. She was fond of him and they remained friends, but divorce was a bitter disappointment for Wolfe. It was at this time, the autumn of 1938, after he had spent a fifth consecutive season in the Alps, that Alice introduced him to Wiessner.

In February 1939 Wolfe wrote to his brother Clifford:

> I have made 30 major climbs including the descent of the north face of the Breithorn, which according to my guide, is the first time it has ever been done. A steep, difficult, and dangerous ice wall on which several people have been killed, but which we got down safely. Last spring I traversed Mont Blanc with skis, the highest mountain in Europe under very difficult conditions—a traverse that has been very seldom done. Please do not think that I am blowing my horn; you will understand when you see what I am leading up to.
>
> A short time ago I received an invitation from Fritz Wiessner, leader of the American Alpine Club expedition to the

Himalayas, to join the expedition in an attempt to climb K2, 28,200 ft, the world's second highest mountain. This invitation, after carefully looking into the situation, I have accepted.

Alice was annoyed with Wiessner, telling him he 'shouldn't persuade Dudley to go on such a hazardous trip.' She knew he would say yes, but thought he was too old, and would not be equal to it. Wiessner, however, was obliged to select his team from those who could afford their share of the expedition's cost—some $17,500. The fact that Wolfe could clearly afford a great deal more brought a feeling of security to the enterprise. Wiessner liked his enthusiasm and believed that he would be strong enough for the lower part of the mountain at least. As Alice suspected, her ex-husband saw things differently. The chance meeting with Wiessner, the promise of travelling to a distant land and a fabled mountain, seemed to have provided him with a final opportunity to make his mark on the world. From the very beginning he made up his mind that he wanted to reach the summit.

'All in all I have accepted this invitation for a good many reasons,' he told his brother, but was not prepared to elaborate. Clifford, he knew, would be worried about his younger brother's latest adventure, and Wolfe was at pains to reassure him.

On this expedition there will be no professional guides, but Wiessner is as good as the best guides and will have the complete planning of the climb. As he nearly reached the top of Nanga Parbat and has had much other experience I feel that he will be most conservative. He impresses me as being a most careful climber. Finally, realize that the men taking part in this trip are mature, responsible, professional men and married men, some with families, who will not take foolish risks...

In regard to my personal affairs, let me state that my house is completely in order. I drew up a will just before coming to

Europe. My estate is in good shape and I have no outstanding debts. Do not be alarmed when I speak of my estate. I merely do so as it shows good sense.

He finished his letter by asking Clifford to send three small flags—those of the United States, the State of Maine and Harvard University.

The expedition assembled in Europe and sailed for Bombay via the Suez Canal. A film shot by Wolfe on board the SS *Conte Biancamano* shows a happy group of men lounging by the deck pool, playing badminton, flirting with a couple of attractive female passengers. They were surprised to find on board Dr Hjalmar Schacht, the well-known German financier and sometime confidant of Hitler. Wolfe described him as a 'smooth article' and wondered what his 'government mission' to India entailed, adding 'the British are watching him.' Both Wiessner and Durrance enjoyed his company and his generosity at the bar. In a letter to Alice, Wolfe said the first class accommodation was full of Jewish refugees en route to Shanghai, some of whom would play the piano and accordion and sing for the others: 'They are the only people on board that have any life or personality to them.'

The men were in high spirits. 'Our party,' Wiessner wrote to the President of the American Alpine Club, 'is really exceptionally congenial.' They arrived at Bombay on Easter Monday, took the Frontier Mail train to Rawalpindi and continued on the hair-raising Punjab Motor Express to Srinigar. Here they met the nine Sherpas from Darjeeling who were to serve as high-altitude porters and a liaison officer provided by the British Army, Lieutenant 'Joe' Trench.

Having dusted themselves down, the men enjoyed the luxurious hospitality of the local representative of the Himalayan Ski Club, Major Kenneth Hadow. A landowner and rug manufacturer, he was the grandnephew of Douglas Hadow, killed on the Matterhorn in 1865.

To relax and acclimatize before the long march to the mountain, Wiessner had scheduled ten days of skiing in the spectacular Vale of

Kashmir. Hadow arranged access to a palatial ski 'hut' and provided a team of servants; Wiessner invited two English girls to join them. They were 'not at all interesting' in Wolfe's opinion and it would have been better if they had not come, he wrote in a letter to Alice. 'This trip and the preparation for it are too important. Two girls amongst six men are bound to cause demoralization.'

Nor was he pleased at the time given to social activity following their return from the mountain hut. Dr Schacht had unexpectedly appeared in Srinigar, called on Wiessner, and was now invited to the large party organized by the Americans to thank Major Hadow. Wolfe thought Schacht's presence inappropriate and, having wondered how the British would take it, was disappointed to see Hadow warming to him. It seemed typical to Wolfe of the British attitude to Germany. No one was more relieved when they finally set out for the mountain.

Four weeks later, ahead of a long column of heavily laden porters, they reached the confluence of glaciers known as Concordia and began climbing towards the base of the mountain. In the space of a few moments the clouds thinned and then parted to reveal the gigantic shape of K2. It seemed to fill the sky. George Sheldon's initial reaction was to feel intimidated. They were already higher than any summit in the United States. The air was thin, and even on the glacier, they had been forced to stop every ten minutes, gasping. What was it going to be like on the mountain?

But Wiessner was intensely excited. 'Will this be the crowning achievement of my climbing career?' he wrote in his diary. 'Everything that I have learned in my long years in the mountains; whatever degree of strength, energy, endurance, and instinct that they have given me, is dedicated to this effort—cool and deliberate, but with a warm heart.'

They set up Base Camp on 31 May and the next morning things started to go wrong. At seven o'clock Chappell Cranmer came out of his tent and very quietly said that he didn't feel well. All the men had felt ill at some point during the march, and didn't give it a second thought. But when Durrance checked on him at noon he found that he was coughing profusely and developing a fever and a racing pulse. By the afternoon, Cranmer was close to death. With no doctor in the party it was up to Durrance, who was considering medical school, to do his best with a first-aid book, some codeine tablets, and a hypodermic syringe. As Cranmer's breathing grew weak and his face turned purple, Durrance gave him two hours of artificial respiration. Many years later Durrance recalled:

> Chappell was coughing up a huge quantity of clear, frothy fluid, or mush, from his lungs. I must have collected at least three coffee cups full. Horrible, bubbly stuff. Poor fellow, he was completely out of it, delirious, unconscious, babbling nonsense from time to time about a baseball game he dreamed he was playing back at Dartmouth. I fought a losing battle to keep him and the immediate vicinity clean. But even the tent was becoming a mess and everything inside smelled to high heaven. Then the worst happened: Chappell developed diarrhoea and simultaneously lost control of his body functions... I never knew anyone could be so sick and stay alive—especially here at 16,500 feet.

By dawn he seemed to have passed the first crisis, but remained extremely weak. Wolfe was concerned that news of a serious illness or even a death in the party might reach his brother—mail runners carried letters to and from Base Camp, by arrangement with Major Hadow. That morning he wrote to Clifford and told him 'in the strictest confidence' about the events of the previous night: 'We hope for the best. I think he has an even chance. I am writing this because if the worse comes to the worse and it gets into the US papers *do not worry* about me. I have survived the march in extremely good shape and am in splendid condition.'

Cranmer pulled through, but could take no further part in the expedition. 'My best man seems to be out of it for some time,' Wiessner recorded in his diary. He had expected him to do better than anyone on the mountain. They had not set foot on it yet, but already they were down to five men, one of whom had already stated that he would not climb high.

The assault began on 5 June. Wiessner intended to follow the route and camp positions established on Houston's reconnaissance, and lay siege to the summit. Sheldon summarized the plan: 'Our plan was to establish a series of camps up to within striking distance of the summit. Each of these camps would be stocked with tents, sleeping bags, petrol, and a two-week supply of food, in case a storm should maroon a party. The camps were to be near enough together to permit constant contact.'

The Sherpas ran ahead 'like goats' to set up the first camp on the ridge and the next four days were spent going backwards and forwards from Base Camp, bringing up loads. This exhausting work completed, the party began moving upwards. Initially, everything went well—by 22 June Wiessner, Sheldon and Wolfe were ensconced in Camp IV, at 21,500 feet (6553 metres), just below the 'House Chimney.' They had all read about the famous obstacle in the mountaineering journals and Wiessner was looking forward to climbing it. But that night a fantastic storm engulfed the mountain. The gusts striking the tent sounded like machine-gun fire, and even Wiessner was terrified. He had been in bad weather before, but nothing like this. Sheldon wrote:

> It never did get light that morning. The black night merely turned a pasty grey. We settled back in our sleeping bags to wait it out. We waited eight days. We would lie in our sleeping bags swathed in several sets of woollen underwear, wind suits, gloves and hats. At any moment we expected to be blown into nearby Tibet. We had nothing to read except the labels on food cans... meanwhile the eternal banging and cracking of the tent made us virtually psychopathic cases...

By the time the wind died Sheldon's nerves were so fraught that the sudden quiet frightened him. Sent down to Camp II for more supplies, he made his way uneasily through the new snow, along fixed ropes thickened with ice, while Wiessner shouted advice and encouragement from above. He was looking down from a rocky pinnacle, and long after the swirling mists obscured him Sheldon could still hear his voice, carried on the wind.

Cromwell and Durrance had weathered the storm at Camp II. They were relieved to see Sheldon, but he found them in low spirits: 'The storm left its mark on us. Days of inactivity in the rarefied altitude had drained us of that elusive spirit which gives a man the power to carry on when the body is through.'

The thin air seemed to inhibit sleep, and through the night they suffered frequent fits of coughing. As the weather cleared, the three tired men resumed the laborious task of backpacking supplies from the base of the ridge, but after two days more snow fell, and Cromwell began to worry about the risk of avalanches above them. He decided not to move up to the higher camps until the snow hardened. While they waited, the freezing temperature of the past two weeks took its toll: Sheldon developed severe frostbite in his foot. It began to swell and turn black, and Cromwell had no alternative but to order him off the mountain while he could still walk—or at least hobble. A short time later Sheldon was reunited with Cranmer at Base Camp. The mail runners had been there and in month-old newspapers the two young men read about Hitler and Chamberlain and the crisis in Poland. Nursing his foot and describing the storm to his classmate, Sheldon could not resist the idea that the struggle taking place on the mountain was of far greater magnitude than anything reported in the papers: 'It sounded like a puny world, full of little people.'

Out of six climbers, two were now *hors de combat*. Cromwell and Durrance remained at Camp II, but they were weary and nervous, and talked endlessly of the comforts of home. Other than Wiessner, only one man emerged from the great storm with an undiminished appetite for the work ahead: Dudley Wolfe. He felt strong, and was sleeping well. Although he had found the steep climb to Camp IV awkward and difficult he had not been frightened, and it seemed to him that he had been right about Wiessner in the letter to his brother: he was like a guide, cautious and protective. If he could stay close to him, Wolfe was more certain than ever that he would lead him all the way to the summit.

On 30 June, the day after the storm cleared, Wiessner and the Sherpa Pasang Kikuli climbed the House Chimney—they found the ropes left by Houston's party embedded in the snow—and the next day they carefully guided Wolfe to the top of the cliff. A short distance above it they made their fifth camp and endured another two days of bad weather. While Wolfe remained at Camp V to receive supplies from below, Wiessner and two Sherpas now pressed on to Camp VI, at 23,400 feet (7132 metres).

A long slow passage over rocks and a 300-feet traverse across a steep ice slope brought Wiessner and the Sherpas to the site of Camp VII. Now at nearly 25,000 feet (7620 metres), he was elated by the progress they were making and delighted with the performance of his Sherpas—especially Pasang Kikuli, who seemed to Wiessner to be as strong and proficient as the best Swiss guides. It was time to descend to Camp V and assemble a party for an attack on the mountain's final 3000 feet (914 metres).

Wiessner expected to find the camp stocked with provisions and equipment brought up from below. But Wolfe was alone, and had seen no one since Wiessner had left him there three days before. Each day Wolfe had inched his way down to the top of the House Chimney and peered down on Camp IV, but there had been no sign of life and no answer to his shouts. Wiessner was annoyed, and decided to go down alone and investigate.

'Lo and behold,' Durrance wrote in his diary at Camp II on 10 July, 'Fritz came forth from the hanging fogs of K2 alone yesterday aft.' He had not seen Wiessner for more than two weeks, and was struck immediately by how thin and tired—and irritated—he looked. Durrance could hardly believe that Camp VI had been established and that one load of supplies had been pushed almost as far as Camp VII. As he and Cromwell had considered it too dangerous in the heavy snow even to try for Camp IV, it seemed that Wiessner had 'achieved the impossible.' The leader's unexpected appearance at their camp, and his words of urgent encouragement worked like a dose of adrenaline on the two men. Perhaps the mountain would be climbed after all. But the effect did not last.

The following day Wiessner led the entire party back up the ridge. Leaving Cromwell in charge of Camp IV, he continued to the high camps with his 'summit team' of Wolfe and Durrance, accompanied by seven Sherpas. Cromwell had been too tired to go further, and now Durrance began to struggle—and also to worry. He had not enjoyed being on the same rope as Wolfe. On several occasions the older man had stumbled and almost fallen, threatening to take others with him. It was plain that he could not look after himself. Durrance said later:

> Dudley would have trouble in different places. Trouble in balancing himself and handling the rock. An experienced man knows how to go up it and causes no trouble. Dudley was slow for one thing, very slow, and a bit awkward. He did not do an awful lot of climbing, made one or two trips to Camp I, then he only went up, and never came down, didn't do any trips between camps... The Sherpas refused to carry him on their rope because they were afraid to, and Dudley felt that. I know he knew he couldn't go alone and depended always on someone to take him on a rope.

He felt that Wiessner should not have allowed him to climb so high. They were wasting time and energy 'hauling him about just because he was able to finance the undertaking.'

At Camp VI, Durrance shared a tent with Wolfe. After the performance on the rocky slope that afternoon, he assumed that Wolfe would now accept that he had reached his high point—but he was wrong. The idea had not crossed his mind. In fact, he said how much he was looking forward to the next day's climbing. Durrance decided to try to talk him out

of it. It was an awkward subject to broach: he didn't know Wolfe well, but
he realized how serious he was about the expedition and had seen that he
was sensitive to criticism. Wolfe listened, as he made his point plainly. He
explained that if he went higher it would be his responsibility—he did not
have the skill to descend alone. But the words seemed to make little
impression.

That night, Durrance didn't sleep at all. As for Wolfe, so long as he
had Wiessner's approval to continue, he was satisfied. The next morning he
told him about the conversation with Durrance and said that he regarded
his advice as 'silly'—after all, wasn't *he* coping much better with the altitude
than the young rock climber? Wiessner told him what he wanted to hear:
that he 'could not refuse anyone who could carry a load and keep up with
the party.' He knew that Wolfe was a poor climber, but he was strong—and
he was the only man left who wanted to go higher.

On 13 July they set out from Camp VI. After an hour of climbing
Durrance was unable to catch his breath and could barely keep up with
Wolfe—something that did not escape the older man's notice. For a while
Wiessner took his pack, but he moved more and more slowly and eventually told the others that he could not go on; he did not have the strength.
He unroped and descended to Camp VI, saying that he would try again
the next day. Wiessner sent four of the seven Sherpas with him, with
instructions to help bring up supplies to Camps VII and VIII, with or
without Durrance. Among them was Pasang Kikuli, whose feet were showing signs of frostbite; if he lost his toes, he said, his wife would never look
at him again. It was a further disappointment to Wiessner, who wanted the
most experienced Sherpa to be with him for the final push.

Beyond a long, steep ice traverse the lead party established Camp VII,
stocking it with two stoves, six quarts of fuel, three sleeping bags and
twelve days of food. It was to be the main supply depot on the high
mountain. On 14 July they climbed with 40-pound packs through knee-
deep snowfields for five and a half hours to reach the site of Camp VIII.
While they pitched the tents Wiessner sent two of the Sherpas back to

Camp VII, to bring more food and sleeping bags. Wiessner, Wolfe and the Sherpa Pasang Lama were now at 25,300 feet (7711 metres). The high camps were well provisioned and, below them, out of sight, a moving supply line stretched all the way down to the glacier. All three men felt strong. Wolfe, it seemed to Wiessner, was doing better the higher he went.

For the next two days it snowed and the men rested. On 17 July, in clear weather, they moved towards the top of the snowfield. Less than 300 feet from Camp VIII, the snowfield ended in a crevasse or 'bergschrund'— beyond it was a rocky shoulder leading towards the summit cone. Filled with soft snow, the bergschrund was like a pool of quicksand, and crossing it required all Wiessner's power. He sank up to his chin: 'As we approached the bergschrund the snow became deeper and deeper, and finally bottomless. After two hours of the hardest conceivable work I succeeded, almost by swimming... Pasang Lama followed in my trench but almost disappeared in the snow before he reached me; he too needed an hour.'

In that time they had travelled only 60 feet. Now it was Wolfe's turn. Far heavier than either of his companions, he simply could not do what they had done. With his arms outstretched he made repeated, floundering efforts to reach them and each time came to a halt, the snow packed hard against his chest. Unable to move another inch, he stopped struggling and Wiessner's hoarse encouragement died away. It was impossible. Retreating alone to Camp VIII, he hoped the snow would soon harden and that he could follow with a supporting party the next day, but he was bitterly disappointed.

He watched Wiessner and the Sherpa making their way on to the rocks above. Exhausted, the two men climbed for only an hour before pitching a temporary camp. The following day they moved across a snow slope, below a giant cliff of ice, to reach the site they had chosen for Camp IX. At a little over 26,000 feet (7925 metres), they were at the high point of the previous year's expedition.

From their camp to the easy snow slopes of the summit cone, two routes seemed possible: to the left, over an intimidating mass of black rock, and to the right, following a snow gully that curved around the great white cliff. The gully promised easier climbing, but there was a risk that the ice cliff, more than 200 feet high, could avalanche. Weighing the options, Wiessner decided to trust his skill rather than his luck: they would make their attack over the rocks, difficult as they were. His next decision was less cautious. Anxious that the weather would break, he told Lama that they must strike now and make no further camps—they would try to go all the way to the summit the following day. Both were decisions he would come to regret.

Wiessner and Pasang Lama left Camp IX at nine o'clock on 19 July, and from that moment were climbing where no man had been before. The first stretch of the ridge, some 800 feet, was easy, and they made the distance in two hours. From here the rock grew rapidly steeper, then vertical, and eventually, in places, overhanging. Much of it was coated in a film of ice.

On a mountain half as high, in air far richer, it would have been a demanding route; at 27,000 feet (8230 metres) it tested the limit of Wiessner's ability. Trying one way and then another, securing himself with pitons on the most difficult sections, Wiessner gradually moved upward. The sun was astonishingly warm and he was able to remove his gloves to search for handholds; with the bare rock under his fingers, he felt powerful and confident. Lama, close behind, was belaying him skilfully and copying his manoeuvres. 'Although we could speak only a few words of each other's language,' Wiessner said later, 'it seemed to me as if I were climbing with an old and completely dependable friend.'

They climbed for another seven hours. At the top of a narrow gully an overhanging slab of rock stopped Wiessner in his tracks. He could find nowhere to place his hands and the nails on his boots were now too worn to grip the surface. The only escape from the gully was a traverse across 50 feet of steep rock to his left, leading to far gentler slopes. It would be an awkward manoeuvre but, once there, it seemed to Wiessner, they could practically walk to the summit, now less than a thousand feet away. The

air was still, the sky clear, and the moon would soon be out; he had already
made up his mind to climb through the night. But when he began the traverse, he felt a tug at his waist and turned to the Sherpa. Pasang Lama had
not moved from the gully and was smiling apprehensively. 'No, Sahib,' he
said, 'tomorrow.' He would not pass out the rope:

> I could have threatened to take it off and go on by myself, and
> he probably would have followed. The poor fellow was shaking
> and praying in fear of the devils and the near dark. I tried to
> explain to him as well as I could that we should go on through
> the night to the summit. This would have been so much easier
> and less dangerous than trying to descend the dangerous route we
> had just come up.

Unable to reassure him, and unwilling to leave him behind, Wiessner finally gave in. Throughout the morning he had a good view of the long
sweep of snow next to the ice cliff—the route he had decided not to risk.
It was certainly less difficult than the rocks and now he was satisfied that
it was also safe from avalanches. Resolving to make the next attempt by
this route, Wiessner began the long climb down to Camp IX. The lower
he climbed, the more he regretted his 'softness' towards Pasang Lama; the
summit had been within his grasp, and he had let it go.

As Lama followed him down a difficult overhang, the rope became
entangled in the crampons strapped to his rucksack. He struggled to untie
them and as he did so they slipped from his hand and bounced away into
the darkness. Wiessner paused. He was confident that they could get down
safely, but he knew that unless a supporting party had reached Camp IX
with fresh equipment, the odds of a quick success—so favourable a short
time before—had suddenly turned against them. It was past two o'clock in
the morning when they arrived at the tent, but it was just as they had left it.

The next day they recuperated in the sunshine, so warm that Wiessner lay naked on his sleeping bag. On 21 July, they attempted the new

route. The snow slope, they discovered, had an ice-hard crust. Steep as it was, they could have walked up with crampons; without them, steps had to be cut—four or five hundred of them. In the thin air it was a slow and laborious task, and Wiessner could see that it was too much for one day. They made their way back to camp. As no one had appeared from below, Wiessner reluctantly decided that they would have to descend to Camp VIII—they were running out of food and they had to find new crampons.

Wiessner's first view of Camp VIII alarmed him. The tent seemed partially collapsed and there was no sign of Wolfe. But he must have heard them on the slope, for a moment later he emerged and came towards them, his arms raised in a gesture of helpless frustration. 'Those bastards,' he shouted, 'they never came up here.' Five days had passed since he watched Wiessner and Pasang Lama head off towards the summit. Hoping to catch up with them, he had waited eagerly and then impatiently for the support party. After three days his matches had run out, leaving him unable to heat his food or melt snow for drinking; since then he had been gathering water in a fold in the tent. He was delighted and relieved to see Wiessner, but could not understand why Durrance—or at least the Sherpas—had failed to reach him. The weather had been mostly fine and each day he had scanned the snowfield below. There had been no trace of them.

Wiessner's disappointment was greater. Only four days of rations remained at Camp VIII: it was not enough to resume the attack on the summit. They had no option but to continue their descent to Camp VII and the main body of supplies that they had carried up the mountain ten days before. Another day would be lost, but from Camp VII they would be able to make up for the failure of their support and replenish their higher camps for a sustained assault, perhaps for another two weeks. It was a setback, but Wiessner had no doubt that one way or another he would soon be standing on the top of K2.

After a warm lunch and cocoa, the three men began to descend. Fog blew across the mountain and it was difficult to make out the route. As the slope fell away more steeply, Wolfe, roped between his companions, began to move awkwardly. Wiessner had to change his stance to help him: 'Dudley did not like the technique which had to be applied and the slow moving was annoying and made us cold... As he found it difficult to go down face to the slope and kicking steps in the hard snow, I started to scratch steps, while facing forward. After having prepared the third step, a sharp jerk from the rear pulled me away and I started to slip...'

Wolfe had trodden on the rope. Wiessner fumbled for the head of his ice-axe, but he was sliding, and within a moment the rope had tightened and jerked Wolfe from his footing and then Lama. Before he could bring his own slide to a halt the two men flew past, the rope played out and a second, more violent jolt pulled him downwards:

> I somersaulted and began to slide very fast, the two others sliding ahead of me. I now had a good head-grip on the axe and worked hard with the pick to stop. A little better snow on the ever steeper slope made me succeed and even the next jerk could not throw me off anymore. I had Dud and Pasang on my rope; it was a narrow escape. The two had been stopped on the hard steep slope about 60 feet above the edge of the big ice rim, behind which steep rock and ice slopes fell down directly to the glacier.

All three men had been certain that the moment of their death had arrived. Wolfe could hardly believe he was no longer falling. As he climbed back up the rope to Wiessner, his first words were, 'How did you do that?' Wiessner had kept his head and done everything right, but he knew it was also a matter of luck: had he fallen a little further, where the snow gave way to ice, it would have been impossible to stop.

Tired and bruised, they approached Camp VII at twilight. Suddenly they sensed that something was wrong: no one answered their shouts, and as they hurried towards the tents they could see that one of them was collapsed, its poles broken and the fabric torn. The camp was empty. Food lay scattered in the snow; the sleeping bags had gone. For a few minutes

the men stumbled around the debris, uncomprehending, almost too distressed to speak. The site had been cleared deliberately, the tents left open
to the snow. No one had been there for days: 'The disappointment was
well nigh unbearable. The wildest ideas tormented our minds. We could
find no explanation for this unexpected state of affairs. A great part of
our reserve food and all the sleeping bags, which we ourselves had lugged
up by hard work and which formed the backbone of our expedition, had
vanished.'

At that moment it seemed to Wiessner like an act of sabotage. Wolfe
was incensed and told him that he would take legal action against the
other members of the expedition. They were now in a dangerous position:
it was too late to descend further. The scattered food and stoves could be
rescued and there was a can of oil, but between them they had only the
sleeping bag in Lama's rucksack. Wiessner had left his at Camp IX and
Wolfe's had been lost in the fall. After clearing a tent and heating supper,
the three men huddled together, stretched Lama's sleeping bag across their
knees and waited for the night to pass. 'We were longing for Camp VI,'
Wiessner wrote in his diary, 'some sleep in a warm bag and an accounting
for what had been done to us.'

The dawn was raw and windy. They felt weak, but the thought of
abandoning the summit did not cross Wiessner's mind. At Camp VI, he
presumed, they would find Durrance and the other Sherpas. One of them
could relieve Pasang Lama; he could get the supply chain moving, and
after a day's rest he would be strong enough to begin climbing again.
Wolfe preferred not to descend further and suggested that he remain
behind. With Lama's bag he could sleep and by the time Wiessner
returned—in two or three days—he would be ready to join him in another bid for the summit. He stood by the tent and waved as Wiessner and
Lama slowly disappeared into the fog.

They were descending into a nightmare: Camp VI was deserted. The
tents had been dismantled, the sleeping bags removed:

Our situation now became very serious. We could not go back to Camp VII, since there was only one sleeping bag for Wolfe there, and this would not have been sufficient to keep the three of us from freezing. Camp V, according to the expedition's plans, had not been prepared as a support camp. So only one course was possible, the descent to the big Camp IV. But, a thing inconceivable to us, there too the reserve sleeping bags had vanished! Desperate, and at the end of our powers of resistance, we threw ourselves upon the empty tent platforms. But we had to go on, the fight for our lives had begun.

The next support camp was Camp II. Utterly exhausted and almost in despair, they reached the camp at nightfall. Both large tents were standing and for a moment they thought they were safe—but one was empty, and the other contained nothing but food. Wiessner recorded in his diary: 'We just cannot go further and will have to stay a second night without bags. We take down the second tent and use it as a cover. To describe in words the horrible feelings and thoughts I had during the day, would be futile indeed. Is there any possibility for an excuse for such a condition? Does one sacrifice a great goal and human beings in such a way?'

At daybreak the two men staggered down to the glacier and began dragging themselves towards Base Camp. Both men were frostbitten and emaciated and Wiessner's throat was so painful that he could barely speak. Several times they fell to the ground. In a delirium of exhaustion, they had gone some distance when Wiessner became aware of voices—the sound came from behind him—and four hurrying figures. He could see that one of them was Cromwell, his second-in-command. 'Thank God you're alive!' he was saying. He was smiling.

Wiessner could not contain his rage. He thrust his face at him and in a menacing whisper accused him of attempted murder. Wolfe, he snarled, was going to sue him. He *demanded* to know why they had done it—why they had cleared the mountain—why he and Wolfe and Pasang Lama had been left to die. Cromwell shrank from him in horror.

At Base Camp, it took some time for Wiessner to calm down. Eventually, anger gave way to fatigue and he listened. Piece by piece, from Cromwell and Durrance, he learned what had happened.

The last time Wiessner had seen Durrance was on 13 July, eleven days earlier, when he turned back a short distance beyond Camp VI, exhausted. Wiessner had wanted him to bring supplies to the high camps, but he was suffering badly from the altitude and did not recover that night. Afraid that he would soon be too weak to move, he descended the next day to Camp II, taking two of the Sherpas for assistance, including their headman, Pasang Kikuli. At Camp II he joined Cromwell, who had come down from Camp IV the previous day and would soon return to Base Camp, satisfied that he could be of no further use. Unknown to Wiessner, the descent of Durrance had left the supply chain through the mid-mountain camps entirely in the hands of the Sherpas. They had been given precise instructions, Durrance assured him.

Having established Camp VIII, Wiessner had sent two Sherpas back to Camp VII with orders to bring up more supplies. While he and Pasang Lama pushed on towards the summit, Wolfe had waited in vain for the Sherpas to return—this much Wiessner knew. He now heard that the Sherpas had sat out two days of light snow at Camp VII and when the weather cleared, one of them—Tendrup—persuaded the other that the leading party had perished in an avalanche. They began to descend. The Sherpas at Camp VI did not believe Tendrup and refused to go with him, but he continued down the mountain with his companion until they were confronted by Pasang Kikuli at Camp IV. The headman was furious and ordered them back to the high camps.

On 19 July Tendrup reached Camp VII once more, now with two companions—this was the day, Wiessner recalled, that he had so nearly reached the summit. The next morning the Sherpas tried to climb the steep slope above their camp, but without crampons they were frightened of slipping. When Camp VIII came into view they stopped and called out, but there was no response and they could see no sign of life.

Wolfe, then, must have been asleep in his tent. Wiessner listened unhappily to the remainder of the story. When the Sherpas called up to Camp VIII, his summit party had not been seen for five days. Tendrup was impatient to descend. If they *had* reached the top of the mountain, he had told his companions, they would surely have returned by now; since they had not, the only explanation was an accident. Convinced that his story of an avalanche was true after all, the Sherpas turned back and, as they descended from camp to camp, they took the valuable sleeping bags with them and whatever else they could carry, arriving at Base Camp on 23 July. The next day Cromwell had gone to search the glacier for any sign of an accident above—he had been looking for their bodies when he met Wiessner.

It was not the whole truth, but for the moment Wiessner had heard enough. Later that evening he wrote in his diary: 'The mountain is far away. The weather is the best we have had so far. Will it be possible for me to go up after a rest with some Sherpas and with Jack, if he is in shape, pick up Dudley and then call on the summit? Seven days of good weather will be necessary. Maybe the Gods will be with me and let me have what is due to me.'

Wolfe was now alone on the mountain, 10,000 feet (3048 metres) above Base Camp. The remainder of the expedition was ready to move out. Sheldon and Cranmer were already on their way home, hoping to be back in Dartmouth for the start of the new term. Twenty-five porters had arrived, according to schedule, to begin the return march; there was not enough food at the camp to delay them. Wiessner decided to let eighteen of them leave immediately, with Trench, the transport officer, Tendrup, the disgraced Sherpa, and Cromwell, still smarting from his bitter rebuke. He had no further use for his deputy: 'Tony [Cromwell] offers to stay on but I feel it is better to let him go when I look at his face. For weeks he has been looking forward to this day. I am afraid that if I keep him it would be a great strain for him and there is really no need now.'

As the party prepared to leave, Durrance, with three Sherpas, made his way back towards the mountain. His instructions were to 'meet' Wolfe at Camp VII. Wiessner had told him he would follow in one or two days with Pasang Lama, as soon as they recovered their strength—to lead another attempt on the summit. Durrance, however, did not take the idea seriously. Wiessner was little more than skin and bone and could still barely speak; Lama's condition seemed even worse. It was obvious that neither man would be fit to climb. He was not going to 'meet' Wolfe, as Wiessner put it, but *rescue* him, as he was unable to descend alone. Hadn't he said all along that Wolfe should not have been allowed to go so high?

Two days later Wiessner watched the clouds rolling in across the top of the mountain. The weather seemed to be changing and the pain in his throat and frostbitten feet made it impossible to sleep; he was not getting better. The moment had come, he now accepted, to relinquish his last hope of the summit and he spread word around Base Camp that they would leave as soon as the party returned from Camp VII. To the Sherpas it was like news of an armistice, greeted with relief and delight. He knew that he was alone in his sense of defeat.

The same day, towards evening, he heard the sound of boots approaching camp. It was Durrance and one of the Sherpas, evidently sick; he brought bad news. The Sherpa had become ill at Camp IV and Durrance had been uncertain what to do. He could not leave him behind or send him down alone. The two other Sherpas were afraid of the long ice traverse beyond Camp VI and refused to climb it unaccompanied. He might have taken one of them and tried to make Camp VII himself, but he did not feel strong and was afraid that he would fail to reach it, as he had on his previous attempt; precious time would then have been wasted. He had decided to descend immediately with the sick man and find help.

The men gathered for a meeting. Wiessner declared that he would go himself, but Pasang Kikuli, the Sherpa headman, intervened—he told

Wiessner that he was not fit enough and insisted that *he* could handle the situation. In the morning he would take one man with him and try to reach Camp VI before nightfall. The two Sherpas from Durrance's party were no doubt already there. Between them, Kikuli said, they would climb to Camp VII the following day and bring down Wolfe Sahib. If anything was wrong on the mountain and Wiessner needed to come up, he would make a fire signal. Wiessner agreed to the plan and wrote that night in his diary: 'Good luck for me to have a man like Pasang Kikuli left, he is dependable and always does what he plans. I could not do it better. Hope the weather will be all right. Dudley ought to come down now, he has been up there since the forenoon of July 23rd. It will be six days if Kikuli makes it day after tomorrow.'

On the morning of 29 July, a little over twenty-four hours after Kikuli left Base Camp, Wiessner kept his binoculars trained on the snow slope between Camps VI and VII. At eleven o'clock he made out three tiny figures; they were moving upwards. Pasang Kikuli, evidently, had been as good as his word: he had climbed to Camp VI in a single day, a feat of endurance that seemed to Wiessner almost superhuman. In another hour or so, they would be at Wolfe's tent.

Wiessner resumed his vigil at two o'clock in the afternoon, hoping to see *four* men making their way down to Camp VI. The hours passed slowly and it was not until five o'clock that he detected movement again: the tiny figures were descending. With a shiver of alarm, he counted only three of them. For the first time in his diary, Wiessner admitted that both he and Durrance were beginning to worry that something was wrong. They waited for a fire signal from Kikuli, but none came and by the morning a screen of heavy cloud was drawn across the mountain.

The cloud persisted for two days. On 1 August the view was clear again, but it revealed no sign of activity at Camp VI and no fresh tracks on the snow slope above. At half past seven the next morning Durrance saw a man leaving the tent at Camp VI; a little later there seemed to be new tracks below Camp V and at noon a solitary figure appeared on the glacier, walking quickly towards them. It was Tsering, the Sherpa taken by Pasang Kikuli with him from Base Camp six days before.

Tsering was exhausted and distressed. He was sure that something terrible had happened on the mountain. With the rest of the expedition gathered around him, he told the following story.

He and Kikuli had climbed directly from Base Camp to Camp VI; here they found the two Sherpas from Durrance's party, Pinsoo and Kitar. The next morning, Tsering remained at the camp while Kikuli took the two men up to Camp VII; these were the three figures that Wiessner saw through his binoculars on the morning of 29 July. They reached Wolfe's tent at midday. He was lying in his sleeping bag; he seemed listless, indifferent to their arrival. He didn't read the note that they brought him from Wiessner and when they handed him his letters he flung them away. He complained that he had no matches and apparently had not eaten for several days. It was obvious that he had not been outside the tent in that time, even to relieve himself: he was lying in his own bodily wastes. The Sherpas made him tea and took him outside the tent while they cleaned it, but he staggered around and refused to descend with them that afternoon. They were to come back the next day, he told them—then he would be ready to come down. All this Tsering had learned from Kikuli when the Sherpas returned to Camp VI in the evening.

The weather closed in overnight and the Sherpas were unable to return to Wolfe's tent in the morning. The following day Kikuli decided that they would climb up to Camp VII in spite of the continuing bad weather. He told Tsering, who remained behind once more, to have tea and food ready in the afternoon. If Wolfe Sahib refused to descend, Kikuli intended to drag him down the slope and, if that failed, he would demand that he write a note for Barrah Sahib—Wiessner—explaining that the Sherpas had done everything they could to help him. They would be back before nightfall, Kikuli said, no matter what happened. All three men left their sleeping bags behind.

Tsering prepared tea and waited, but the Sherpas did not return that afternoon. He waited another day, but there was no sign of them. After a second night alone at Camp VI, in a state of great anxiety, Tsering had rushed down to Base Camp. Knowing that his three companions could not have remained at Wolfe's tent without sleeping bags, he was convinced that a dreadful accident had occurred.

Wiessner was worried, but he simply could not believe that an accident was possible:

> A serious situation but we cannot believe that something should have happened to such experienced men as Pasang Kikuli and Pinsoo, also Pasang Kitar, a newer man who was perfectly able to handle a difficult situation safely and had shown good rope technique. If Dudley had really not recovered and the Sherpas had transported him down the mountain they certainly would have been well roped up and would have taken all precautions with belaying each other to judge from the good belaying which they had done throughout the trip. No, it seems impossible that anything should have happened to such an able group.

As Durrance could not cope with the altitude, and the other Americans had already left, Wiessner had no choice but to return to the mountain and search for the missing party himself:

> Now nothing else remains for me to do… until we know what the situation is. I am really not in shape to do it, my throat will certainly cause me trouble and I may lose my toes. Tomorrow I shall go to Camp I or II with Tsering and from there up as quickly as possible. I would prefer Pasang Lama in place of Tsering, but Pasang Lama says that it is absolutely impossible for him to accompany me no matter how much he feels that he ought to go.

Before he left, Wiessner dismissed the porters who had been waiting at Base Camp. He sent a note with them to Cromwell, explaining 'the seriousness of the situation.'

Wiessner and Tsering spent the night of 3 August at Camp I, hoping to reach IV the following day. As Wiessner began to climb the mountain for the last time, his legs felt strong enough, but the breath seemed to stop in his throat. Gasping painfully, he moved slowly and by the time they reached Camp II most of the day had gone and he was almost exhausted. Tsering shouted up the ridge towards Camp VI. The evening air was still and the mountain silent; Wiessner had no doubt that if the men were up there, they would have heard him. Looking down across the glacier towards Base Camp, he hoped to see a fire signal. It would have meant that Durrance had seen movement on the ridge above them, but there was nothing. 'I am now very much afraid,' he wrote, 'that an accident has occurred.'

The next morning snow fell steadily from the grey sky and the wind gathered strength. It was impossible to move on from the camp. The following day brought darker skies and deeper snow and they waited again, but by the morning of 7 August the storm had entirely engulfed the upper mountain and Wiessner knew it was the end: 'Two feet of snow outside and storm above, we must retreat. It is hopeless to get higher and supplies are getting low. We leave around 11 A.M. The rocks are deeply covered; my toes suffer again. It is better on the glacier with the temperature around freezing. Arrive at Base Camp feeling desperately low.'

On 9 August, Wiessner, Durrance and the remainder of the expedition began the long walk back to Srinigar. The nearest telegraph station was at Skardu, eleven days into their march, and from here Wiessner wired news of the disaster to Cromwell, care of Major Hadow in Srinigar, to the American Consul in Calcutta, Wolfe's secretary in New York and the Himalayan Club in Darjeeling, the point of contact for the Sherpas' families. The message he wrote for Alice Wolfe read:

DUDLEY WITH THREE SHERPAS LOST VICINITY CAMP SEVEN ACCIDENT CAUSE UNKNOWN AS SEVERE CONDITIONS PREVENTED RECOVERY OF BODIES THIS SEASON STOP DEEPEST SORROW FELT BY ALL AIRMAILED COMPLETE REPORTS TODAY STOP.

Before he handed it to the operator he deleted 'bodies' and wrote simply 'severe conditions prevented their recovery.'

When the news reached Cromwell in Srinigar, he was not only horrified but enraged. Since the day Wiessner staggered off the mountain with Pasang Lama, accused him of attempted murder and berated him in front of the other men, he had seethed with resentment. A month had passed, he had had time to reflect and as he did, his resentment hardened. Back in New York he had liked Wiessner and counted him as a friend, but he had seen a different side of him on the expedition: his arrogance, his egoism, his determination to reach the summit at any price; his *German* side, it seemed to Cromwell. In his impatience to succeed, Wiessner had rushed to the top of the mountain before the supply line was properly established and when it broke down he had abandoned Wolfe in his eagerness to repair it—and to find a culprit. How many times had they told him that it was dangerous to take Wolfe so high? It was a catastrophe that he and Durrance had foretold. If anyone was guilty of murder, it was Wiessner.

Cromwell said as much to his face when he met Wiessner and Durrance outside Srinigar on 27 August. Durrance urged Cromwell to show restraint; if he did not, there would be a public scandal. The older man, however, was set on his course. He had already made his feelings plain to Major Hadow and the British community in Srinigar. In a letter to Joel Fisher, Treasurer of the American Alpine Club, he complained bitterly about the conduct of the expedition and repeated the accusation that Wiessner was personally responsible for all four deaths. Knowing that

Trench shared his resentment, he urged the transport officer to send his own account of the expedition to Fisher. Trench claimed that Wiessner had been unable to account for his movements high on the mountain, was incoherent and unsure of the date when he returned with Pasang Lama, that he *ordered* the Sherpas to go up and rescue Wolfe, while he rested and planned another summit attempt. He too implied that Wiessner had cared only about reaching the top of the mountain as fast as possible. His letter concluded: 'It is not for me to make comments, nor is it desirable that I should, but having given you the facts as best I can I'm sure you will agree, even with such a novice as myself, that if Camp VIII had been consolidated initially and any summit attempt deferred until the camp was fully stocked, the lives of four first class fellows would not have been needlessly wasted.'

For the time being, Wiessner concentrated on presenting a factual account of the expedition for the American Alpine Club, the State Department and the families of the bereaved. He did not apportion blame, but he had no doubt where it lay. The failure of the expedition to reach the summit and the subsequent disaster were the direct results of the premature clearing of the support camps. There was no need to look elsewhere. If the sleeping bags had been left on the mountain according to his plan, he would have conquered the second highest mountain on earth and brought everyone down safely. Cromwell and Durrance had told him that the Sherpas acted on their own initiative, misled by Tendrup, but he knew now and had known for some time that this was not the whole truth.

For Pasang Kikuli had given him a different story. It was while Durrance was on the mountain, attempting to reach Wolfe, and after Cromwell had left Base Camp for Srinigar, that Kikuli spoke to him. He said that he had received orders from Durrance to remove the sleeping bags from Camp IV downwards, in readiness for the expedition's departure. He had been doing this when Tendrup appeared from above with his story that the summit party had been killed in an avalanche. He had admonished Tendrup and sent him back to the high camps, but a few days later, when Tendrup persuaded the other Sherpas that his story was true, they had followed Kikuli's example, taking all the sleeping bags with them from Camps VI and VII. It seemed to be what the white men wanted. Kikuli added that as the Sherpa headman he should have been allowed to remain at one of the higher camps, in charge of his companions, but when Durrance fell ill at Camp VI he had insisted that he help him descend. *He could have prevented the disaster.*

Durrance had made a casual and fatal mistake in assuming that the descending summit party would carry bags with them. Both he and Cromwell had been in too much of a hurry to clear the mountain and go home.

Resting in Srinigar, enjoying the comforts of Major Hadow's hospitality once more, Wiessner could find no appetite for a quarrel. He was depressed. War, as everyone knew, was imminent; it seemed that the world was collapsing around him. His conspicuous German origins made him unpopular in the colony, as if Cromwell's public recriminations were not enough. Some local rumours suggested that he was an enemy agent—after all, he had been seen in the company of the mysterious Dr Schacht. Wiessner was at Hadow's weekend retreat when news arrived that war had begun. The following day he wrote to Alice Wolfe:

Again, I want to express to you, for myself and also for the expedition, our deepest felt condolence. It was a terrible shock to me when I realized that Dudley had had an accident, and I cannot get over this dreadful disaster. The whole story of the happenings seems still like a nightmare. I am also so depressed about the fact that I could not take a more active hand in the rescue attempts, and that we were forced to leave the mountain without knowing the exact cause of the accident and could not recover the deceased. I have never been hit so hard in my life, first to lose the summit which seemed in my hands, then the terrible realization of Dudley's and the Sherpas' deaths, and now a war.

Enclosing the final draft of the expedition report, composed with the help
of Durrance, Wiessner reminded Alice that it was written by 'the only two
members left on the mountain during the time of the accident.' He knew
that a different version of events would emerge from Cromwell.

When he applied for a permit to leave India in Bombay, the local
CID insisted on interviewing and searching him. They knew that he had
held a commission in the German Army in the last war and were suspicious that he had been in Bombay earlier in the year asking questions
about ports, roads and conditions in Northern Kashmir. After an 'annoying and costly' delay, he was allowed to take the Imperial Airways flight
from Karachi to Alexandria. From Egypt he sailed for New York and was
eight days from home, trying to sleep while the ship rolled in heavy seas,
when he felt a sudden pain in his back—he had wrenched a joint. Arriving on 28 October he was met by a doctor and taken straight to the
orthopaedic hospital, where he remained for several weeks.

A letter was waiting for him from Bill House. It warned him to be
careful in his explanation of the accident:

> I think I know you pretty near as well as anyone except members
> of the expedition and some of your friends in New York. I think
> it is quite likely that you have rationalized everything that hap-
> pened and are convinced that everything that was done within
> your power was right. I don't question this, but an appearance of
> righteousness is sometimes dangerous. There is a possibility that
> the conflicting and confusing reports which reached this country
> may have been misunderstood and that some people may have
> jumped to conclusions—as they have from time immemorial
> when an accident happens in the mountains. No matter how
> thoroughly convinced you are that your judgements were right
> please realize that you may have to convince other people and
> that to convince them you must be patient and understanding. I
> am writing this in the hope that it will not alarm you...

Wiessner was indeed convinced that he was right and paid little attention to his friend's advice. In November, a committee from the American Alpine Club visited him. They showed him the letters written by Cromwell and Trench and a copy of a report compiled by the British Srinigar Residency, based on comments made by Cromwell before Wiessner's return from the mountain. The report had already been distributed among members of the Club and its contents incensed him. It stated that he and Pasang Lama had left Wolfe behind in their bid for the summit because he was too ill to go further and, when they descended, they had left him at Camp VII for the same reason. In short, he was accused of abandoning a sick man. The report concluded with words of praise for the Sherpas and 'several members of the expedition' for attempting to rescue Wolfe in such difficult circumstances. Wiessner insisted that Wolfe had been perfectly well at that time, that the report was 'absolutely untrue' and that Cromwell, in any case, had no first-hand knowledge of events. The committee, however, told him that considering the gravity of the charges made against him and the controversy that was now breaking out in the Club about the conduct of the expedition, there would have to be a formal inquiry.

Many members had already heard enough to convince them that Wiessner had made serious errors of judgement. Some of them had never liked his style and found it all too easy to believe that the general thrust of Cromwell's criticisms was true. He *was* the kind of climber who would risk everything for the summit and make no allowance for the weakness—or even illness—of others. It was the opinion of his critics that whatever condition Wolfe was in, Wiessner should not have split his party and left him alone so high on the mountain. Nor was it accepted practice to have unaccompanied Sherpas in charge of supply camps. Members of the expedition had complained that they did not know what the summit party was doing. Morale had obviously declined, there had been a series of misunderstandings and the Sherpas had panicked. It sounded like poor leadership. Charlie Houston was particularly angry:

Pasang Kikuli had been on his 1938 reconnaissance and the two men had become friends.

As the inquiry proceeded, the Secretary of the American Alpine Club wrote to Wiessner:

> There is as you naturally know, Fritz, a tendency to gang up against you on the part of some. This I strongly object to. Your restraint since landing has been more dignified than the rather loose talk of other members of the party. Both because of my official position and because I don't think it wise or profitable I am not going to get involved in the controversy, but I do want to see fairness all round. There were, I'm sure you agree, some things on the expedition that shouldn't have been. Don't you think you would strengthen your position now by a frank statement as to what errors there have been in judgement? You see, some people now think that your desire to attempt the summit got the better of your otherwise good judgement—that you hoped all would be well with the rest of the party, but that you stretched their margin of safety so thin as to leave yourself open to much criticism.

But Wiessner was not prepared to concede an inch of ground. A *wide* margin of safety had been created, he insisted, through a line of well-supplied camps. He could not have foreseen their destruction by other members of the expedition and the consequent series of events that led to disaster.

Anxious to douse the flames of the controversy, the committee of inquiry was determined to produce, as far as possible, a conciliatory report for its members. A second investigation, conducted by Wolfe's brother Clifford and his team of lawyers, was more hostile. Clifford wanted to discover precisely what had happened to his brother, if his body could be recovered, and if anyone was culpable in his death. He conducted interviews with each of the climbers.

Confronted with a lawyer and a stenographer, Cromwell distanced himself from the report which stated that Wolfe had been ill when Wiessner left him at Camp VII. He conceded that the report had been based on his comments, but claimed that he in turn had relied on what Durrance had told him in his letters from Base Camp at the time of the crisis. He now understood that Wolfe had been in good health, having acclimatized better than anyone except Wiessner.

Clifford heard that at some point over the next six days, while his brother lay alone in his tent, he had suffered a mental breakdown. All the climbers agreed: it was the only possible explanation for the condition in which the Sherpas found him. He appeared to have given up the will to live. Clifford asked Durrance if his brother had been depressed on the expedition, but he could only answer that he had seemed withdrawn: 'I had the idea that something was worrying him but he wanted to climb the mountain. I did not know him well enough to know what it was. He kept very much to himself the whole time and I only know he wanted to climb the mountain—regardless of what happened.'

Clifford was astonished to hear that his brother was considered a poor climber. So poor, in fact, that the Sherpas were afraid of being on the same rope. Durrance told him: 'I think Dudley's ambition got away with him. I don't think he should have attempted to climb it. He was always guided. He never guided a rope himself. He was always taken up—and Wiessner did it. I think it was a frightful mistake.'

Wiessner acknowledged that the other men had criticized him for allowing Wolfe to go up the mountain, but told Clifford that his brother was very determined and had made his own decisions: 'He did all the things he wanted to do.' Wolfe, he said, had asked him several times during the ascent, 'What do you think? Shall I go higher?' Each time he had replied: 'I cannot tell you that you should not go higher if you feel in good condition.'

Clifford wanted to know exactly why Durrance had given up on his rescue attempt and questioned him closely. He explained that he was 'way underweight' at the time, that he was certain that he would have failed to reach his tent, having failed to climb the same slope—above Camp VI—earlier in the expedition. One of the Sherpas had become ill and the other two simply refused to obey his commands to go to Camp VII unaccompanied. Clifford was now becoming angry, firing questions at him, but Durrance was adamant that his decision to bring the sick man down and 'get Fritz' was the best solution. At this point Clifford snapped: 'Of course in my viewpoint the life of a Sherpa is nothing compared to Dudley's,' and Durrance, clearly stung, replied, 'Of course it isn't. We didn't treat it as such.'

The precise circumstances of Wolfe's death were a mystery, but each of the men interviewed had arrived at the same conclusion. When Pasang Kikuli and his two companions set out from Camp VI for the second time, they reached Wolfe and in all probability were attempting to bring him down the slope when all four of them fell. His body, Wiessner told Clifford, would be preserved in the snow as it was at the moment of death; he had heard of such cases before. But there could be no hope of recovering it. Cromwell surmised that it was already buried under tens of feet of snow.

Clifford was reaching a conclusion of his own: his brother had not perished in some freak mountaineering accident. The circumstances of his death appalled him. Dreadful mistakes had been made, and when he pressed the men, they blamed each other. Durrance blamed the mutinous Sherpas. Both he and Cromwell blamed Wiessner for taking Wolfe up the mountain in the first place. Wiessner, meanwhile, insisted that he had been let down by the others. He said that Durrance was 'unable to stand up under the strain when he was alone'; that Cromwell was excitable and argumentative and wanted to get away from the mountain as fast as he could; that both men had been jealous of Wolfe because an amateur was out-performing them. In Clifford's opinion, such criticism of the morale and commitment of his team raised an obvious question about Wiessner's leadership. When he asked Durrance if he considered him 'qualified' to lead an expedition of this kind, he had refused to answer. In the end it didn't matter to Clifford where the truth lay in all the recriminations he had heard. He was bitter and angry. It was clear to him that his brother had died either because he should never have been there in the first place or as a result of the collapse of the expedition. Either way, it seemed to him that the final responsibility rested with the leader. Dudley had trusted his safety to Wiessner and it had proved a terrible mistake.

Clifford appears to have kept his thoughts to himself. He abhorred the idea of any further publicity surrounding his brother's death and took no further action. Many years later, when another American expedition travelled to K2, he contacted the Alpine Club and asked the Secretary for an assurance that nothing would appear in the newspapers if Dudley's remains were found. 'All we want to know,' he said, 'is where he is buried and to have any small mementoes which could be brought out and a photograph of the grave.'

The American Alpine Club Committee completed its report in early 1940. The stated purpose of the document was to point the way forward for future expeditions but, in the context of a rumbling controversy, it amounted to a judgement on the conduct of the expedition. A draft copy was sent to Wiessner and he did not like what he read. The premature removal of the sleeping bags, it said, 'probably had no effect on the final tragedy.' He was flabbergasted. He had said repeatedly that it was the *only* cause. In the margin of his copy he scribbled, 'How can you say this? These remarks are typical of the Committee's attitude of excusing mistakes of Durrance and blaming Wiessner.' The clearing of the camps, the report continued, was indicative of the lack of clear understanding between members of the party, which it attributed to 'weak human administration'; in other words, his leadership. Combined with bad weather, weakened personnel and too much responsibility 'thrust on Sherpas,' the expedition's margin of safety was 'pared to the limit.' It only required a break in the weather, the Committee concluded, to precipitate disaster. Against this Wiessner scrawled 'It had nothing to do with it!'

Wiessner demanded a long list of amendments and several senior climbers at the Club wrote to the Committee to complain that the report was a whitewash of the action taken by Durrance and a serious injustice to Wiessner. 'To my mind,' wrote Al Lindley, 'the action taken by Durrance and the Sherpas in evacuating the camps was so much the major cause of the accident that the others are insignificant.' Robert Underhill was of the same opinion and concluded his letter with an eloquent tribute:

> What impresses me most is the fact that throughout all the bad weather, the killing labour and the grievous disappointments, Wiessner still kept up his fighting spirit. Except Wolfe, the rest of the party were, excusably enough, finished and through—quite downed by the circumstances: toward the end they wanted only to get out and go home. Wiessner, with Wolfe behind him, was the only one who still wanted to climb the mountain. Far be it from me to blame the others; I know well that if I had been there myself I should have come to feel exactly the same way, and probably much sooner. But this leads me to appreciate Wiessner the more. He had the guts—and there is no single thing finer in a climber, or in a man.

The Committee made some adjustments to the report, but eventually decided that it was best left unpublished. Feelings were running high on both sides. Wiessner received a visit from the FBI. Investigating claims that he was a Nazi, the officers admitted that they were acting on information supplied by members of the American Alpine Club. Wiessner had had enough, and on Boxing Day, 1940, resigned his membership.

The controversy began to recede. Wiessner spent the war as an adviser on mountain equipment to the US Army, and when peace broke out he married and started a family. He continued to climb. In 1960, he realized an ambition by completing a list of ascents of all sixty-nine 4000-metre peaks in the Alps. He was nearly seventy years old when he reached the top of Popocatapetl in Mexico, and at the age of eighty-six was still climbing cliffs of moderate difficulty in the Shawagunks and Eldorado Canyon. Eventually, he climbed the tree in the garden.

He always said that the 1939 expedition was the greatest disappointment of his life. From time to time, it would lurch back into his life. In 1955, the English professor Kenneth Mason published a history of mountaineering in the Himalayas in which he equated Wiessner's attempt on the summit with the German 'suicide climbers' on the North Wall of the Eiger: 'It is difficult to record in temperate language the folly of this enterprise.' When another author repeated the accusation that he had abandoned a sick man, he heard from Wiessner's lawyers. As the years passed Wiessner only grew more adamant in his view that the disaster was caused by 'the fantastic errors of others.'

In 1965, two members of the American Alpine Club ran a successful campaign to bring him back into the fold—but it was not easy. Resignations were threatened, but the majority took the view that the shadow of 1939 had hung over the Club long enough. It was like Banquo's ghost, one member wrote, 'destined to return again and again until it is exorcized in some fitting manner.'

THE CRITICAL VIEW OF WIESSNER HAS FADED with the passing of time. Most of his critics are dead. The context has changed. Mountaineers take more risks, and many more die. If the events of 1939 were repeated today, it is unlikely that they would provoke a storm of protest. Charlie Houston maintains to this day that Wiessner was a poor leader and bears responsibility for the deaths of four men, but it is an unfashionable view. Yet, reading Wiessner's diaries and letters, his published accounts of the expedition and his interviews with Clifford, it is impossible to ignore the impression that he consistently overestimated his fellow climbers' fitness, both physical or mental, for the continuing struggle on the mountain. His optimism was also a kind of blindness.

But how far back should one trace the cause of an accident? The immediate cause of the 1939 disaster was the clearing of the camps. And it might have been averted by chance: if Wiessner had chosen to make a further camp with Pasang Lama, if the Sherpa had not spilled his crampons, if Wolfe had been awake, standing by his tent, when Tendrup called up to him...

CHAPTER 8

Houston's Last Expedition

'I still think about poor Dudley lying up there in the snow,' Alice Wolfe wrote to Wiessner in 1941, 'and I probably will until I die.' After the disaster, the snow fell undisturbed on K2 for fourteen years.

Had Wiessner stood on the summit, he would have broken the four-minute mile of mountaineering by making the first ascent of any of the world's fourteen 8000-metre peaks. In spite of prolonged sieges, an invisible barrier seemed to defend them. By 1939 the British had sent no fewer than seven expeditions to Everest without improving on the high point reached by Mallory in 1924. The death toll in the Germans' grim ongoing struggle with Nanga Parbat stood at twenty-six. Kangchengjunga, the world's third highest mountain, had repelled every effort to climb it for nearly forty years. When Wiessner turned back, 800 feet from the top of K2, it was the closest any climber had come to defeating one of the giants but, before he left Kashmir, the Second World War began, expeditions ceased and Himalayan mountaineering was suddenly frozen in time.

More than a decade passed before it resumed in earnest, but when it did, in a fresh climate of optimism and public interest, an 8000-metre peak was conquered almost immediately. The dramatic ascent of Annapurna in 1950, by Maurice Herzog's French expedition, seemed to herald the beginning of a second 'Golden Age' of mountaineering. A century after the British romped through the Alps, claiming all the great peaks, few doubted that something similar was about to happen in the Himalayas.

Dr Charlie Houston was certain of it. Even before Annapurna he knew that there was no 'barrier' defending the highest peaks. It was not a question of oxygen. He had proved it in a laboratory in 1947—by acclimatizing a group of men over thirty-five days, in a special chamber, to the atmospheric conditions of 30,000 feet (9144 metres) of altitude. 'Operation Everest' was sponsored by the US Navy. The Navy brass were interested to know if their pilots might benefit from a pre-flight acclimatization process, while Houston's discreet agenda was to find out if a man could ride an exercise bicycle on top of the world's highest mountain. Two of his volunteers managed twenty minutes of pedalling before passing out. The film of the experiment shows a very tired man pedalling more and more slowly, like a marathon runner staggering towards the tape, until finally he slumps on to the handlebars. At this point Dr Houston rushes forward with an oxygen mask. The unfortunate volunteer had demonstrated that a climber could function on the summit of Everest—but getting there was another matter.

It was a different matter in another sense. Before the war, Tibet had allowed a series of British expeditions to approach the mountain from the north, while to the south Nepal remained closed to foreigners. The situation was now reversed: Tibet was closed, the borders of Nepal open. For the first time a route to the mountain from the south was a possibility for expeditions. Houston was quickly off the mark. While the climbing of Everest was not for him a priority, exploring an unknown route through a mysterious Asian kingdom was precisely the kind of work he liked to do. In 1950, with his father Oscar, Houston's was the first party to make a reconnaissance of the southern approach to the mountain.

The following year the British, inspired by the conquest of Annapurna, sent a full-scale reconnaissance expedition by the route Houston had explored. Meanwhile the Germans were planning to take up where they left off on Nanga Parbat. If there was an American mountain in the Himalayas, it was K2. Charlie Houston preferred not to think in such terms—he had a record of organizing international expeditions—but what he did have was a personal stake in the mountain. K2 was unfinished business.

On his reconnaissance expedition in 1938, he had decided to retreat at 26,000 feet (7925 metres) when at least one member of the party believed they should press on for the summit; indeed they might have done, had they not *run out of matches*. It was a rather absurd conclusion to an otherwise brilliantly executed expedition and there were some at the American Alpine Club who felt that Houston had been over-cautious, even that he had 'chickened out' when the mountain was there for the taking. Houston was aware of their opinions, and while he accepted that he had been cautious, or that he had been cautious too soon, he has always said that he was comfortable with the decision he made. Climbing was, after all, a sport, and at least they had all got back alive. It had been a wonderful adventure, the happiest and most exciting of all his expeditions. He had found the route and demonstrated that the mountain could be climbed, if the weather allowed it. These were two good reasons to go back, but there was a harder edge to Houston's determination to return. The spectre of the 1939 disaster lingered around the American Alpine Club. It had cost the life of his friend Pasang Kikuli and he had lent his own weight to the controversy. Houston wanted to close the book.

It was going to need all his tenacity. Just as the changing political landscape offered new opportunities for the climbing of Everest, it presented new problems in reaching K2. The partition of the subcontinent in 1947 led to a bitter struggle between India and newly created Pakistan over Kashmir. When the United Nations brokered a truce, the resulting ceasefire line bisected the long marching route to the mountain from Srinigar, now in Indian territory. Crossing the line was out of the question and the prospects for any climbing expedition looked distinctly unpromising. Houston, however, had made friends in high places, among them the American Ambassador to Pakistan. Houston learned that an airstrip had been constructed by the Pakistanis at Skardu, within 150 miles of K2. If permission could be secured from the Pakistan government, it was now feasible for a party to fly into Skardu from Rawalpindi without crossing the sensitive frontier and to reach the mountain in less than two weeks of marching, when before it had taken four. Persuading the authorities to allow it was a different proposition, but Houston persevered, the Ambassador pulled strings and in the spring of 1952 a permit was agreed. It was time to assemble a team.

In the wake of the 1939 disaster, another American diplomat, the Consul in Calcutta, had interviewed Wiessner and sent an official report on the circumstances of the accident to the State Department in Washington. Wiessner's responsibility, he wrote, lay in the fact 'that he should have exercised far greater care in selecting the members of the party and in studying their temperaments.' The Consul was not a climber and he went on to make an unlikely and extended comparison between expedition leaders and opera impresarios:

> The leader must be an impresario, a person of great tact and patience, but also firmness. The difference between an opera company and a mountaineering expedition lies, however, in the fact that while, if there is a clash of temperaments in an opera company, the impresario is in a position to change the cast, or the opera; in the management of a mountaineering expedition the leader is neither able to change the cast nor the opera. He has to put up with the singers and if these happen to have particularly delicate temperaments, his touch must also be delicate—but firm.

In Charlie Houston's opinion, 'there were some notable prima donnas' in American mountaineering and he had no intention of inviting them to K2. He had a very clear view about the kind of men that he wanted to recruit. They did not have to be among the best climbers in the country; Houston did not put himself in that category. Courage, expedition experience, all-round competence on both rock and snow were essential, but what he looked for beyond that—with the help of his friend and climb-

ing partner from 1938, Bob Bates—was a good temperament. 'High altitude dispositions,' Bates wrote, 'are notoriously bad.' It was once said of
the British mountaineer, Frank Smythe, well known at sea level for his
tantrums, that he was one of few men whose temper improved at altitude.
Most did not. Houston and Bates wanted to find men with whom they
would be comfortable sharing a tent in a storm; agreeable companions, the
sort who would come up smiling. A compatible party would pull together
and have a better chance of success—but of more immediate importance
to Houston and Bates was their intention to enjoy the expedition and
make new friends.

They read applications, studied references, conducted interviews and
asked around. Many of the candidates were invited to the Houston family home for inspection: 'My children looked at them,' he recalled, 'the
dogs looked at them, we looked at them.' By the end of the year they had
a team with a sense of humour and a wide range of talents. George Bell
was a tall, quiet, theoretical physicist from Los Alamos; he had made first
ascents in Peru and was working at the time on the development of the
hydrogen bomb. Bob Craig, of Aspen, Colorado, a ski instructor and
trained philosopher, had climbed Mt McKinley and made national news
by his first ascent of the Devil's Thumb in British Columbia. His friend
Dee Molenaar was an artist and geologist with an impressive climbing
record that included Alaska's Mt St Elias. Pete Schoening, a chemical engi-
neer from Seattle, had led a successful expedition to the Yukon and earned
a reputation as an immensely powerful and skilful mountaineer. The least
experienced member of the party was Art Gilkey, a postgraduate student
from Wyoming who had made several difficult rock climbs and run a geological research project in Alaska.

Craig and Molenaar could hardly believe their luck. As Craig says:

We were just western boys—Charlie Houston and Bob Bates
were these luminary figures from the eastern United States who
had done a lot in Alaska and had already been on K2. This was

the big league. K2 was certainly one of the three or four hardest mountains in terms of extreme altitude, steepness, and technical difficulty. It was a once in a lifetime opportunity to go to the Himalayas, which very few people had a chance to do—and with a group of people that were respected and liked.

The seven climbers left for Pakistan on 25 May 1953; at that time Hillary and Tenzing were just a few days from the summit of Everest, while the latest German expedition was closing in on Nanga Parbat. They flew into London—the city was preparing for the coronation of Eliza-beth II—and continued via Frankfurt and Beirut to Karachi. A day later they were in Rawalpindi, after three nights of travelling—a journey that had taken Wiessner's party a month to complete. Here they were met by the Pakistani liaison officer who was to accompany them to the mountain, Colonel Mohammad Ata-Ullah, and by Captain Tony Streather of the British First Gloucestershire Regiment, appointed as the expedition's transport manager. The ebullient Streather had served with the Pakistan Army since partition, spending most of his time on the high mountain border with Afghanistan, the fabled Northwest Frontier. In 1950 a Nor-wegian climbing expedition to the 25,000-feet (7620-metre) peak of Tirich Mir had asked him to help with their transport arrangements, for Streather knew the local languages and had many contacts. To pass the time, the Norwegians taught him some mountaineering techniques and when one of the party fell ill, Streather found himself climbing in his place—all the way to the summit:

> So my first mountain was 25,000 feet plus. When I came home to England at the end of the year, I found quite unexpectedly that I was a bit of a name in mountaineering. Apparently I had been higher than any other Brit since way before the war, and was even considered for the Everest party of 1953. At about this time I had a letter from someone I had never heard of called

Charlie Houston. He said that he was arranging an expedition to
K2 and would I like to go with them? I could climb as much as
I liked or felt I was able.

A plummy-voiced Englishman, living a life of adventure on the Northwest
Frontier, Streather seemed like a character from a book to his new American friends and they pulled his leg at first. But both he and Ata-Ullah
were soon among the most popular members of the expedition.

The men spent a week in Rawalpindi making preparations, while
Ata-Ullah introduced them to the local great and good. Craig wrote later:

> Our evenings were spent in a round of wonderful dinner parties,
> where we met some of the most brilliant and capable of Pak-
> istan's leaders. We ate enormous amounts of strange and deli-
> cious Pakistani dishes, and in the cool evenings on the lawn of
> the colonel's house we talked. We learned about the birth of Pak-
> istan and talked about the problems faced by this the youngest of
> the world's great nations, and we came to admire deeply the
> courage, patience, and the energy with which the people are solv-
> ing these problems.

On 1 June an Orient Airways plane took them on to Skardu, a distance that cost Houston and Bates two weeks of marching in 1938. The
one-and-a-half-hour flight, skimming high mountain passes, plunging
between the walls of deep ravines and skirting the giant peaks of
Haramosh and Nanga Parbat, was one of the world's most spectacular and
least relaxing. The passengers' nerves were strained a little further by the
sudden appearance of a second airliner that flew alongside for most of the
journey, wing to wing. A more pleasant surprise awaited them in Skardu.

Most of the small town's 7000 inhabitants seemed to have turned out
to welcome them. Diplomats of both nations hoped that the visit of the
expedition would help promote a friendly relationship between America

and Pakistan, and the people of Skardu were making the most of the opportunity. Western visitors were rare. Cheering crowds lined the streets and garlands of roses were hung about the climbers' necks. 'Pakistan zindabad!' they shouted—'Long live Pakistan! America zindabad!'

Four days later the march through the mountains began. Dee Molenaar knew some of the mountains from photographs: 'It was just like a hick walking up Broadway and seeing all these famous skyscrapers coming into view.' George Bell remembered the walk as 'marvellous, terrific, beautiful'; to Houston it was a 'tremendous privilege and a great joy.' As the mountains got bigger and bigger, each day brought a vista more magnificent than the last. There were vertical rock faces that dwarfed anything they had seen in the United States. No climber had attempted them and many were unnamed. But the view that all of the men were waiting for, one of the most dramatic in the Himalayas—the view that had stopped Abruzzi, Spoleto and Wiessner in their tracks—was a disappointment. When they reached Concordia and looked up the glacier, K2 was invisible. The scenery dissolved into a wall of cloud. Floating above it like a moon was the disembodied summit cone—a seemingly impossible distance from the ground. Like their predecessors, they paused to take stock.

'For me it was magic,' Houston says. 'I think for all of us it was magic. We thought we could climb it, if we got the weather. I think we were quite confident. We didn't make any big boasts about it because we knew by then that it was a very difficult mountain.'

They began their assault in clear weather on 26 June. Houston's confidence seemed well-founded. Climbing in pairs, taking turns at leading, they made good progress: 'It was working very well. Nobody had been sick, nobody got hurt; we were having a good time. The weather was no better and no worse than we expected. We were climbing well, we were climbing safely, and things looked very good.'

The locations of their camps followed the pattern established by Houston in 1938 and repeated by Wiessner; there were few alternatives. In some other respects it was a different kind of expedition. There were no Sherpas. Most of the Nepalese high-altitude porters lived in Darjeeling and were regarded by Pakistanis as Indian—and therefore unwelcome. In their place Streather and Ata-Ullah had recruited six porters from Hunza—they were mountain men, but not climbers, and it was agreed that they would carry loads only as far as the lower camps on the ridge. Once these were established, they would remain at the base of the mountain with Ata-Ullah. Houston's men were to do their own packing to the high camps. This time they had the benefit of radios, the use of which had been recommended by the American Alpine Club committee in their report on the 1939 disaster. The climbing party spoke regularly to Ata-Ullah at Base Camp, who in turn relayed the latest weather forecasts for the Karakoram from Radio Pakistan.

The unremitting steepness of the Abruzzi Ridge required constant concentration from the climbers, but in the back of their minds was the uneasy thought that they might come across the bodies of Dudley Wolfe and the three Sherpas who had tried to rescue him. As they approached the site of Camp VI, they saw the frozen remains of a tent and Streather had 'a nasty feeling' that he was about to see something gruesome.

To Bob Bates the memory of that moment is as clear as a photograph: 'Pete Schoening and I came across the tents, two tents, one of them in almost perfect condition inside. The top part of the tent had mostly eroded away but in it, very, very neatly placed, were these three packs, with this can of tea and everything all set for when they came down. It was so neat and looked just as if it had been left the day before, and that hit me very hard.'

One of the bags belonged to Pasang Kikuli, who had climbed with Bates and Houston on the 1938 reconnaissance; the Sherpa had been Houston's personal attendant and then his friend. There was no sign of the bodies and there seemed little doubt that the accident had happened as Wiessner and his men supposed, somewhere on the slope above the camp as the Sherpas were on their way up to Dudley Wolfe or attempting to bring him down.

The men cleared the remains of the camp to make room for their own on the ledge. They found letters from Dudley Wolfe that he had never had a chance to dispatch and a bill from a laundry in New York. 'We should have brought that back with us,' Molenaar says, 'and paid it off for him.' Pete Schoening knocked the ice from one of the sleeping bags and decided that he preferred it to his own and for several days the men brewed fourteen-year-old Ovaltine from a can they found in the snow.

By 2 August all eight climbers were established in Camp VIII, at 25,500 feet (7772 metres). The plan was for two men to advance in the first spell of clear weather to a ninth camp at around 27,000 feet (8230 metres). The following day they would attempt the final 1300 feet to the summit, and while they did, another pair would climb to Camp IX, ready to make a second attempt if the first had failed. The men were in good condition and had all the equipment and stores they required. What they needed now was a break in the weather. Just two clear days would be enough.

That evening a storm began, the latest of several they had endured on the way up the ridge. Making themselves comfortable in their tents, they held a ballot to select the teams for the summit attempt. Molenaar recalls: 'We had a silent vote. Charlie Houston and I were the only ones with children, so we eliminated ourselves right away. By that time I was realizing that I probably shouldn't even be up there, worrying all the time. You can't go on these mountains and think about your family.'

Having chosen the teams—Bob Craig and George Bell for the first attempt, Art Gilkey and Pete Schoening for the second—they settled down and waited for the weather to break.

But it got worse. The wind rose to a level of violence that the men could scarcely believe. They could not hear themselves speak above the straining and cracking of the tent fabric. Streather was sharing with Bates:

The tent banged against our heads, and banged against our shoulders. At one stage we crept across to put our weight on one side of the tent because we were frightened that the whole thing would be blown away, and we would be blown off the mountain inside it. When we got a slight lull we went out and drove our ice-axes in as hard as we could and belayed the tent to them. The most difficult and dangerous thing was that it was impossible to keep the primus stoves alight, and so we couldn't produce water. At those altitudes, because you are puffing a lot and breathing dry air, you need an immense amount of liquid.

On the second night the tent shared by Houston and Bell suddenly ripped apart and they were forced to crawl in with the other men. Unable to heat their food and without sufficient water, the men knew that they were slowly deteriorating. On the morning of 7 August, after five days of confinement, the wind dropped and they were able to move around outside, prepare breakfast and discuss the prospects of continuing the ascent. But in one stroke, ten minutes after breakfast, everything changed.

Art Gilkey climbed out of his tent and fell forward on to the snow. He had fainted. For some time he had complained of a pain in his calf, which he took to be cramp. Houston examined him and found that his leg was swollen and tender. He applied a bandage, reassured him and a short time later broke the news to the others: it was thrombophlebitis, blood clots in the leg. Gilkey was seriously ill. Houston had encountered the condition at his medical practice, but never in one so young and never, to his knowledge, had it afflicted a climber. As Bates said later, smallpox would have been no more surprising. There was a possibility, Houston explained to the men, that the clots in Gilkey's leg would break off and enter his lungs. But when he told them that he might improve, he was trying to shield them from the truth: in the cold of Camp VIII, dehydrated and anxious, he would only get worse.

From the moment he made the diagnosis, Houston sensed that Gilkey was doomed. He would not be able to walk and a man could not be carried down a mountain like K2. When Houston talked to Schoening and Craig, both of whom were experienced in mountain rescue work, they assured him that somehow they would find a way: 'Both said we could somehow manage to get Art down, but their statements lacked conviction. I did not believe them. I knew, *we all knew*, that no one could be carried, lowered, or dragged down the Black Pyramid, over the dreadful loose rock to Camp V, down House's Chimney. My mind's eye flew over the whole route. There was no hope, absolutely none.'

But they were going to try. They wrapped Gilkey in the remains of Houston's tent and immediately started down by the route they had climbed nearly a week before.

Within a few hours, however, they were back at Camp VIII, defeated. The slope below was now waist-deep in new snow. Wading through it, pulling Gilkey behind them, they had persevered for several hundred yards before Schoening and Bell realized that the entire expanse was about to avalanche. They had no choice but to return. Exhausted by the struggle, Houston could see no way out of their position. It was now desperate. Their retreat was cut off, the wind was gathering force and all of them were getting weaker by the day.

Craig and Schoening now suggested that they reconnoitre a route over the steep rocks to the east of the ice slope. They returned two hours later with the news that it looked difficult and dangerous, but feasible, as far as they could see through the driving mist. At least it offered a chance. They decided to attempt it in the first reasonable weather.

At Base Camp, Ata-Ullah was receiving Houston's radio messages with increasing anxiety. 'I do strongly urge,' he now said to Houston, 'that I come up to help you. After all, you have two or three frostbite cases besides Art and I can share your burden.' It brought tears to Houston's eyes, but there was, of course, nothing that Ata-Ullah could do—except pray. He and the porters had been praying for many days, he told Houston, and concluded 'you are fighting now for all your lives.'

On 9 August the storm screamed down on their tents, beating wildly at the fabric. Gilkey, having rallied the day before, now took a turn for the worse. His other leg had developed clots and he was coughing, his face turning bluish-grey. It was obvious to Houston that the clots had reached his lungs: 'He looked dreadful; his pulse was pounding at 140 per minute. But his courage never faltered... Art said nothing of himself. He had never talked about his death, though he was too wise not to see its imminence. He apologized for being a burden upon us. He encouraged us, spoke of another summit attempt—after we got him down.'

The next morning Houston told the others—he had to shout to be heard—that unless they descended immediately, Gilkey would die. In all probability he would die on the way down the mountain, but they had to *try* to save him. All the men felt the same and they began to pack without further discussion. Leaving him was unthinkable and they had already expressed their reluctance to split the party, despite Houston's and Streather's suggestion that they stay with him while the others tried to regain their strength at a lower camp. The descent that they now prepared for would have been testing for fit climbers in clear weather. In a storm, manoeuvring a helpless man, after a week of thirst and hunger, some kind of accident was inevitable.

They wrapped Gilkey once more in the tent, Houston gave him a sedative to subdue the pain from the bumping he was bound to receive and they set out. The driving snow froze on their goggles—they could barely see, nor, before long, could they feel their own hands and feet, such was the cold. A short distance below Camp VIII they began to lower Gilkey, accompanied by Craig, down a snow couloir. George Bell was helping to belay them: 'I can remember sitting up there and feeling the wind go through my windproof clothing and gradually getting colder and colder and less and less functional. At one point a small avalanche swept over Craig and Gilkey. It was a desperate struggle, the storm was continuing, the mountain was mercilessly steep, and it couldn't come to a good end.'

When the snow roared over him Craig thought he was going to die; Bates, looking down from above, was 'very relieved and a little surprised' to see both men still there. They moved on slowly: by mid-afternoon they had descended only 400 feet. The relative security of Camp VI had been their objective, but at their rate of progress it was out of range; they would have to spend the night on the cramped ledge that supported Camp VII. A long traverse across an ice slope separated them from it. Craig had unroped and gone ahead to prepare the site when the inevitable happened.

The pitch of the ice slope was 45 degrees. The plan was to swing Gilkey in stages across it, from anchor points some 60 feet above. While Schoening belayed him, the other men moved along the ice at Gilkey's level searching for a place from which they could safely pull him across. Bell and Streather were roped together, as were Houston and Bates. Molenaar, who had been climbing with Craig, attached himself to the ropes that held Gilkey. George Bell was moving downwards when he missed his footing: 'The wind and the storm blew snow on our glasses and we couldn't really see very well. I thought I saw a nicely chopped out step, and I put my foot out. My crampon came off the step and I was soon head over heels down the mountain.'

He flew past Streather, and when the weight came on the rope, the Englishman was instantly jerked downwards. Bates saw him swept off the slope 'as if by a giant hand' and crash towards the rope that attached him to Houston:

> He was obviously going to slam into the rope between Charlie and me in just a second and I got my ice-axe and slammed it into the ice just as hard as I could... and of course the next second I was flipped off, the axe was left sticking in the slope, and I went head backwards. My jacket pulled up over my head and the rope was wrapped around my hands. I knew there was nothing below to stop me, and there was nobody belaying me so I said well, we did our best and this is it, and that was the only thought I had.

The last thing he saw before his own fall was Houston's. All of them hurtled into Molenaar's rope and now he too was flung helplessly from his stance.

Molenaar's rope, attached to Gilkey, played out. Above them, with his back turned, Schoening held Gilkey in a secure belay, his ice-axe wedged behind a small rock. He had looped the rope around the axe handle, back across his hips and through his right hand. When he felt the first tug he braced himself and a series of violent jolts followed. He lent with all his power against the axe head. The rope stretched and thinned. For a moment it ran out through his hand but then it was still, as thin and taut as wire across his body. He didn't dare move.

Schoening didn't know it, but he was holding the fall of all five men. When Bell slipped, the five were on three separate ropes. As they fell, the ropes had crossed and tangled and the weight of all the men had come on to the rope holding Molenaar to Gilkey and eventually on to Schoening's anchor.

Two hundred feet below, Bates realized that he was no longer falling. As he struggled to free his head from his jacket he heard a gasp underneath him and discovered that he was lying on top of Molenaar: 'His hair was standing on end, a little blood dripping off his moustache. He looked absolutely astonished.' Some 25 feet below lay Houston, apparently unconscious, and still further down they could see Bell climbing up 'from the edge of nothingness.' He had lost his mittens and was stumbling up the slope, his white hands raised towards them.

Bell had found himself dangling by his rope over a precipice. He didn't know that the other men had fallen: 'I thought I had better get myself out of this because nobody can possibly rescue me. I couldn't climb the rope with my pack on, so I threw it off. I couldn't see anything so I threw my glasses off, and I couldn't climb with my mittens, so I threw them off. So the three things that you would never abandon, except in the most desperate circumstances, I abandoned.'

Bates found some spare gloves for Bell and scrambled down to Houston. He was mumbling and seemed unable to comprehend where he was or what had happened. Bates urged him to climb up the rocks, but he would only repeat, 'What are we doing here?' But when Bates took him by the shoulders and told him that if he didn't get up he would never see his wife and daughter again, 'a look of fear came over him' and he sprang to his feet.

Those who were able helped the injured men to Camp VII, while Craig anchored Gilkey to the ice slope with two axes: 'I think he was very cold. I talked with him and I said we'll be back for you, Art. We've had an accident. We're going to take care of the guys that are hurt and I hope you'll be OK, and he said, "Yes, I'll be fine, I'm OK." So I left him out on the slope.'

As soon as they had pitched their tents, Bates, Craig and Streather made their way back towards Gilkey. They were close to exhaustion. For much of the day they had climbed without goggles in order to see better in the storm and were beginning to be affected by snow blindness. When they approached the place where they left Gilkey, Streather wondered if his eyes were deceiving him: 'There was an extraordinary sight. Everything looked a bit misty, but Art wasn't there. We couldn't believe this initially. I went over to the spot where he was and it looked completely different. There was a gully running down and the snow was all soft round about. We concluded that an avalanche must have come down and taken him away.'

'We just couldn't believe this had happened,' Craig recalls. 'We thought: is there anything that we can do? And we looked at each other and shook our heads and said this is it, he's gone.'

On the cramped ledge at Camp VII, battered, stunned and still in grave danger, the men were in no condition to reflect on the loss of their friend. They faced a battle for their own survival. They recognized that his death delivered them from a situation in which they could neither abandon him nor proceed with any hope of success; they could only *try*. Try-

ing to save him involved huge risks for the whole party and had already
brought them within an inch of disaster. 'In so far as we were capable of
feeling anything,' said Bell, 'we felt a sense of relief.'

In two small tents the seven men spent a desperately uncomfortable
night. Their feet were hanging over a precipice. Molenaar had cuts and
broken ribs, Bell's hands and feet were frostbitten, Schoening was badly
bruised from the effort of arresting the fall and Houston, concussed,
blind in one eye and injured in the chest, was delirious. He asked continually if everyone was all right. 'How's Art?' he repeated. Unable to breathe
comfortably, he demanded a knife so that he could cut a hole in the tent
and get some fresh air. When the others restrained him, he reminded them
that he was an expert in oxygen and if they didn't do as he said, they would
all suffocate in three minutes. He would drift off to sleep and then suddenly rear up, shouting for air.

At dawn they began to inch their way down the mountain. Bates
likened the journey to Camp VI to descending a steeply angled house
roof, 1700 feet long, over tiles coated with ice and snow. One slip might
bring all the men down. Houston was concussed and unable to reason, but
seemed otherwise strong. The greatest worry to Bates was George Bell. His
hands were blistered and his feet so swollen that he could barely squeeze
them into his boots. Without spectacles, his eyesight was poor: 'The
weather continued foul and I didn't have my glasses. I didn't have an ice-
axe either for a while. Then an axe was found sticking out of the snow
somewhere, and passed to me. That was a great benefit because I could use
it like a blind man uses a cane, except of course that I was climbing down
steep rocks.'

At about 1000 feet below the scene of the accident they began to see
traces of Gilkey: a broken ice-axe, fragments of cloth and tangled rope.
Bates picked up a small bag of personal effects. They climbed silently past
two or three rocks splattered with his blood. Houston's recollection of the
descent is incomplete, but he remembers the bloodstains 'all too well. It
was a very bad experience and one that really seared me.' He could not

bring himself to talk about what he had seen—what they had all seen—
until the expedition held a reunion, twenty-five years later. If there was any
consolation, it was that Gilkey had evidently died in an instant.

At Camp VI they were in relative comfort and could use the sleeping
bags left by Wiessner's Sherpas in 1939. Although Houston had occasionally sunk to his knees during the day's climbing, an expression of
bewilderment on his face, he had always responded to a few sharp words
from Schoening. It was an unfamiliar sensation for the youngest member
of the expedition: 'Charlie was like a dad to you, and you didn't speak to
your dad in that fashion. He was a hero of mine and I always looked up
to him, but there were times when it was necessary to speak sternly to keep
him on the route and keep him coming down.'

He had climbed safely. Bell remained in constant pain from his frostbite, but his morale was about to benefit from a minor miracle. The bag
Bates had picked up among the wreckage of the accident did not belong
to Gilkey after all—Bell immediately recognized it as his own. Inside it
were the expedition accounts ('the least of my worries') and his spare pair
of spectacles, unbroken. He let out a whoop of delight.

One more barrier remained the next day: House's Chimney. If they
could negotiate the cliff, they knew that the worst would be over. They
reached it as darkness fell. Houston insisted on going down last. One by
one the men descended safely and waited, but there was no sign of
Houston. A hundred feet above them he was facing a personal crisis. He
could not distinguish between the new fixed rope and the old—Wiessner's rope and his own from 1938 were embedded in the ice at the top
of the cliff. He suddenly lost confidence: 'It was my moment of truth,
and I had begun to realize that I couldn't do it. It was dark and I was
still hurting. I remember saying that I'm going to jump off, because if I
fall I'll knock them down—they're waiting for me at the bottom. I stood
there for a while—while they were shouting up to me—and I said the
Lord's Prayer.'

Although he has no recollection of it, in the next instant Houston began to climb, and within a few minutes had caught up with his colleagues. Nothing would stop them now.

From Camp IV they were able to radio Base Camp. Having begun to fear the worst, Ata-Ullah was lost for words and could only repeat, 'Thank God.' On the slope above Camp II, they heard the cries of the Hunza porters and a minute later saw them clambering eagerly over the ice towards them. The porters had tied themselves together with what looked to Bates like string and when they threw their arms around the climbers he was momentarily terrified: the slope fell away sharply for some 1500 feet. 'Such a place,' he wrote later, 'is not suited to an uninhibited heart to heart embrace.'

But it was a wonderful reunion. 'It was a very emotional experience,' said Craig. 'There were a lot of tears. They cared a lot about us and they expressed it, and they tried to help us across.' Tony Streather wrote:

> When we had eaten and drunk all our unaccustomed stomachs would take, we settled down to talk quietly among ourselves for the first time in many days. There was an almost tangible feeling of relief in the air. I told the Hunzas about Art, and they offered a most touching prayer in his memory and asked me to translate their feelings to the others. Although no sentimentalist, I found it hard to prevent my voice from breaking as I translated their thoughtful wishes of condolence to the Americans. No people from our so-called civilized countries could express themselves with such complete and unaffected sincerity as those six men from the remote Central Asian State of Hunza.

At Base Camp, Mohammad Ata-Ullah continued to shake his head and murmur, 'Thank God. Thank God.' The porters built a memorial mound on a rocky promontory above Base Camp and a metal box containing what remained of Gilkey's possessions was placed on top. Bob Bates said a few prayers, but only three of the men were fit enough to walk to the cairn.

George Bell had to be carried back to Skardu. His feet would recover from their frostbite, but he believed that his life would never be the same again: 'We felt lucky to be alive, very privileged to have had that experience and survived, and that it would make a difference forever after. I think we told each other and ourselves that after that, why, most things will seem trivial.'

Walking alongside him, Houston had the same thought: that nothing would ever upset him, that he would be all right for the rest of his life. He was wrong.

Back home in New Hampshire, he and Bates immediately submitted an application to return to K2 in 1955. But it never happened. Almost exactly a year after Gilkey's death, Houston suffered an attack of complete amnesia. A policeman identified him by calling the store on the label of his necktie. He took a holiday and was driving along a road in New England when the black top suddenly turned to the colour of blood. It was then that he decided never to climb again.

Gilkey's death was the first on any of his climbing expeditions and he speaks of bearing 'a heavy burden of guilt.' During the remainder of his professional career Houston became one of world's leading authorities on high-altitude medicine. Although he has not climbed for nearly half a century, he is still regarded as the grand old man of American mountaineering, an inspirational figure to younger climbers. He holds strong opinions about the risks taken by contemporary climbers on dangerous mountains.

Bob Bates lost some of his appetite for climbing after 1953, but none of his love for the mountains. He continued to teach at the idyllic Phillips Academy in New Hampshire until his retirement. This year, approaching his ninetieth birthday, he was visiting Nepal. Dee Molenaar never returned to the Himalayas. In 1963 he declined an invitation to join Norman Dyhrenfurth's American Everest party. He didn't want to disrupt his family life 'and besides, it would have meant coming up with $10,000 just to join the expedition and I didn't have that kind of money.' A painting he did at Camp VIII on K2 remains a world altitude record in fine art.

George Bell, Bob Craig, Pete Schoening and Tony Streather returned to further adventures in the Himalayas. In 1955, only five years after he climbed his first mountain, Streather made the first ascent of Kangchengjunga, the third highest in the world.

IN THE SPRING OF 2000, we interviewed Tony Streather and all six American climbers from the 1953 expedition. For nearly fifty years they had remained close friends and whenever they had a reunion it was just as if they were back in the Karakoram. 'We had gone over as strangers,' Bell told us, 'and returned as brothers. It was a depth of fellowship that we would never relinquish and we would cherish all our lives.' Three months after we visited him in Los Alamos, George Bell died.

CHAPTER 9

The Jealous Mountain

W hen, at the end of August, Charlie Houston's battered and bruised team arrived at Rawalpindi, they were surprised to encounter another pretender to K2's crown—a professor from Milan, Ardito Desio. He was a short man and, at the age of fifty-six, much older than any of them, but what he lacked in height he made up for in ambition. They all met at Colonel Ata-Ullah's house at an official reception for the returning climbers. He commiserated with them over the death of Art Gilkey and quizzed them about their recent experiences. A couple of days later he set off for Skardu.

For the last twenty-five years he had been trying to drum up support for an Italian expedition to K2 and was at that very moment waiting to hear back from the Pakistani government about his application for a climbing permit. A few months later he was given official approval, and in the summer of 1954 he returned to Pakistan with a small army of climbers to lay siege to K2. As he would later write of this campaign, it was different from anything that had gone before because 'it was undertaken with the specific aim of *conquering* K2, and not merely of *making an attempt* on it.' These were proud words, from a very proud man.

Ardito Desio was different from all the others who had set their hearts on K2. He was a geologist who had done some climbing, but he was not a world-class mountaineer like Houston or Wiessner. His first experience of the Karakoram had come many years before when, in 1929, he had been part of an expedition led by the Duke of Spoleto, a nephew of the Duke of Abruzzi. Spoleto had originally planned to make an attempt on K2 himself, but he was discouraged from doing so by those in the Italian government, who weren't keen on anything so risky. A year earlier an Italian airship had crashed on an expedition to the North Pole and Mussolini had been severely embarrassed by the ensuing publicity. So Spoleto had to be content with continuing the mapping and general exploration of the area that his illustrious uncle had begun. Ardito Desio was enthralled by the Karakoram and particularly fascinated by K2. As soon as he got back to Italy he contacted the Italian Alpine Club and sounded them out about financing another expedition, but nothing came of his efforts until the early 1950s.

After intensive personal lobbying, Desio had obtained permission from the Pakistan government to visit the Karakoram on a reconnaissance mission in 1953, with a view to coming back with a full-scale expedition a year later if Houston's party didn't succeed in reaching the summit of K2. As soon as he heard that the Americans had been unsuccessful he knew that he was in with a chance to realize his greatest ambition. Desio wasn't planning to climb the mountain himself, but he was determined to be remembered as the conqueror of K2. He was the man who would put the expedition together, the man who would organize all the logistics, select the climbers and talk to the press.

Desio invited Riccardo Cassin, then considered Italy's leading mountaineer, to accompany him on his reconnaissance mission. From the beginning, though, Cassin felt that he was treated like a second-class citizen. Both men flew to Pakistan. but whereas Desio then took an internal flight from Karachi to Rawalpindi, Cassin had to make the thirty-six-hour journey by train. Desio went alone to meet Houston's team at Ata-Ullah's house and Cassin had to make do with seeing the Americans off at the airport.

The two Italians reached K2 at the end of September after a brief diversion to make an examination of a nearby glacier for the Pakistani government. Originally they had planned to go as far as Windy Gap, the pass to the north-east of K2, but in the end they managed to get only as far as Houston's advance base camp at the foot of the Abruzzi Ridge. After taking a lot of photographs, they were chased back to Skardu by bad weather. Both men were excited by the prospect of returning with a full-scale team the following year and were overjoyed when, a month later, Desio was told that his application had been successful. Now the planning started in earnest. The Italian Alpine Club put forward an initial list of 200 climbers to be considered for the expedition. This was whittled down to twenty-two men who were then sent for medical examinations in Milan.

To his astonishment, Riccardo Cassin was rejected after the first round. He couldn't understand this—he had never previously had any problems with his health and he was very confident that he would cope well on K2. At one stage there had been talk of officially appointing him as the leader of the climbers; now it looked as if he might not be able to go at all. In desperation, he went for a second series of tests in Rome. These contradicted the first set of results and confirmed that he was in top condition. At this point, Desio persuaded Cassin to resign from the official organizing committee, and shortly afterwards it declared that he was not fit to take any further part in the expedition. It was a terrible blow for him: in his autobiography, he later commented on the sorry episode in a chapter entitled 'An Unfair and Bitter Exclusion':

> I was bitter at the dishonesty of the way I had been treated...
> Professor Desio was afraid that his reputation might be obscured
> by mine: in fact when we were on the way out from the Baltoro,
> the journalists, reporters and climbers preferred to talk to me, a
> climber, not a geologist... Even if the committee did not want
> to publicize the real reason for my exclusion, they should not
> have based it on the fabrication of 'physical unfitness'—a very
> serious accusation that was a real shock to me and which affected
> me for a long time.

When he came to writing the expedition book, Desio barely commented on the Cassin episode, but you do get a very clear sense that he didn't want to share the leadership of the expedition with anyone else. His was never going to be like Houston's expedition where everyone had a stake in the action. In a submission to the Pakistani government, Desio outlined his philosophy:

> The expedition will of necessity be organized along military lines, in a sense that will be familiar to all who have spent some part of their lives—especially under wartime conditions—in our Alpine regiments. The need for rigid discipline will become apparent to every man once he has grasped the essential fact that everything must be subordinated to the attainment of the final goal, which is the conquest of K2. Everyone must be prepared to sacrifice all for the sake of the others, and all must be ready to sacrifice themselves for the sake of the individual.

Desio didn't just want to make an attempt on K2 though: on the same expedition, he intended to conduct a very ambitious scientific exploration programme and planned to take along a team of scientists who would work independently of the climbers. This would become an important source of tension later on when it came to financing the expedition. It also reflected an ambiguity on Desio's part: strange though it sounds, he never seems to have felt quite at home with the mountaineers. In his expedition book their names and their photographs came after those of the scientific staff and he added details about their heights on to their potted CVs as if they were racehorses or prizefighters. Readers were informed that Paolo Grazioso, scientist, had published more than 200 scientific works, but one of the most important things about Pino Gallotti, climber, seemed to be that he was '6 feet tall.'

Of twenty-two climbers who went through the first round of medical tests, six were rejected straight away and a few more were weeded out after

more prodding and poking in Turin. In January 1954, the remainder were
sent to a training camp at the Klein Matterhorn in the Alps where they were
observed by an officer from the Italian Army. A committee of experts decided that two of them weren't up to scratch and the final eleven-man team
was confirmed. Most of them were full-time mountain guides, though only
one of the men had climbed outside the Alps. They all had to agree to work
for no pay, to submit to a draconian disciplinary code and not to talk to the
press. Nevertheless, there was huge excitement within Italian mountaineering over the expedition and there was no shortage of people volunteering to
take part. Eventually, two of these eleven men would make the final attempt
on the summit of K2: Achille Compagnoni and Lino Lacedelli.

At forty, Compagnoni was the second oldest member of the team.
He was a prize-winning skier and marksman and had served in an
Alpine regiment during the war. Today he is a quiet, reflective elder citizen of Cervinia, the small Italian town at the foot of the Matterhorn,
but in his prime he was a very well-known local 'character,' famous for
chopping off his customers' ties and hanging them over the bar in the
hotel he still owns. In his own account of the K2 expedition, he began
with the story of a strange dream he had in December 1953, in which
he found himself standing on the edge of a huge mountain: 'It looked
like the Matterhorn but it wasn't; it was much higher, monstrous and
unnaturally big. The summit was hidden in clouds, its flanks were fur-
rowed by enormous gullies.' The very next morning a letter from the
Italian Alpine Club arrived in the post inviting him to come to Milan
for their expedition to K2.

Lino Lacedelli was a young ski instructor from the Dolomites. As
soon as he heard rumours that an expedition was being planned, he and
some other climbing friends went into training; ultimately he was the
only one selected to go to Pakistan. For Lacedelli the expedition was an
incredible opportunity: 'I was so happy because I never dared to hope
that I'd be chosen because there were so many other good men who were
also up for it.' The youngest member of the team was Walter Bonatti, then

the rising star of Italian Alpinism. He too was overjoyed to have been chosen but ultimately this expedition would become one of the great regrets of his life.

While the team was being chosen, Desio got on with organizing the other aspects of the expedition. There were problems getting money for such a big project in a period of political and economic instability, but he was a tireless fundraiser and eventually secured considerable financial commitments from the Italian Olympic Committee and a scientific body, the National Council for Research. Desio did his homework well; he went to England to meet Sir John Hunt, leader of the successful British Everest expedition, and look at the equipment they had used, and talked to Swiss and Austrian climbers about their recent trips to the Himalayas. He corresponded with Charlie Houston and spent three days with Fritz Wiessner in Italy discussing everything from what to eat to where to place camps. Desio decided that his would be a much larger-scale enterprise than either of the American efforts, a 'heavy' expedition that would lay siege to the mountain until it was conquered. Although Wiessner advised him that K2 could be climbed without oxygen, he decided that, like the British, his men would take oxygen sets for the high-altitude climbing. For all their equipment, he cherry-picked the best items used on recent Himalayan expeditions and, when he found something that could be improved, he had it specially manufactured in Italy.

In April 1954 the expedition got under way. Desio flew out to Pakistan where he was warmly greeted by the Prime Minister, and 16 tonnes of equipment was sent out by ship from Genoa, shortly followed by the climbers. At the end of the month everyone reassembled in Skardu where they were honoured with the customary polo match. Once again, Colonel Ata-Ullah had been appointed as the head liaison officer. Desio presented him with a badge and a membership card for the Italian Alpine Club and in return he gave Desio a Pakistani flag to take to the summit.

Originally Desio had investigated the possibility of airlifting most of their supplies to K2 base camp, but it had proved impossible to get the

planes from Italy. He did however manage to persuade a Pakistani airline
to make the world's first aerial reconnaissance of K2, quietly ignoring the
fact that this would take them into Chinese airspace. There were two
problems though: first of all, there were no maps available of the Chinese
side of the mountain and, second, the only plane available had a maximum
altitude ceiling of 23,000 feet (7010 metres), which was going to make
things a little tricky when it came to flying around a mountain that was
5000 feet (1524 metres) higher. Fortunately Desio was one of the few
men in the world who had made a topographical survey of the area and
he was confident that he could direct the pilot to get them safely to the
mountain and back.

Desio set off with the expedition's two cameramen and its oxygen
expert. The plane was unpressurized so they had to use the masks and canisters brought along for high-altitude climbing. The plane flew along the
Baltoro Glacier and then turned left at Concordia; in a few minutes they
were able to pass over what would take them many days on the ground.
Desio told the pilot to head for Windy Gap, the pass between K2 and
Broad Peak; after that he would look for a familiar landmark on the other
side of the mountain to guide them back. The pilot managed to take the
plane all the way up to 24,000 feet, giving them a little extra margin, but
it was still a hair-raising trip. At first they didn't need to use the oxygen
sets, but when Desio started to hear a buzzing sound in his head he realized that now was the time to put one on. Ironically, having been amazed
at how quick the journey was, they now began to regret that the plane was
so fast: 'We barely had time to survey the rock walls of K2 before we
found ourselves face to face with the monster—too close to it, in fact, to
be able to take in the whole of our route from the foothills to the summit.' Nevertheless they were able to take the first aerial photographs of K2
and get a unique glimpse of its ferocious north face.

After this unexpected privilege, the next couple of weeks were ago-
nizingly slow. It took a full month to get the climbers and all their equipment from Skardu to Base Camp. There were two basic problems: the

weather and the size of the expedition—at one stage they were employing no fewer than 600 porters. For some reason, the men they hired were much more rebellious than those who had worked for previous expeditions and on several occasions the porters put down their bags and refused to continue. The problems started at Askole when they demanded a rest day. Desio refused: 'When a caravan is on the move, the best way to avoid trouble is to keep going day after day.' When they reached Urdukas, the halfway point along the Baltoro Glacier, things took a turn for the worse. In 1929, this had been the base camp for the Duke of Spoleto's expedition and Desio had lived here on and off for four months. He remembered it as a beautiful spot, but this time round all its vegetation was covered in snow and it was clear that difficulties lay ahead. They had not brought along sufficient quantities of snow goggles and blankets to properly equip everyone, so once again the porters refused to leave. The Pakistani liaison officers cajoled most them out of the camp and somehow persuaded them to go as far as Concordia, but at this point most of them unceremoniously dumped their loads and headed back to Skardu. Desio and Ata-Ullah continued on to K2 base camp but it took another fortnight to finally get all of their supplies transported there, even though it was less than a day's walk away from the point where everyone left.

In spite of all these organizational problems, for most of the Italian climbers the journey itself was a hugely memorable experience. Lino Lacedelli was shocked by his first sight of K2: 'I thought, how are we going to get up there? We were a day's walk away and we still had to strain our necks upwards just to see it properly—it was stupendous.' Achille Compagnoni had a strange sense of déjà vu: 'I suddenly stopped and felt the blood rushing to my head with emotion. It was a real effort to hold back the tears: why were my feelings so intense? It was because straight away I felt that it was like the Matterhorn for me. A Matterhorn magically transported here and magically enlarged, a mountain fit only for super-humans. It was just like the mountain I had seen in my dreams back at home in December.'

They settled into Base Camp, which was dubbed by Desio 'the new Italopolis of K2.' In addition to their personal accommodation, it consisted of four large tents: a mess tent, a wireless room, a food store and an office for Desio. Outside in a nice grotto they installed a Madonna that had been presented to them by the Archbishop of Milan. Having determined to lay siege to the mountain, they had packed for a long stay and been provided with all mod cons. They had walkie-talkies to communicate with each other on the mountain and a large wireless set that would eventually enable them to send messages to the outside world. Taking a cue from Houston, they brought along a couple of rope and pulley sets that made it much easier to transport supplies to and from their various smaller camps on the mountain.

Desio had decided to follow the same route that Houston had taken, but whereas the previous year's expedition had moved en masse up the Abruzzi Ridge, he had quite a different plan. Base Camp would be the nub of operations and he would do no climbing himself. His men would steadily progress up the mountain, setting up a series of smaller camps that would, as far as possible, all be connected together by fixed ropes, which would allow them to go up and down at will. Desio realized that long stays at high altitude had caused problems for previous expeditions and hoped that by keeping a path constantly open between base and the upper camps, his climbers would be able to descend if they felt ill or exhausted and then reascend once they had sorted out whatever problems were ailing them. In addition to the large team of climbers that he had brought from Italy, Desio hired a team of Pakistani high-altitude porters to do as much as possible of the load-carrying.

Each man was given a pocket guide to the mountain, which summarized the experiences of previous expeditions and listed all the supplies left by Houston's team on the mountain. They were told that at Camp II they could look forward to tins of marmalade, meat and biscuits. There would be more at Camp III and a very small quantity of food at Camp VIII. Desio brought along a set of Vittorio Sella's photographs, taken on the Duke of Abruzzi's 1909 expedition to K2, and all the climbers had already been required to attend lectures back in Italy on the history and topography of K2. As Desio wrote: 'By the time they came within sight of the Abruzzi Ridge everyone felt as if they had been there several times before, so clearly were even the most trivial details of the terrain impressed on them.' In the early stages at least, Desio was a harsh disciplinarian and made sure that everything happened according to his carefully worked out plans. He knew that some of the men might have done things differently, but he was always sure that he was right: 'To the Italian temperament an expedition conducted along the lines of a commando raid might have been more congenial. But it would have failed.'

The only thing that Desio knew he couldn't control was the weather. They were able to get reports from outside, but these provided little comfort—at one stage they heard over the wireless about torrential rain in Lahore, and a couple of days later snow storms arrived at K2. As ever, Desio had reviewed all the literature in order to devise the optimum climbing schedule, but things didn't turn out as he had expected. The weather was consistently inconsistent; Desio pinned his hopes on a window of opportunity at the end of July, but in order to take advantage of it he knew that they would have to be able to get high up the mountain.

Their early progress was slow but steady. In the middle of June they reached the site of Houston's Camp III and found abandoned an embroidered umbrella that he had brought along a year earlier. A couple of days later they made their first tentative foray on to House's Chimney, the rock feature that had always been such a test for previous expeditions. Then, suddenly out of nowhere, disaster struck. Everyone thought that Mario Puchoz was one of the strongest members of the team, so when one day he complained about a throat infection, no one took it that seriously. Instead of going down to base camp, he elected to stay at Camp III with Lino Lacedelli and wait for Guido Pagani, the expedition doctor, to come up to him.

The doctor was delayed by the weather. When he arrived he realized straight away that it was more serious than everyone had thought, but at first Puchoz reacted well to the medicine he was given. Pagani stayed with him for the next few days until suddenly, on the morning of 21 June while he was preparing some medicine for him, Puchoz died 'after a brief agony.' Afterwards Pagani diagnosed the illness as pneumonia, though modern experts suspect that it may have been a case of high-altitude pulmonary oedema. Puchoz was wrapped up in his sleeping bag and placed outside the tent. The doctor and all the remaining men descended to Base Camp to deliver the shocking news. For five more days the storm raged and they were unable to retrieve the body. Finally, on 27 June, almost a month after they arrived, Puchoz was buried in a crack in the rocks next to the monument erected by Houston's 1953 expedition as a memorial to Art Gilkey.

On the following day they resumed their attack on the mountain with renewed vigour. Now they were climbing not just for themselves or for Italy but in honour of Mario Puchoz. There were further setbacks. Their high-altitude porters all went on strike and three of them were dismissed. One of the Italian climbers, Cirillo Floreanni, took a fall after trying to climb down on a fixed rope left over from Houston's expedition. The weather remained stormy and unpredictable. As de Filippi had noted fifty years earlier on Abruzzi's expedition, the worst periods for everyone were when they were confined to their tents.

Sometimes conditions got so bad that their radios didn't work properly, so Desio would send up written messages to men in the high camps. These ranged from gung-ho exhortations to veiled threats. Message 11 warned them not to get despondent about the weather and added: 'If we were to return home before we had exhausted all the possibilities that remain to us of reaching the summit of K2, or without at any rate making a serious attempt on the peak, we should be breaking faith with the nation.' Message 12 informed them of the huge international press interest in what they were doing and reminded them that they had a moral responsibility to do their best: 'If you succeed in scaling the peak the entire world will hail you as champions of your race and your fame will endure long after you are dead. Thus even if you never achieve anything else of note you will be able to say that you have not lived in vain.' For the men on the mountain, Desio's notes were taken with a pinch of salt. Lacedelli didn't pay much attention: 'What someone writes sitting on a chair down in Base Camp is one thing but high up on the mountain you have to think for yourself and your companions. So the messages would go in one ear and out the other. We had more important things to think about.'

In the middle of July things started happening more quickly. Down at Base Camp, they made the first outgoing transmission on their wireless set while up on the mountain the climbers reached the shoulder of K2. One day, Compagnoni and one of the other climbers, Ubaldo Rey, came across what for a moment they thought was the body of Art Gilkey. Compagnoni recalled:

> I saw the wind was making something move and I thought it
> might be Gilkey because his body had never been found. They had
> left him anchored to the slope but when they came back he had
> disappeared. We all thought he had deliberately cut himself free
> in order to save the lives of his companions. It looked like two
> arms, swinging stiffly in the wind. I told Rey to wait there because
> I knew that he was still in shock after the death of Puchoz, but
> when I got over there I discovered that it was Gilkey's duvet
> jacket and his sleeping bag.

Nearby there were a few of his possessions; Compagnoni left them there.

On 28 July, after almost two months of climbing, they reached Camp VIII where Houston's expedition had been trapped by a ferocious storm the previous year; they found a couple of his tents and a small quantity of food. By now they had lost radio contact with Base Camp; Desio and the others below had to be content to scour the upper slopes with binoculars and to occasionally fire rockets into the air to remind the men above them that they should make every effort to stay in touch. Desio had appointed Compagnoni as the leader of the climbers and he chose Lacedelli to accompany him on the final assault.

There was a real sense that it was now or never: Lacedelli and Compagnoni were 3000 feet from the top, and if they could pitch one more high camp they knew that they would be close enough to make a bid for the summit. All they needed was a couple of days of good weather and for the oxygen sets to be brought up from below. They had managed to climb without artificial oxygen up to this point, but everyone agreed that for the final assault on the summit it would be vital. So on the following day, 29 July, it was planned that while Lacedelli and Compagnoni pressed on up from Camp VIII to establish the next camp above them, the four climbers in the camp below them would haul up their precious oxygen. At this stage Walter Bonatti became a key player in the final drama.

Though the youngest member of the team, Bonatti was already a skilled climber. He had been thrilled to be accepted on the expedition, but he was very ambitious and wasn't at all fazed by the company he found himself in. He had only just recovered from a stomach bug but, in spite of this, on the morning of the 29th when he and the three other climbers left Camp VII Bonatti was feeling the strongest of them all. Things started badly: Erich Abram and Ubaldo Rey were forced to turn back very early on, and soon after, Gallotti began to feel exhausted. He and Bonatti decided that instead of going back, they would cache the oxygen sets in the snow and carry on to the next camp where they would meet the others and devise a new plan.

When they reached Camp VIII they discovered that Lacedelli and Compagnoni had also had a bad day and hadn't succeeded in making their next camp. When they heard Bonatti's news they were very disappointed: without the oxygen sets everyone knew that they would not be able to make a bid for the summit. A new plan was devised: Bonatti and Gallotti would go down the next day and somehow try to retrieve the oxygen sets, while Compagnoni and Lacedelli would make a second attempt to set up Camp

IX. If everything went smoothly, Bonatti and Gallotti would carry on to deliver the oxygen sets to the upper camp themselves. No one was that optimistic, though; Bonatti sensed that Compagnoni was close to exhaustion point and commented later that he almost volunteered to take over: 'I was in fact torn between the feeling that I would have to take Compagnoni's place, the scruples which in our present situation prevented me from doing so and the fear that, in my place, Compagnoni would not succeed in bringing the oxygen up to Camp IX.' For the moment he held his peace.

The next day they all set off on their allotted tasks. After they had reached the oxygen cylinders, Bonatti and Gallotti met a revived Abram who told them that he now felt strong enough to come up with more supplies. He was accompanied by two of the Pakistani high-altitude porters, Mahdi and Isakhan. All five men pressed on upwards to Camp VIII, sharing the loads, but at this point Gallotti and Isakhan declared that they could go no further. Bonatti realized that all three able men would have to carry on if they were to have any chance of delivering the oxygen to Compagnoni and Lacedelli, who had already left camp, but he knew that Mahdi would need some persuasion. They offered him a bonus and, best of all, an opportunity to become famous: 'We put the proposal to Mahdi giving him the impression that he might be able to go on up to the summit with me, Lacedelli and Compagnoni. It was a necessary deception which had however a grain of truth in it.'

When they set off again there were just four hours of daylight remaining. It was hard work carrying the oxygen cylinders and harder still when they discovered that Compagnoni and Lacedelli weren't where they thought they were going to be. Abram turned back at 6:30, exhausted and sure that he was getting frostbite in one of his legs. Bonatti and Mahdi pressed on but it grew darker and darker and there was still no sign of Lacedelli and Compagnoni. Mahdi started to get very worried. Bonatti called out and heard distant shouts from above but all they had to direct them was a line of tracks in the snow. Finally they had to stop. It was too dangerous to carry on and too dangerous to turn back.

As Bonatti vividly remembered, Mahdi was in a terrible state: 'His excitement and his hysteria made him do the most unreasonable things. Sometimes he went up, sometimes he went down, sometimes sideways. He was no longer conscious of the burden on his back and swayed violently.' Bonatti began to hack out a platform in the ice for them to sleep on but even he had to fight back despair: 'Suddenly I surprised myself by shouting and breaking into violent threats: "No, I don't want to die. I must not die! Lino! Achille! Can't you hear us? Help us, curse you!" When this fearful crisis was over I felt as if I had awakened from a nightmare.'

Then, to their amazement, they saw a light up on the ridge above them: it was Lacedelli. He asked if they had the oxygen and then told them to leave it there and go down at once. Bonatti shouted back that Mahdi was in no state to do anything. At this point the controversy began: according to Bonatti, he made it clear that they needed help and he expected the others to come down and join them. According to Lacedelli and Compagnoni, it was very different. They understood that Bonatti and Mahdi had decided to turn around and go back down, so they returned to their tent: '"Go back! Leave the masks! Don't come any further!" we shouted. It did not even occur to us that our colleagues could be thinking of spending the night at such an altitude without a tent or even a sleeping bag. Now Bonatti's voice was no longer audible. Obviously, we thought, he's taken our advice and gone down below.' But he hadn't gone down at all and, as Bonatti would later write: 'We waited in vain for our friends to reappear. We began to call again, to implore them, but no one gave a sign of life all night long. I felt as if a fiery brand were being seared into my soul.'

There was no choice but to spend the night out in the freezing cold. All they had to eat were three caramel sweets but as soon as they put them in their mouths they started choking because they had no saliva. It was an awful night; periodically Bonatti would beat himself with his ice-axe when he felt that a part of his body was getting frostbite. At one stage he had to physically restrain Mahdi when he looked as if he was about to throw himself off the edge. The wind grew worse and worse until they felt that they were being suffocated by a blizzard. 'Like shipwrecked men in a stormy sea we hung on to life with every fibre of our being so as not to be overwhelmed.'

Just before dawn, Mahdi stood up and tottered down the mountain. Bonatti waited for the sun to warm him and then, shortly after six, he pulled himself up and after dusting off the snow that had accumulated over the oxygen sets, he too began to descend. Bonatti heard a shout from above but when he turned round he still couldn't see anything behind him except the oxygen cylinders. The shout came from Lacedelli and Compagnoni, who were bemusedly staring at the scene below them. They saw a small figure receding into the distance but they had no idea whether it was Bonatti or Mahdi and didn't know what had gone on the night before. 'We called out to the man at the top of our voices. He stopped and turned around, but he did not answer, and after a moment he resumed his halting progress down the precipitous slope.' But they didn't have time to dwell on it; below them most of the mountain was covered in mist and they knew that if they still wanted to make an attempt on the summit they would have to descend first to pick up the oxygen sets. Above them was almost 2000 feet of rock and snow and a chance to make history.

These were anxious moments, but the two climbers decided that even though the weather seemed to be getting worse, they would press on. When they put on the oxygen sets, they found that it did make a huge difference but, to their surprise, after a few hours the first cylinders ran out. When they reached the snow slope just below the summit, the second cylinders ran out, leaving each of them with just one. They weren't unduly worried at first because they thought that the top was very close, but somehow the slope never seemed to stop and the snow conditions got even worse. Then suddenly Compagnoni felt the last of his oxygen running out. He dropped to his knees: 'I tried to breathe but the air was freezing cold and I couldn't. I thought that I was about to die or that I was going mad. "What's my name?" I called out to Lacedelli.'

Lacedelli's oxygen also ran out and he had no idea what was going to happen next. He looked around him and began naming the surrounding peaks just to make sure that he could still think straight. 'There's Broad Peak, 8047 metres—see, our brains are still functioning!' Through sign language he and Compagnoni told each other that they were both still alive and still in with a chance of making it to the top. Even though the oxygen sets were painfully heavy, they both decided to keep them on because it was just too complicated to get rid of them. For Compagnoni the whole experience was very odd: 'I had the strange sensation that there was someone behind me, a woman, a large woman—but I couldn't tell who it was. And this person said to me, "Compagnoni, go on, you're near the summit, you can do it."'

A few moments later the clouds dramatically opened below them and they were able to look down on Camp VIII and see their friends moving around, tiny shadows on the snow. Lacedelli remembers this as a key moment for both of them: 'It was the most wonderful thing... we felt morally obliged to go on now—at any cost.' But it wasn't going to be easy: 'You're pulled in two directions. If you're well trained you have this voice inside you telling you that you must go on. But there's also another voice telling you to go back. I said to myself you must go on, because if you're strong enough you can succeed.'

Finally, at six o'clock in the evening, after almost twelve hours of climbing, they reached the summit. Forty-five years after the Duke of Abruzzi had declared it an impossibility, an Italian expedition had reached the summit of K2. Compagnoni was all but done in: 'I didn't arrive on my feet, I arrived on my knees. It was a very emotional moment, so amazing to think that we had finally made it. Whatever happened next we had made it to the top. We put a flag up on our ice-axes and I hugged Lacedelli and we cried like babies. It is impossible to describe our emotions at that point.' Lacedelli was overjoyed at getting to the top but he was already thinking about the return journey and knew that the real celebrations could start only when they got back to Camp VIII. 'We were too high up to feel really satisfied, we couldn't relax because we knew that we had to get down.' He took a bit of dried meat out of his pocket and chewed it to get some saliva back in his mouth and then cautiously lent over the north face of the mountain to look down into China. 'That looks like a big wall—someone's going to make a name for themselves if they can climb that,' he thought, but he knew that their priority was to get down. The mist had cleared further and they were able to see right down to Base Camp.

'The sky wasn't just blue, it was dark navy... If we had stayed a little bit longer we would have seen the stars,' remembers Compagnoni. 'In front of us lay the whole Karakoram chain, Nanga Parbat 120 kilometres away, all the Gasherbrums, and I have to say—it was just marvellous.' Lacedelli was less emotional but equally excited: 'It was a truly exceptional view, a sea of mountains and the Baltoro Glacier, which looked just like a motorway from up there...' They had brought along a cine-camera and a stills camera and felt duty bound to take pictures. As soon as they took their gloves off to record their victory, their fingers turned to ice. From first thing that morning when he had put his crampons on, Compagnoni had felt his hands getting colder and colder and now he knew that frostbite was inevitable: 'I had to change the roll of cine film so I took off my gloves and I watched as my hands turned black in front of me. I started to bang them against my ice-axe to bring back the circulation. Then I stopped and I said, "God forgive me, let me die here, I don't want to go home with my hands all frostbitten and be useless for work. What will my children say?"'

Lacedelli realized that he would have to act decisively:

Compagnoni wasn't thinking straight because of the altitude. He said, 'I'll stay here and come down tomorrow morning.' I said, 'No way, we must go down. And if you don't move, I'll hit you with this ice-axe!' I had to be tough with him. So he said, 'OK, OK, help me put my gauntlets on,' because we were both finding it difficult. Then one of his gloves slipped off so I gave him one of mine.

After about half an hour they took out their pocket torches and, as darkness began to fall, they headed down the mountain. Their return journey had more the quality of an escape than of a descent. Compagnoni was the first to slip: he came off on one of the rock slabs below the summit but was lucky to fall on to soft snow. Then, just before they reached a dangerous crevasse they had noted on the way up, their torch batteries ran out. Illuminated only by the light from the stars, they managed to get across this dangerous obstacle, but Lacedelli lost his ice-axe in the process. Finally, just above Camp VIII where they knew their friends were waiting for them, Compagnoni lost his footing for a second time coming down an ice wall. He flew 50 feet through the air before landing in a patch of soft snow, narrowly avoiding another crevasse. As he lay there, he confidently expected to feel the sharp points of Lacedelli's crampons come tumbling down on top of him, but somehow his partner had stopped himself. Compagnoni got up and discovered that, astonishingly, he hadn't even broken any bones. He shouted up to Lacedelli, trying to guide him over to a safer spot, but Lacedelli also lost his footing and fell down. Amazingly, he too emerged unscathed.

A few minutes later they stumbled into their colleagues' tents at Camp VIII. At first they were so overcome and their throats were so sore that they were barely able to speak, but then bit by bit it all came out. The radio set was working but they couldn't call down to Base Camp because the huge shoulder of K2 was in the way. As they began to warm up in the tent, their fingers started to thaw slowly and excruciatingly. The next day when they headed down towards Base Camp straight away, Compagnoni slipped yet again and plunged 650 feet down the shoulder before miraculously stopping. At Camp VI he met three of the Pakistani porters praying on a rock. 'K2 finished,' he told them and showed them his frostbitten hands. 'They looked at each other and they took my hands and they kissed each finger and then they lifted them up to the sun, told me to say a prayer and then said a prayer themselves.'

At Base Camp, everyone was getting anxious. Nothing had been heard from the climbers for four days; they had sent up rockets to try to encourage them to use their radios but there was no reply. Then, on the evening of I August, Floreanni and Rey stumbled into camp to announce that the summit had been conquered. The next day Compagnoni and Lacedelli arrived and on the 3rd all the climbers were reunited at Base Camp. On 4 August the news was telegraphed to Italy. Desio knew that he was going to stay on in the Karakoram for several more months to complete the scientific part of the expedition and so he composed a final message for his men:

> Lift up your hearts, dear comrades! By your efforts you have won great glory for your native land, whose name, following the announcement of your triumph over our camp radio, is on the lips of men throughout the world… When you get back home, try to remain calm and modest in the midst of the celebrations which will be held in honour of your achievement, for by doing so you will add further to your glory.

Base Camp was dismantled and the men added two inscribed tablets to the rocks of the Gilkey memorial, one to commemorate Puchoz and all the others who had died on K2, and another to the Duke of Abruzzi. They headed back to Skardu and then on to Italy. Compagnoni and Lacedelli were still in acute pain because of frostbite but at least they were able to walk out. After his night out in the cold, the high-altitude porter Mahdi had to be carried back on a stretcher.

Most of the climbers took a ship to Genoa, but because of his frostbite, Compagnoni flew back to Rome. He was ushered away to a private area of the airport and not allowed to speak to anyone or give interviews, but when he reached Milan he was greeted by huge crowds. The Archbishop of Milan ordered that the lights on top of the Duomo should be turned on and Compagnoni's plane circled it twice to see its famous Madonna. After an emotional meeting with his family, he was rushed away to a TV studio for several hours.

The excitement continued for months. There were civic receptions, audiences with the Pope and interviews with the world's press. Charlie Houston came over to Italy and was presented with the embroidered parasol he had left on K2 the previous summer. Desio published his account of the expedition in 1955 and in spring that year a documentary film of the expedition was released in cinemas all over Italy. Then, slowly at first, the arguments started.

In October 1955, Compagnoni was photographed for a popular magazine holding his frostbitten fingers out to the camera under a headline that read 'I want justice for this hand.' For the next three years he pursued a court action against the company that produced the K2 movie, demanding a share of the profits in compensation for the fingers that had been frost-bitten while filming on the summit. He eventually lost his case but, in the meantime, Desio became embroiled in a number of wrangles with the Italian Alpine Club over who should pay for the scientific portions of the expedition. Things got so bad that the Italian Alpine Club initiated a second, even more bizarre court case over a prestigious trophy that had been awarded to Desio's team by the city of Genoa. He wanted it for the Science and Technology Museum in Milan but the Italian Alpine Club demanded that it should be placed in their museum in Turin. Eventually they won their case.

The general atmosphere of ill feeling rumbled on inconclusively until a new and much more bitter controversy started. Walter Bonatti had always felt that his role in the expedition had not been sufficiently acknowledged, and that there were still many unanswered questions about why he and Mahdi had been forced to sleep out on the mountain on the night before Compagnoni and Lacedelli's summit bid. It was barely touched on in Desio's expedition book and Bonatti had to insist on it being mentioned in the official film. In 1961 he told his side of the story for the first time in his autobiography, *My Mountains*. Bonatti added many new details, including one that would come back to haunt him a couple of years later. As they were struggling to carry the heavy oxygen sets up the mountain towards the final camp, he remembered thinking in an idle moment:

> We were carrying pure oxygen, 45 pounds of precious freight which in a few moments could restore us to the same conditions as those 7000 feet further down. How simple it would be to turn on one of those valves! What did it matter that we had no masks? The air around us would soon become impregnated with the precious gas. I could not help thinking upon what a slender thread the conquest of K2 depended.

Then in July 1964, on the tenth anniversary of the climb, two articles appeared in a Turin newspaper that brought everything out into the open. Under the headline 'After 10 years the truth about K2,' the author, a journalist called Nino Giglio, alleged that far from saving the day, Bonatti had behaved totally selfishly. He claimed that Bonatti had planned to try to reach the summit before Lacedelli and Compagnoni and that during his night out on the mountain he had used up some of their precious oxygen. Furthermore, he accused Bonatti of abandoning the frostbitten porter Mahdi and descending to Camp VIII ahead of him.

Bonatti reacted with fury: 'It appeared that my conduct during the expedition had been treacherous, lying, incompetent and generally vile. What worse could be said of a man?' To Bonatti, it was all preposterous: no sane person would deliberately spend a night out on the top of K2, and without a mask it would have been impossible for him to have used any of the oxygen. Giglio defended his story, claiming that it was backed up by Compagnoni and the respected Pakistani liaison officer Ata-Ullah. Bonatti sued for libel and two years later he won his case.

It didn't stop there, though. Bonatti had a burning sense of injustice and was appalled that neither Desio nor the Italian Alpine Club had seemed willing to let the truth come out. His reputation was at stake and he fought back with three books and countless articles and interviews. He demanded recognition for what he saw as his crucial role in the success of the expedition and turned on Lacedelli and Compagnoni. Now he openly criticized them for moving the position of the final camp and accused them of ignoring his cries for help. Sensationally, he claimed that their dramatic story of the oxygen running out was pure fabrication. According to his calculations, they had in fact set off at 8:30, not 6:30, A.M. and there would have been enough oxygen to get them all the way to the summit. In Lacedelli and Compagnoni's account of these events, they said that they kept their sets on all the way to the top because they were too difficult to remove and because they wanted to leave something up there as proof that they had reached the summit. Bonatti said that this wasn't true and that they had kept them on because they were still using them all the way up.

Then in 1994, on the fortieth anniversary of the ascent, there were two seeming breakthroughs. The president of the Italian Alpine Club made a speech apologizing for the way that Bonatti had been treated and a story appeared in the mountaineering journal *Alp*, which was widely covered by Italian newspapers. It was written by an Australian doctor, Robert Marshall, who had followed Bonatti's career for many years. He had found two photographs that had appeared in a respected climbing journal, *Mountain World*, in 1955 which hadn't been reproduced in Desio's official book. They showed Compagnoni on the summit of K2, wearing a respirator which was still connected to his oxygen tanks. Clearly visible on Lacedelli's face were frost marks, implying that he had only just taken his mask off. Marshall claimed that all this proved that Bonatti had been telling the truth and, though Compagnoni publicly refuted all Bonatti's accusations, to many people it seemed as if he had been finally vindicated.

In the end all the arguments over the Italian 1954 expedition pall into insignificance compared to the scandals surrounding Wiessner's attempt fifteen years earlier. No one died on the night of 30 July and, although Mahdi suffered severe frostbite, Bonatti emerged relatively unscathed. If Compagnoni was the principal source for Nino Giglio's article, then it could be argued that he brought all the problems on himself; but, in his defence, perhaps it was Bonatti's insinuations in *My Mountains* that Compagnoni wasn't really up to the climb that caused him to lash out. The whole issue of the oxygen is very strange. Compagnoni and Lacedelli are both adamant that the cylinders did run out before they reached the summit and there doesn't seem to be any reason why they would lie. To reach the top of K2 with or without oxygen would have been considered heroic enough. Maybe they did move the site of their final camp higher than they had agreed earlier, but according to their version of events, the conditions they found meant that they had no choice. It would not have been in their interest to risk the lives of the men who were supposed to be bringing up their oxygen supplies and, after Mario Puchoz's death a couple of weeks earlier, it's hard to think that they would be so deliberately callous as to have risked their colleagues' lives.

Later on, Riccardo Cassin, the climber who had been so badly mishandled by Desio on the reconnaissance expedition in 1953, commented that if he had been taken on as the leader of the climbers then perhaps many of the problems that came up would never have happened. Ultimately he went on to reaffirm his reputation as one of the greatest climbers of modern day. In 1957 he led an expedition that made the first ascent of the legendary Gasherbrum 4, and four years later he made an epic ascent of the North Face of McKinley. Not bad for someone who had been rejected as unfit a few years earlier.

TODAY, IN SPITE OF ALL THE ARGUMENTS, Lacedelli and Compagnoni remain the grand old men of Italian mountaineering, even if Walter Bonatti has far eclipsed both of them in terms of his achievements as a climber. Achille Compagnoni still lives in the shadow of the Matterhorn where he runs a quiet hotel. His upstairs room is filled with trophies, citations and awards, many of them connected to K2. Lino Lacedelli lives in the 'Villa K2' in Cortina d'Ampezzo, a chic resort in the Dolomites. In the summer of 2000, Ardito Desio celebrated his 101st birthday, proving that mountaineering is good for you. Though he claimed that K2 didn't change him at all, for Compagnoni and Lacedelli it was clearly one of the defining moments of their lives. When we interviewed Compagnoni in February, he was very generous with his time but slightly reticent. He finished:

> I must say this. Tonight I'm sure I won't sleep, because when I talk about K2 something always happens inside me, I'm not sure what it is but it always stops me sleeping. It is the mountain which gave me the most joy but it called for big sacrifices and I suffered a lot. There were moments when I just didn't think I could carry on but a voice within me told me that I had to. K2 is a jealous mountain, a mountain which doesn't want to be climbed.

CHAPTER 10

Why Climb?

4:25 A.M. The Hornli Mountain Hut, just below the Matterhorn. Head torches flare in a darkened room; quiet figures shuffle between tables laid for breakfast, trying to avoid each other's rucksacks and ice-axes. In five minutes' time the lights will come on, coffee will arrive and, after a quick swig, the first climbers will venture out of the door and start heading up the Hornli Ridge towards the summit. But for now, everyone behaves as if there's a power cut and waits for the hut masters to declare an end to the curfew and let there be light.

4:40 A.M. The Matterhorn stands proud against a starry sky as a queue begins at the fixed rope that takes climbers on to the ridge. It steadily grows over the next half-hour. It's still a race to get to the top, but for most climbers their rivals are coming from the same side as they are, and one of the greatest dangers is people kicking stones down on top of them. After half an hour there's a chain of lights snaking its way up the mountain, almost like a religious procession. In Knock in Ireland, every year Catholic pilgrims climb a holy mountain on their bare knees, hoping to redeem their sins and find a spouse; here Gore-Tex-clad pilgrims come to worship mountains for their own sake and seek personal fulfilment rather than any religious goal. After four hours, the first climbers are visible on the summit, though others may take a couple of hours more to make it.

EVERY YEAR AROUND 3000 MOUNTAINEERS come to Zermatt to climb the Matterhorn and most of them try it via the Whymper route.

About half of them are guided. For the local guides, it's a production line: foreigners arrive in town with dreams in their pocket and the guides service them as efficiently as possible—hauling them up and down, congratulating them at the top or sometimes pulling them off early if conditions get too dangerous or if they think that someone isn't up to it.

Today the Alps are no longer just 'The Playground of Europe,' as Leslie Stephen christened them—they're the playground of the world. Those Matterhorn mountaineers are among the 1.5 million or so tourists who visit Zermatt every year, and about the same number visit Chamonix. A staggering 8000 of these reach the summit of Mont Blanc every year, but most of the tourists are interested in other things. Hiking, skiing, snowboarding, paragliding, micro-liting, mountain biking, 'fat-biking,' canyoneering—the list goes on and on and grows from year to year and the Alps get ever more popular.

Although, compared to skiing, it's still a minority sport, there are more people who enjoy climbing and mountaineering than ever before. In 1858 the British Alpine Club started with around 100 members; today it has 1118 and the Continental clubs are even bigger. Today it's even possible to make your living as a 'professional' mountaineer, either by working as a mountain guide or, if you're very talented and lucky, getting commercial sponsorship. Other lifelines include lecturing, media work and journalism. As a last resort, furniture-making seems to do for mountaineers what painting and decorating does for out-of-work actors. For a few top names, a new sideline has emerged in recent years as motivational speakers. Since the 1980s boom in management consultancy, when business gurus wrote books with such titles as *Climbing the Corporate Matterhorn*, a few lucky mountaineers have found themselves in high demand, leading seminars and occasionally guiding businessmen up mountains in order to give them a unique insight into the mysteries of goal-setting, team-building and getting to the top.

Mountaineering has always been about numbers, the most important of which has usually been number one. Whymper, Cook, Hillary and Tenzing—they were all spurred on by the magical possibility of being the first person to get to the top of a particular mountain ahead of anyone else. In the early days, the prizes were all at the top of Alpine peaks; then mountaineering spread out around the world and the Himalayas became the new Holy Grail. Today, all the big Himalayan mountains have been climbed many times and there are fewer and fewer parts of the world whose mountains remain untouched. So what are young climbers meant to do if they want to make a name for themselves?

First of all, they can climb an old mountain by a new route. In the 1930s a new generation of German and Austrian mountaineers headed for the Alps, where they scandalized the Establishment, particularly in Britain, by attempting to climb the north faces of familiar peaks, including the Matterhorn and the Eiger. Until this time, these had been considered impossible routes: because they get no direct sunlight, north faces tend to accumulate more snow and ice, which makes them more visually attractive but much more dangerous to climb. Those young climbers were derided as 'suicide climbers' but today, for any serious mountaineer, the north face of the Eiger is considered a 'classic' climb—though it is still a real test.

Second, mountaineers aspiring to fame can climb an old route at a new time of the year. Again, in the northern hemisphere, mountaineering was traditionally a summer sport for the very practical reason that in winter most mountains are much colder—and therefore much more challenging. In the European Alps temperatures can drop below minus 20 degrees Celsius, while in North America it can get very much colder. Winter mountaineers need to carry much more equipment and therefore everything takes more time and is that much more difficult. Walter Bonatti crowned his climbing career with a solo ascent of the north face of the Matterhorn in February 1965. Vern Tejas amazed America's climbing community in 1988 by making the first solo winter ascent of Mt McKinley, where temperatures have been recorded as low as minus 56 degrees Celsius.

Third, they can join a different numbers game. In 1985 an American climber, Dick Bass, became the first person to have climbed all the highest peaks of each continent—the 'Seven Summits': Everest in Asia, McKinley in North America, Aconcagua in South America, Elbrus in Europe, Kilimanjaro in Africa, Mount Vinson in Antarctica, and finally either Mount Kosciuszko in Australia or Carstenz in Indonesia (depending on whether you think that the relevant continent is Australia or Australasia). Since then, about seventy other people have matched his feat.

A much more exclusive club is made up of the climbers who have managed to reach the summit of the world's fourteen 8000-metre peaks. Though some consider fourteen to be rather an arbitrary number and argue about what should and shouldn't be included, this is a considerably more difficult test than the 'Seven Summits.' All these mountains are located in the Himalayas and the Karakoram in Asia. The first man to achieve this was Rheinhold Messner, the Italian climber who is widely considered to be the greatest climber of the modern age and maybe the greatest climber ever. In 1986 Messner got to the top of his last 8000-metre peak with Polish climber Jerzy Kukuczka hot on his trail, and by 1999 five other mountaineers matched his achievement.

On the other hand, today there are many serious climbers who are cynical about the numbers game and are more interested in climbing lower, 6000-metre, peaks which are often just as technically challenging and where the goal of getting to the summit may be replaced with the goal of getting up a particularly big rock wall. In the 1950s, when during 'The Golden Age of Himalayan Climbing' all the big Himalayan peaks were climbed for the first time, large-scale expeditions were the norm. In the 1980s there was a move to bring what is known as 'Alpine-style' climbing to big mountains all around the world.

In the Himalayas, going 'Alpine-style' meant putting together small-scale expeditions that didn't employ lots of Sherpas as high-altitude porters and didn't require huge armies of people to carry tonnes of supplies to base camp and thence to lay siege to a mountain. The idea was to arrive at a mountain in a small team and then to keep on going until the summit had been reached, without putting up lots of fixed ropes or keeping other climbers in reserve. At the same time there was new thinking on the best way to acclimatize. In the 1950s it was thought that the best thing to do was to sleep as high as possible for as long as possible and to get used to the altitude by slowly progressing up a mountain in very definite stages. Today, it is recognized that above a certain point it is impossible to acclimatize and so the new philosophy is for climbers to spend a long period at lower altitudes and then make a dash for the summit. In 1986 two Swiss climbers, Erhard Loretan and Jean Troillet, made what is considered to be a classic 'Alpine-style' ascent of Everest. They spent five weeks acclimatizing at the foot of the mountain at 21,325 feet (6500 metres) before ascending and descending the world's highest mountain in two days!

The recent history of Everest exemplifies many of these trends in mountaineering. Since Hillary and Tenzing's first ascent in 1953, top climbers have come from all around the world to open up new routes on the mountain or break the established patterns of doing things. In 1978, Rheinhold Messner and Peter Habler got to the summit without using oxygen, and three years later Messner repeated the feat in a solo climb that took him just three days. In 1988, the Frenchman Jean Marc Boivin paraglided from top to bottom in eleven minutes; and on 8 October 2000, a Slovenian extreme-sports enthusiast, Davo Karnicar, became the first man to ski down Everest, getting from the top back to Base Camp in just five hours.

Everest has also been making headlines of a different kind, though, and it's all basically to do with the sheer number of people who are willing to take on the world's highest mountain.

Until the 1980s, nearly all the attempts on Everest were made by national teams who usually needed to raise large amounts of money to finance their expeditions. In recent years, there has been a huge growth of professional guiding, which has allowed many more people to realize their dreams—and their worst nightmares—on Everest. Again, the numbers are very telling: between 1921 and 1979 there were forty-four deaths on the mountain; between 1979 and 1991 seventy-five more people died; in the last nine years another forty-two have been added to that total. In 1997 there were so many dead bodies on Everest that the Nepalese authorities announced that they were going to begin a special operation to bring them all down. There was an international outcry and they agreed to leave the climbers where they had fallen.

In 1996 the sceptics who had been warning that Everest was no place for rich amateurs had their worst predictions realized: in one infamous season, twelve people died on Everest, including two professional guides and several inexperienced clients. The press leapt on reports that one of the survivors, a wealthy New York socialite called Sandy Pittman, had arrived at Everest laden down with two laptops, five cameras, two tape recorders, a CD-rom player and a printer—and insisted on having them carried most of the way to the top. As we saw in Chapter I, the prospect of danger and death has never deterred aspiring climbers—in fact the threat seems to enhance the appeal. This Everest disaster was chronicled by John Krakauer in his book, *Into Thin Air*, which became a best-seller. When we were filming in Alaska, our guides told us that after the success of Krakauer's book, they were inundated with calls from scores of absolute beginners who wanted to have a crack at Mt McKinley. You might have thought that Krakauer's inside story—filled as it was with hapless amateurs dying at high altitude—would have acted as a caution. Far from it: *Into Thin Air* only inspired more and more people with a desire to go up mountains.

Though Everest is most likely to appear in the headlines, the three others that we have concentrated on in this book are still regarded as iconic mountains. The Matterhorn is one of the most famous mountains in the world. Its silhouette has graced everything from chocolate bars to muesli packets and it has even been replicated in wood at Disneyland. As we have come to expect, the disaster of 1865 only attracted more visitors than ever to Zermatt, and within two years the British climber Crawford

Grove had made the third ascent of the Matterhorn after Whymper and Carrel. The Italians continued to hope that the lure of the Matterhorn would turn Breuil into an important centre for Alpine tourism, but Zermatt has always been much bigger and, in mountaineering terms, the Hornli Ridge has always been more popular than the route from the Italian side. In the 1930s, Breuil was redeveloped and renamed Cervinia; today it's a popular ski resort.

It is estimated that 500 climbers have followed Douglas, Hadow, Hudson and Croz to their graves, trying to reach the summit of the Matterhorn. In one of the most famous incidents, in 1879, an American doctor from Boston, Dr William O. Mosely, died while descending from the summit after insisting on untying from his guides. Crossing a large piece of rock, he slipped, let go of his ice-axe and flew down the east face to his death. In his honour the rock has been known as the Mosely slab since then. On the Italian side, a small memorial marks the spot where Whymper's old sparring partner, Jean-Antoine Carrel, perished on his way down the mountain in 1890. He had been leading a party on the Italian ridge when they were caught out in a storm. After heroically leading his clients back down to safety, he stopped close to the bottom and a few minutes later he died. According to a much repeated local story, years later his son was taking a party of foreign mountaineers past this spot when they asked him if this was the place where his famous father had fallen. 'He did not fall—he died,' was the indignant reply.

Like the Matterhorn, Mt McKinley continues to attract more and more climbers, and more and more statistics, every year. In 1973, 203 of them made attempts; in 1984 the figure rose to 695, and in 1999 no fewer than 1183 climbers from 39 different countries pitched their tents on McKinley's slopes. On average, they were aged between 35 and 37; 90 per cent of them were men and 43 per cent of them reached the summit, or so they claimed.

Most expeditions fly in to a landing strip 7200 feet (2194 metres) up McKinley and make their attempts from the west. Hardly anyone uses the Sourdough route from the north, and most people aim to be in and out within a month. Brad Washburn, the renowned cartographer, is the grand old man of McKinley. He pioneered the route from the west in 1951, was responsible for the first proper map of the mountain, and for the last fifty years has been offering advice, challenges and the loan of excellent aerial photographs to anyone interested in the mountain. He has also been one of the prime movers in the continuing saga of the Cook controversy. At the venerable age of ninety he is just about to publish his latest salvo in his ongoing battle with the Cook Society, a book entitled *The Lie that Wouldn't Die.*

Amazingly, almost ninety years since Parker and Browne came back from McKinley with proof that Cook had faked his summit photograph, there are still people who fervently believe that he did make the first ascent. Most of them are part of the Cook Society, an organization dedicated to preserving the memory of the man who, they claim, was one of the greatest American explorers of all time. They are a small group, but increasingly they have been prepared to put their money where their mouth is, organizing conferences and even sponsoring expeditions to McKinley to retrace Cook's footsteps. The sceptics remain unmoved, and over the years nearly all of Cook's photographic evidence has been shown to be false. No one has ever succeeded in duplicating Cook's supposed route up McKinley and barely a dozen climbers have even attempted the east ridge. For his diehard supporters, though, it is an issue of faith, not of reason, and whenever anyone comes up with anything against Cook they invariably cry conspiracy and claim that it is really just Peary extending his tentacles from the grave. No trace has ever been found of the Sourdoughs' flagpole but in the late 1930s two of the men—Charlie McGonogall and Billy Taylor—were interviewed for the first time about their expedition. They confirmed that Lloyd's original version of their story was indeed economical with the truth and that in fact only two of them had gone all the way up to the north summit. Archdeacon Hudson Stuck's wish that McKinley should revert to its original native name has never been fulfilled, but in 1980 the land that surrounds it was renamed the Denali National Park.

There have also been attempts to rename K2. In the 1980s, the Pakistani government mooted the idea of calling it Jinnah Mountain after the founding father of their country. So far nothing has come of their plans and K2 continues to attract devotees from all over the world under the name it was given in the mid-nineteenth century. Perhaps it is fitting that such a stark mountain should have such a stark name. Today it still has a reputation as one of the most dangerous mountains in the world: by 1995, a hundred climbers had reached its summit and thirty had died trying, a death rate of almost one in three.

After the Italian triumph in 1954, for many years, as India and Pakistan continued to argue about their northern borders, K2 was closed to foreign mountaineers. In 1975, the Americans came back and attempted to climb the north-west ridge—leaving with nothing but regrets. Three years later, three US climbers finally reached the summit. One of them, Jim Wickwire, was forced to spend a night out in the open just below the summit at 8460 metres.

In 1986 a strange controversy began over the height of K2. An American astronomy professor, George Wallerstein, measured K2 with state-of-the-art satellite techniques and announced to the world that it was in fact taller than Everest. Ironically, it was the man who stood to gain most, the Italian geographer Ardito Desio, who conclusively rebutted his claims a year later. At the age of ninety, he led yet another expedition to Pakistan to conduct new and even more detailed measurements of both Everest and K2. Ultimately they came back with news that Everest was actually 49 feet higher than previously thought and K2 actually 13 feet lower.

Nineteen eighty-six was K2's annus horribilis. That summer, thirteen people died on the mountain. At that time no one had seen anything like it; unlike Everest, K2 is not a mountain where there are lots of professional guides who will take you to the top if you have sufficient commitment and sufficient cash. It is still the 'mountaineer's mountain,' so it was a real shock for thirteen world-class climbers to die on K2. Again, that didn't put too many people off and in 1995 another seven perished.

The memorial to Art Gilkey still stands on a rocky promontory overlooking Base Camp, but today it has become a memorial to all the men and women who have died on K2 in the years since his death. It is festooned with plaques commemorating climbers from all around the world. Some of these are professionally done, while others have a more improvised quality: old camping plates, tin boxes, pitons—all pressed into service to remember the dead. As you get closer, you hear them jangling in the wind. It was one of the most haunting places we filmed, a place that threw up more questions than answers. The plaques are shiny and bright, in contrast to a different kind of reminder down on the glacier below. Here, every so often, an unidentified and unidentifiable bone or rib cage appears, tossed down by an avalanche or simply carried down by the slowly moving snow and ice. It is easy to miss them, as the brown, mottled bones blend in with the rocks next to which they lie.

Which brings us back to the vexed issue of 'Why?' Why does anyone put themselves at risk of death for the sake of climbing a mountain? It's a question that is both inevitable and unanswerable. Occasionally we put it to our interviewees directly; at other times the answer came out more by inference than by actual statement. Here we've put together some of their replies. Looking at this selection as a whole, there is one thing missing that we always sensed as interviewers even if no one actually came out and said it: mountaineers go mountaineering because of the simple fact that they are good at it. Climbing mountains is not a natural act, but there are some people who find themselves on a mountain, for whatever reason, and discover that they are 'natural' climbers and so they keep coming back again and again. Maybe that's the answer to the question. But then again...

ED WEBSTER, *mountaineer*

Why climb? God, I've been dreading that question—one of my friends used to say, 'to lose weight,' and yes, I can confirm that you do lose weight... I actually like going to the high mountains because it is the greatest view on earth... It is for most people a very unnatural thing to do. But for a trained mountaineer, it's the opposite, because climbing at altitude is the greatest challenge that a climber can have. I always felt that when I've been in the Himalayas, there's always been a certain point when my body has become acclimatized to be at high altitude. I would reach what I guess I would call a state of grace, where I felt that we were living amongst these great tremendous mountains and that somehow they were our friends—there wasn't this adversarial relationship. And when I reached this state of co-existence, as it were, then I'd think, OK, now we can try for the summit, now we can try the serious climb.

LINO LACEDELLI. *He made the first ascent of K2 in 1954 with Achille Compagnoni*

I was born in Cortina in the Dolomites and here all the boys want to get out into the mountains. My aunt never liked me climbing, she always told me to go walking instead. One day I was out with my father and I saw a mountain guide taking two English clients up a mountain, so I followed them all the way to the summit and then I let them see me. The guide was angry, he said that he was going to give me a smack—he didn't do it but he was right! My father caught me at the bottom though... After that I always tried to escape on Sundays. I always told lies—I said I was going walking but instead I went climbing. They say that the mountains are dangerous—it isn't true. It's people who cause accidents, not mountains. Sometimes it's just a silly mistake but what about all those car accidents? We went to K2 because we were passionate about finishing something that we knew was difficult. You get to the top for personal satisfaction.

CHARLIE HOUSTON, *expedition leader on K2 in 1938 and 1953*

My own fascination has been more with explo-ration and trying to see what lies beyond, going a little bit further, and so most of my expedi-tions have been to places that were not well known. I think the attitude that you can go and conquer a mountain, to me that's wrong because I don't think that you ever do conquer them. To test yourself, to see how strong you are, how brave you are, how bold, how much you can endure—yes, that's a nat-ural human phenomenon and perhaps that's what Aristotle meant when he said, 'The un-risked life is not worth living'—but that's not neces-sarily the best reason for going to a mountain.

STEVEN VENABLES, *World-Class Mountaineer*

It's that sense of complete, total engagement with a mountain that attracts people. Mountaineering takes you into situations which you would not achieve in any other way. You experience just extraordinary emotions, at a purely aesthetic level, at dawn or sunset, and you're feeling a sense of total, total commitment to what you are doing. At the back of your mind, yes, there's always that awareness of danger, that something might go wrong, that you might even die. And perhaps if you removed completely that element of danger, the thing would lose some of its edge. But to suggest that moun-taineers are deliberately seeking danger, or have some kind of death wish, is simply ludicrous. I mean, there's a sense of living intensely and being intensely alive, which is the complete opposite of having some kind of death wish.

ED DOUGLAS, *Editor of* The Alpine Journal
The laws that get passed make our lives more and more prescribed and, in a sense, that fuels the need to take risks because there is a small group of people who feel more and more hemmed in. You wake up in the morning, you go to work and everything you do is governed by legislation—the car you drive, the way it's built, the way it's put together, the way the road is made, you know, the things you have for breakfast, they're all covered by legislation to make it safer. You can go into the mountains though and you can behave exactly as you want, you are responsible for your own survival, you are in control of your life, and that is extremely liberating. But it comes with the proviso that if you mess up then you could pay an extremely high price.

KEN WILSON, *Publisher*
I think the companionship and the shared adventure is the most important thing in climbing—I look back on some of my climbs and the ones that were the most rewarding were not the ones that on paper were prestigious but the ones where a very good entertaining day has been had doing battle with a difficult route, often with a companion who I had a good time with.

HANNES TAUGWALDER, *author—a distant relative of the guides who climbed the Matterhorn with Whymper in 1865*

You have the feeling, you see this huge mountain and then you want to use your strength, your courage, your power, you want to measure yourself against the mountain—it calls to you, 'Come on, try, try to climb me'—it's like an exclamation, and you feel it in your soul and you have to go.

NIGELLA HALL, *granddaughter of Edward*
Whymper—she climbed the Matterhorn by the Hornli Ridge
at the age of sixteen

It's an entire package which makes it why we want
to do it, and why we go on doing it. You get back
what you give, so that the more difficult and dangerous and challenging the climb is, the greater the
satisfaction and the pleasure. It sharpens the senses and sort of accelerates
the feeling of everything, and the depth of feeling that comes when you
overcome something—it's difficult to answer because it's different for
everyone.

VERN TEJAS, *who in 1988 became the first climber*
to make a winter ascent of Mt McKinley

My very first memory of Mt McKinley is very distinct
today, even though it was almost twenty-five years ago
now. My third day in the state I camped at Wonder Lake
and it was very stormy at the time. Storm subsided, the
clouds lifted like a veil or a curtain being raised on a
piece of art. And slowly, by increments, the mountain was revealed to me. And by
two o'clock in the morning, which means that the sun's in the north, it came out
in its full glory. It was so spectacular that as a nineteen-year-old, I decided there
and then that I was going to climb the mountain.

BRAD WASHBURN, *mountaineer and cartographer. His wife Barbara became the*
first woman to reach the summit of McKinley in 1947

I know Barbara has frequently said that we lived above the clouds an awful
lot of the time... you feel detached from the world below. The view from
the summit is a great sight—it's not beautiful, it's just endless, endless
country. The most interesting part everyone mentions is to the west.
When you get up the mountain in the late afternoon and you look west-

ward, there's millions of little lakes with the sun glittering on them—that's the one thing I brought back every time. I know the last time Jim Gale and I left the top in 1951, I was forty-one and he was forty-two and we both knew we would never be there again, and we both admitted that night that the tears streamed down our cheeks as we saw that view, turned around and came down.

NORMAN ELLIOT, *former Archdeacon of the Yukon,*
the same post held by Hudson Stuck, conqueror of McKinley

When I was appointed, the Bishop said, 'I'm nam-ing you the Archdeacon of the Yukon and there's the mountain there.' My reply to him was, 'Forget it' ... I've flown around McKinley many times in my plane when I've needed to and I was always impressed by the mountain. It's a mountain that a lot of tourists never see—it's so often clouded in. In fact one tourist was supposed to have said it's the greatest hoax that's ever been played on the American people, because there is no Mt McKinley.

JONATHAN WATERMAN, *author and mountaineer*

The pleasure of mountaineering has a lot to do with a hard-to-define aesthetic experience, the people you're climbing with and the sanctity of nature. Of course there is the pleasure of taking on a challenge and self-actualization, and for the last twenty years I've been able to get that by climbing to the tops of mountains. And, you know, the power of those moments I'm certain will sustain me until I'm a very old man.

GALEN ROWELL, *mountaineer and photographer*

I think risk is very much part of the process for me. That doesn't mean it has to be for everyone, but I feel in my life I want to know what those edges are and I want to find them and explore them and only by getting up right on the edge and understanding it do I know how valuable life is to live. I feel that a lot of my most important moments have been those moments where I was on the thin edge of risk.

JIM WICKWIRE, *one of the first four American mountaineers to reach the summit of K2 in 1978*

I think climbing is like flying in small planes—there are bold pilots and there are old pilots but there are no old bold pilots... If you are going to do this over a lifetime, you have to do it on the basis that sure, the objective is important and you're going to do everything to get to the summit, but you're going to

turn back when things ain't right. Now on K2, I don't think I had that, I think when I got to the summit of K2 in 1978 that I had abandoned that philosophy and I think it was the only time in my whole climbing career that I just let it go because I was going to get there and nothing was going to stop me.

BOB BATES, *Mountaineer, veteran of K2*
1938 and 1953

I still enjoy climbing—I mean, if I were young and I could run around I would but I'd keep away from K2. I learned something from that, I don't want to get into anything that tough. I think we got ourselves into a jam that I wouldn't ever want to get

into again, where I thought the odds were against us. And I would follow the same thing I told myself before: if I were married I wouldn't do this because I think that I shouldn't risk somebody else's life along with my own—somebody else's happiness if you wanted to call it.

LUCA BICH, *climber and film-maker, he lives in Cervinia on the Italian side of the Matterhorn*
You wake up in the morning and it's there in front of you. You go out for a walk and sometimes you just stop and look up at the Matterhorn for a few minutes. Sometimes I wonder what it would be like to see it for the first time, to see it maybe through Whymper's eyes,  to imagine the first time he comes here and stands at the foot of the mountain with it there in front of you, a big enormous mountain. Sometimes it still amazes me to see it now, it must really be something for anyone who sees it for the first time.

ANONYMOUS
If you need to ask you'll never know, and if you know already you'll never need to ask.

BIBLIOGRAPHY

Chapter 1

Engel, Claire, *Mountaineering in the Alps*, Allen and Unwin, London, 1971

Fitzsimons, Raymund, *The Baron of Piccadilly*, Geoffrey Bles Ltd, 1967

Hansen, Peter, *British Mountaineering, 1850–1914*, PhD Thesis, September, 1991

Phillips, Francis, *A Reading Party in Switzerland*, Manchester, 1851

Ruskin, John, *Modern Painters 4*, Smith Elden, 1856

Smith, Albert, *The Natural History of Stuck-Up People*, Bogue, London, 1847

Smith, Albert, *The Natural History of the Gent*, Bogue, London 1847

Smith, Albert, *The Story of Mont Blanc*, Bogue, London 1853

Stephen, Sir Leslie, *The Playground of Europe*, Longmans, London, 1871

The Alpine Journal, London, 1863 onwards

Thorington, J. Monroe, *Mont Blanc Side Show*, The John C. Winston Company, Philadelphia, 1934

Chapter 2

Clarke, Ronald, *The Day the Rope Broke*, London, 1865

Kernahan, Coulson, *In Good Company*, London 1917

Lun, Sir Arnold, *Matterhorn Centenary*, London, 1965

Lyall, Alan, *The First Descent of the Matterhorn*, Gomer Press, Llandysul, 1997

Rebuffat, Gaston, *Men and the Matterhorn*, London, 1967

Rey, Guido, *The Matterhorn*, Unwin, London, 1907

Smythe, Frank, *Edward Whymper*, Hodder and Stoughton, London, 1940

Taugwalder, Hannes, *Nearer the Truth*, Aarau, 1990
Tyndall, John, *Hours of Exercise in the Alps*, London, 1871
Whymper, Edward, *Scrambles in the Alps*, John Murray, London, 1871
Whymper, Edward, *Travels in the Great Andes*, John Murray, London, 1892

Chapter 3

Abruzzi, the Duke of, *The Karakoram Expedition*, Rivista del Club Alpino
    Italiano, Milan, 1909
Crowley, Aleister, *The Confessions of Aleister Crowley*, Bantam, London, 1971
Curran, Jim, *The Story of the Savage Mountain*, Coronet, London, 1995
di Filippi, Filippo, *The Expedition to the Karakoram and the Western Himalaya*,
    Constable, London, 1912
Houston, Charles, *Going Higher*, The Mountaineers, Seattle, 1998
Sella, Vittorio, *The Diary of Vittorio Sella*, Unpublished, The Sella Institute,
    Biella
Shandrick and Tenderini, *The Duke of the Abruzzi*, Baton Wicks, London,
    1997
Whymper, Edward, *A Right Royal Mountaineer*, London, 1909

Chapter 4

Brooks, Alfred, 'Mountain Exploration in Alaska,' *Alpina Americana*, 1914
Brooks, Alfred, *Blazing Alaska's Trails*, University of Alaska Press, Fair-
    banks, 1973
Bryce, Robert M, *Cook & Peary, the Polar Controversy Resolved*, Stackpole
    Books, 1997
Cook, Frederick A, 'America's Unconquered Mountain,' *Harper's Monthly
    Magazine*, 1904
Cook, Frederick A, *To the Top of the Continent*, Hodder and Stoughton,
    London, 1909
Dunn, Robert, autobiographical manuscript, Dartmouth College, NH,
    unpublished
Dunn, Robert, *The Outing Magazine*, January–May 1904

Dunn, Robert, *The Shameless Diary of an Explorer*, The Outing Publishing Co., New York, 1907

Dunn, Robert, *World Alive*, Hale, 1958

Moore, Terris, *Mt McKinley: the Pioneer Climbs*, The Mountaineers, Seattle, 1981

Steffens, Lincoln, *Autobiography*, Harrap, 1931

Chapter 5

Browne, Belmore, *The Conquest of Mt McKinley*, New York and London, 1913

Cole, Terrence (ed), 'The Sourdough Expedition,' *Alaska Today*

Cook, Frederick A, *Harper's Monthly Magazine*, May 1907

Dean, David, *Breaking Trail*, Ohio University Press, 1989

Solka, Paul, *Adventures in Alaskan Journalism*, Commercial Printing Co., Fairbanks, Alaska, 1980

Stuck, Hudson, 'On Denali,' *The Spirit of Missions* magazine, 1913

Stuck, Hudson, *The Ascent of Denali*, Wolfe Publishing Co., 1989

The Fairbanks Daily News-Miner, 1906–1914

Chapter 6

Kempson, E G H, expedition diary, 1935, The Alpine Club, London, unpublished

Roberts, Dennis, *I'll Climb Mount Everest Alone*, Hale, London 1957 (most of the information about Wilson's life prior to his flight to India is taken from this book)

The Daily Express, 27–29.4.36

Warren, Charles, expedition diary, 1935, The Alpine Club, London, unpublished

Wigram, Edmund, expedition diary, 1935, The Alpine Club, London, unpublished

Wilson, Maurice, original diary, The Alpine Club, London, unpublished

Chapter 7

Cromwell, Oliver Eaton, 'Spring Skiing in the Vale of Kashmir' *Appalachia* magazine, 1940

Cromwell, Oliver Eaton, Dudley Wolfe obituary, *The American Alpine Journal*, 1940

Houston, Charles, and Bates, Robert, *Five Miles High*, Dodd, Mead and Co., 1939

Kauffman, Andrew, and Putnam, William, *K2: The 1939 Tragedy*, The Mountaineers, Seattle, 1989

'Report of the American Alpine Club Second Karakoram Expedition,' unpublished

Rochester, Dudley, private papers, unpublished

Sheldon, George, 'Lost Behind the Ranges,' *Saturday Evening Post*, March 1940

Smith, Clifford, private papers, unpublished

Wiessner, Fritz, and Cranmer, Chappell, 'The Second American Expedition to K2,' *American Alpine Journal*

Wiessner, Fritz, 'The K2 Expedition of 1939,' *Appalachia* magazine, 1956

Wiessner, Fritz, private papers, unpublished

Chapter 8

Bates, Robert, 'The Fight for K2,' *The American Alpine Journal*

Houston, Charles, and Bates, Robert, *The Savage Mountain*, Collins, 1955

Streather, H R A, 'The Third American Karakoram Expedition,' *The Alpine Journal*, London, 1954

Chapter 9

Bonatti, Walter, *On the Heights*, Rupert Hart-Davis, London, 1964

Cassin, Ricardo, *Fifty Years of Alpinism*, Diadem, London, 1981

Compagnoni, Achille, *Men on K2*, Veronelli Editore, 1958

Desio, Ardito, *Ascent of K2*, Elek Books, London, 1955

K2 1954, Museo Nazionale Della Montagna

Chapter 10

Fanshawe, Andy and Venables, Stephen, *Himalaya Alpine-Style*, Baton Wicks, London, 1995

Salkeld, Audrey, *World Mountaineering*, Beazley, London, 1998

INDEX

271